Mathematics Education and Students with Autism, Intellectual Disability, and Other Developmental Disabilities

Edited by Drs. Emily C. Bouck, Jenny R. Root, and Bree Jimenez

© 2021 by Division on Autism and Developmental Disabilities (DADD)
All rights reserved.

Acknowledgments

We would like to acknowledge the Council for Exceptional Children Division on Autism and Developmental Disabilities (DADD) **Board of Directors** for their support of this book.

We would also like to thank **Jim Thompson**, DADD Publications Chair, for his time and expertise in the publication of this book.

About the Editors

Dr. Emily Bouck is a Professor in the Special Education Program within the Counseling, Educational Psychology, and Special Education Department at Michigan State University. Her research focuses on mathematical interventions for students with disabilities and those at-risk of a disability and response to intervention in mathematics. Emily is a Past President of DADD and the current Executive Director.

Dr. Jenny Root is an Assistant Professor of Special Education in the School of Teacher Education at Florida State University. Her research focuses on instructional methods—particularly in the area of mathematics—to promote academic learning for students with autism and intellectual disability. Jenny is a Past Student Representative of DADD and current Member-at-Large.

Dr. Bree Jimenez is an Associate Professor of Special Education at the University of Texas at Arlington. Her research focuses on math, science, and STEM instruction for students with extensive support needs. Bree is currently the Communications Chair and Critical Issues Chair for DADD.

About the Authors

Emily C. Bouck
Professor
Counseling, Educational Psychology, and Special Education
Michigan State University

Jessica Bowman
Research Associate
TIES Center, Institute on Community Integration
University of Minnesota

Amy M. Clausen
Doctoral Student in Special Education
Department of Special Education and Child Development
University of North Carolina at Charlotte

Sarah K. Cox
Assistant Professor of Special Education
Department of Special Education and Communication Sciences
Eastern Michigan University

Gail Ghere
Research Associate
TIES Center, Institute on Community Integration
University of Minnesota

Bree A Jimenez
Associate Professor of Special Education
Department of Curriculum and Instruction
University of Texas at Arlington

Holly Long
Doctoral Student
Special Education
Michigan State University

M. Addie McConomy
Doctoral Student in Special Education
School of Teacher Education
Florida State University

Jenny R. Root
Assistant Professor of Special Education
School of Teacher Education
Florida State University

Alicia Saunders
Research Scientist
Project IMPACT- Inclusion Made Practical for All Children and Teachers
University of North Carolina at Charlotte

Fred Spooner
Professor of Special Education
Department of Special Education and Child Development
University of North Carolina at Charlotte

Table of Contents

Introduction: *Mathematics Education and Students with Autism, Intellectual Disability, and Other Developmental Disabilities*   pp. 1-6

Chapter 1: Contextualizing Math Standards   pp. 7-29
    Alicia Saunders

Chapter 2: Using Data to Design and Evaluate Math Instruction   pp. 30-75
    Sarah Cox, Jenny Root, & Addie McConomy

Chapter 3: Multi-Tiered System of Supports in Mathematics   pp. 76-103
    Jessica A. Bowman & Gail Ghere

Chapter 4: Manipulatives and Manipulative-Based Instructional Sequences   pp. 104-134
    Emily C. Bouck & Holly Long

Chapter 5: Teaching Problem Solving Using Modified Schema-Based Instruction   pp. 135-168
    Jenny Root, Amy Clausen, & Fred Spooner

Chapter 6: Embedded Instruction   pp. 169-188
    Bree Jimenez

Appendices   pp. 189-193

Glossary   pp. 193-199

Introduction: *Mathematics Education and Students with Autism, Intellectual Disability, and Other Developmental Disabilities*

Mathematics education is important for all students, including students with disabilities. Included in the value of high-quality mathematics education are students with autism spectrum disorders, intellectual disability, and other developmental disabilities (ASD/IDD). Mathematics education supports access and success in advanced mathematics, careers, as well as independent living skills (Browder et al., 2018; Saunders et al., 2018).

Despite the importance of mathematics, mathematics research and teaching has received less attention than literacy for students with disabilities (Fuchs & Fuchs, 2005; Fuchs et al., 2007), including students with ASD/IDD. Historically, research on mathematics education for students with ASD/IDD primarily focused on functional mathematics, such as purchasing skills (Bouck, 2009) and basic number sense (e.g., number identification; Spooner et al., 2019). However, more recent attention on academic mathematics expanded the research base for students with ASD/IDD (Knight et al., 2019; Spooner et al., 2019). Over the past decade, researchers replicated evidence that students with ASD/IDD can acquire, generalize, and maintain meaningful grade-aligned mathematics skills (Root et al., 2020).

Focus of Book

In this book, the authors provide educators with research-based interventions and instructional approaches to supporting students with ASD/IDD in mathematics. Each chapter provides educators with accessible resources that provide research-supported practical strategies and guides to educate students. Each chapter, written by scholars whose work focuses on mathematics education for students with ASD/IDD, provides examples and materials teachers can use with elementary and secondary students with ASD/IDD. Throughout the book, research-supported mathematical interventions and instruction will be presented: contextualizing mathematics standards, modified schema-based instruction, manipulatives and manipulative based instructional sequences, embedded early numeracy instruction across mathematical domains, instructional decision-making in mathematics, and multi-tiered systems of support in mathematics.

This book from the Division on Autism and Developmental Disabilities (DADD) is built upon previous publications of the division. In other words, the conceptual framework for examining mathematics education, interventions, and instruction for students with ASD/IDD is that learning occurs across stages. Learning for students with disabilities—inclusive of students with ASD/IDD—exists in four stages, although they are not necessarily sequential (Shurr et al., 2019; see Figure 1). The first stage of learning is acquisition in which students are originally exposed to a skill or concept (Collins, 2012; Snell & Brown, 2011). When students independently achieve 60% accuracy (or 100% with support), they enter the next phase: fluency. In fluency, students both become more accurate as well as increase the rate at which they are able to complete the task or skill. Next, students work towards maintenance, which means they can successfully engage in the task or demonstrate the skill without instruction proceeding (Alberto & Troutman, 2009; Shurr et al., 2019). While the final phase is generalization (i.e., consistent demonstration of the skill or concept with different people, in different settings, or with different materials), generalization can and should be factored into the other phases (Collins, 2012). Research-based instructional strategies or pedagogical approaches exist to support students in each of the phases (see Table 1).

Figure 1
Stages of Learning

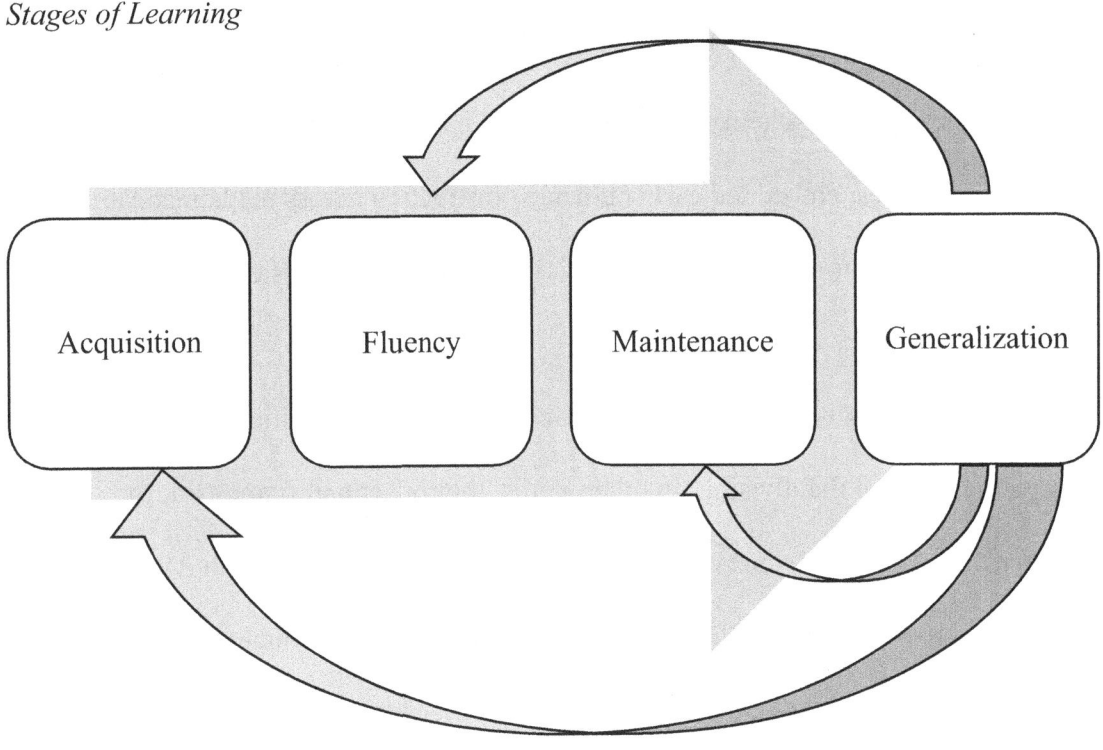

Note: *Adapted from Shurr et al., 2019)*

Table 1
Research-Supported Instructional Strategies Across Stages

	Acquisition	Fluency	Maintenance	Generalization
Task Analysis	✓	✓		
Modeling	✓			✓
System of Least prompts	✓	✓		✓
Visual supports	✓			
Constant time delay	✓			
Distributed Trials		✓		✓
Overlearning		✓	✓	
Support fading		✓	✓	✓
Simulations				✓
Community-based Instruction				✓

Note: Please see the glossary at the end of the book for definitions of these terms as well as others used throughout the book.

Although more research and attention is needed on mathematics education for students with ASD/IDD, multiple effective interventions for students at the acquisition phase have been identified; many of these will be discussed throughout this book (cf., Barnett & Cleary, 2015; Hudson et al., 2018; King et al., 2016; Spooner et al., 2019). However, less attention has been paid to fluency, maintenance, and generalization in mathematics (Spooner et al., 2012; Park et al., 2020). We encourage educators to assess, plan, and teach across the stages of learning of mathematics for students with ASD/IDD, which will likely mean an intervention package (i.e., multiple interventions or practices).

This book is also built upon a commitment from the Division with respect to supporting evidence-based and/or research-based instructional practices (Cook et al., 2008). Educational practices are classified by the amount of research that supports their use; in other words, using evidence to determine the quality of the practice (Shurr et al., 2019). The highest distinction is given to those practices deemed evidence-based, which means positive data exists from a sufficient quantity of methodologically-sound studies involving appropriate design to suggest efficacy (Cook et al, 2012; Cook et al., 2009). In the field of special education, we often now apply quality indicators and standards to situate a practice as being evidence-based (Council for Exceptional Children, 2014; Cook et al., 2014). Others use meta-analyses to determine the quantity and quality of a practice's research base (Kretlow & Blatz, 2011). Research-based practices are those in which efficacy research exists supporting their use, but sufficient quantity of studies or with sufficient number of participants does not rise to the level of evidence-based. Throughout this book, evidence-based practices will be highlighted. However, to the extent that evidence-based practices do not exist, research-based practices will be highlighted throughout the book.

Organization of the Book

This practitioner-focused book on teaching mathematics to students with ASD/IDD consists of six chapters. Chapter 1, written by Alicia Saunders, focuses on contextualizing math standards when considering students with ASD/IDD to ensure they are receiving grade-aligned and personally relevant instruction. Chapter 2, written by Sarah Cox, Jenny Root, and Addie McConomy, explores data-based decision making for teaching mathematics to students with ASD/IDD. Chapter 3, written by Jessica Bowman and Gail Ghere, discusses multi-tiered systems of support and their application for students with ASD/IDD relative to mathematics. Chapter 4, written by Emily Bouck and Holly Long, discuses manipulatives as interventions in and of themselves and as part of an instructional sequence to support students with ASD/IDD accessing and learning mathematics. Chapter 5, written by Jenny Root, Amy Clausen, and Fred Spooner, explores how to support students with ASD/IDD in mathematical problem solving through modified schema-based instruction. Chapter 6 concludes the book with a focus on embedded early numeracy instruction within grade-aligned mathematics, written by Bree Jimenez.

References

Alberto, P., & Troutman, A. (2009). *Applied behavior analysis for teachers* (8th ed.). Pearson.

Browder, D. M., Spooner, F., Lo, Y., Saunders, A. F., Root, J. R., Davis, L. L., & Brosh, C. R. (2018). Teaching students with moderate intellectual disability to solve word problems. *The Journal of Special Education, 51*(4), 222–235. https://doi.org/10.1177/0022466917721236

Collins, B. C. (2012). *Systematic instruction for students with moderate and severe disabilities*. Paul H Brookes Publishing.

Cook, B. G., Buysse, V., Klingner, J., Landrum, T. J., McWilliam, R. A., Tankersley, M., & Test, D. W. (2014). CEC's standards for classifying the evidence base of practices in special education. *Remedial and Special Education, 36*(4), 220-234. https://doi.org/10.1177/0741932514557271

Cook, B. G., Smith, G. J., & Tankersley, M. (2012). Evidence-based practices in education. In K. R. Harris, S. Graham, and T. Urdan (Eds.), *APA Educational Psychology Handbook: Vol. 1. Theories, Constructs, and Critical Issues* (pp. 493-525). Washington, DC: American Psychological Association. https://doi.org/10.1037/XXXXX.XXX

Cook, B. G., Tankersley, M., Cook, L., & Landrun, T. J. (2008). Evidence-based practices in special education: Some practical considerations. *Intervention in School and Clinic*, *44*(2), 69-75. https://doi.org/10.1177/1053451208321452

Cook, B. G., Tankersley, M., & Landrum, T. J. (2009). Determining evidence-based practices in special education. *Exceptional Children*, *75*(3), 365-383. https://doi.org/10.1177/001440290907500306

Council for Exceptional Children. (2014). Council for Exceptional Children: Standards for evidence-based practices in special education. *Teaching Exceptional Children*, *46*(6), 206-212. https://doi.org/10.1177/0040059914531389

Fuchs, L. S., & Fuchs, D. (2005). Enhancing mathematical problem solving for students with disabilities. *The Journal of Special Education*, *39*(1), 45-57.

Fuchs, L. S., Fuchs, D., Compton, D. L., Bryant, J. D., Hamlett, C. L., & Seethaler, P. M. (2007). Mathematics screening with progress monitoring at first grade: Implications for responsiveness to intervention. *Exceptional Children, 73*(3), 311-330.

Knight, V. R., Heartley, B. H., Kuntz, E. M., Carter, E. W., & Juartz, A. P. (2019). Instructional practices, priorities, and preparedness for educating students with autism and intellectual disability. *Focus on Autism and Developmental Disabilities, 34*(1), 3–11. https://doi.org/10.1177/1088357618755694.

Kretlow, A. g., & Blatz, S. L. (2011). The ABCs of evidence-based practice for teachers. *Teaching Exceptional Children*, *43*(5), 8-19.

Park, J., Bouck, E. C., & Josol, C. (2020). Maintenance in mathematics for individuals with developmental disabilities: A systematic review of the literature. *Research in Developmental Disabilities, 105*(2020) [Advanced Online Publication]. https://doi.org/10.1016/j.ridd.2020.103751

Root, J. R., Jimenez, B. A., Saunders, A. F., & Stanger, C. (2020). Replication research to support mathematical learning of students with extensive support needs. *Exceptionality*, *28*(2), 109-120. doi:10.1080/09362835.2020.1743708.

Saunders, A. F., Spooner, F., & Davis, L. L. (2018). Using video prompting to teach mathematical problem solving of real-world video-simulation problems. *Remedial and Special Education, 39*(1), 53-64. https://doi.org/10.1177/0741932517717042

Shurr, J., Jimenez, B., & Bouck, E. C. (2019). *Educating students with intellectual disability and autism spectrum disorder: Book 1 Research-based practices and education science.* Council for Exceptional Children.

Snell, M. E. & Brown, F. (2011). *Instruction of students with severe disabilities* (7th ed.). Pearson.

Spooner, F., Knight, V. F., Browder, D. M., & Smith, B. R. (2012). Evidence-based practice for teaching academics to students with severe developmental disabilities. *Remedial and Special Education, 33*(6), 374–387. https://doi.org/10.1177/0741932511421634.

Spooner, F., Root, J., Saunders, A. F., & Browder, D. M. (2018). An updated evidence-based practice review on teaching mathematics to students with moderate and severe developmental disabilities. *Remedial and Special Education, 40*(3), 150-165. https://doi.org/10.1177/0741932517751055

Chapter 1: Contextualizing Math Standards

Alicia Saunders

It is critical for students with autism spectrum disorder and intellectual and developmental disabilities (ASD/IDD) to not only be able to complete a math skill, but also to truly understand what they are doing while performing the skill. In addition to understanding what they are doing, they must learn *when* and *where* to apply these skills. This chapter will emphasize the development of conceptual understanding in mathematics, as well as contextualizing mathematics to make it generalizable for students to their everyday lives.

Building a Conceptual Understanding

Often in special education, there is an emphasis on drill-and-practice type exercises in math, such as math fact recall, number recognition, telling time using Judy© clocks and flashcards, and counting coins. For example, if a student is shown a flashcard that says "3" and states "three" this is a focus on memorization without connection. This is "naked math," or math without context. Students may learn to state the answer, but many do not have a connection between the word "three" and the quantity of three to truly understand what they are doing or meaningfully apply the skill in their everyday lives. Figure 1 gives an example a student who does not have a connection between the word and an image, such as three dots in a row. Students with disabilities need explicit instruction in mathematics but they also need help making the link to conceptual understanding in order to develop the "picture in their head."

It is not surprising to find that most special education teachers use drill-and-practice strategies, often with skills taught in nonsequential order. Special education teachers report feeling uncomfortable teaching mathematics and unprepared to teach the content (Lee et al., 2016). The later chapters in this book offer detailed strategies for how to teach specific

Figure 1
Example of a Student Without Conceptual Understanding

Carlos, an elementary student with ASD, was given a set of addition and subtraction word problems to solve. Carlos quickly circled the numbers in the problem and used mental math to add the numbers together. He did not read the problem, nor did he comprehend and represent what was happening in the problem. The teacher noticed this. She read one of the subtraction problems aloud to Carlos and asked him to solve the problem using manipulatives. Carlos was unable to represent the quantities in the problem with manipulatives and use them to show the subtraction action. In this scenario, Carlos had fact recall and was able to get some addition problems correct by default but lacked conceptual understanding of the actions happening in the problem.

mathematics content. This chapter aims to answer questions like: How do teachers know what to teach? How do teachers prioritize content? How to teachers ensure they are teaching both academic and functional mathematics? How do teachers select appropriate IEP goals?

Contextualized Math

Saunders et al. (2019) discussed how to plan mathematics content across the years of schooling. In elementary school, there should be a heavy emphasis on teaching early numeracy skills (see Chapter 6 on embedded instruction), followed by mathematical problem solving (see Chapter 5 on modified schema-based instruction), to build a strong foundation for later mathematics. As students move into middle and high school, math skills become much more complex, and there should be a greater focus on teaching ways for students to apply them in their everyday lives (Root et al., 2018; Saunders et al., 2019). This is known as *contextualized math*. This approach varies from traditional functional math in several ways. Contextualized math begins instructional planning with grade-aligned standards versus discrete skills such as counting coins and telling time, which are overemphasized in functional math. The traditional functional math approach is task driven. Goals or activities are selected that are thought to increase independence, perhaps based on information gathered in an ecological inventory (Trela &

Jimenez, 2013). These skills are task analyzed and taught to mastery. Sometimes, community-based instruction is built into the plan, such as learning to make a purchase using mixed dollar amounts and then going to a grocery store to make the purchase. A more contemporary *contextualized* approach has evolved as students with ASD/ID demonstrated they can learn more skills, specifically showing tremendous progress in grade-aligned math skills and use these skills within real-world applications. This allows the teacher to address multiple instructional priorities within the mathematics lesson. Targeted skills may be still be selected from ecological inventories and can include traditional functional skills, but the skills should align with grade-level standards or extended content standards if the state has them. Figure 2 provides an example of how educators can use the contextualized mathematics approach to prioritize and plan instruction for students with ASD/IDD.

In contextualized math, there are three essential steps (Root et al., 2018). First, grade-level standards are selected to target. Second, real-life applications for how this skill could be used in real life are identified, such as the natural routines in which this event would occur. Third, the skill is taught explicitly, such as in the classroom environment, with planned opportunities to build generalization within natural routines or real-life contexts. As illustrated in Figure 2, this contextualized math approach considered Tom's strengths as well as the grade-level standard:

CCSS.MATH.CONTENT.7.EE.B.3
Solve multi-step real-life and mathematical problems posed with positive and negative rational numbers in any form (whole numbers, fractions, and decimals), using tools strategically. Apply properties of operations to calculate with numbers in any form; convert between forms as appropriate; and assess the reasonableness of answers using mental computation and estimation strategies. Common Core State Standards Initiative, 2010)

Figure 2
Example of Contextualized Mathematics Approach

Tom was a 13-year-old boy with ASD and comorbid moderate ID. Alicia served both as Tom's 7th grade middle school teacher and as his home support therapist after school. One of Tom's community goals was to make a purchase, and one of Tom's IEP goals also was for making a purchase using mixed dollar amounts. Alicia took Tom to Walmart to make a purchase. She handed him a $5 bill. Tom slid the $5 bill through the credit card machine, clearly mimicking something Tom had seen with his parents in the past. This made Alicia think hard about what was really functional for Tom. He was great with a calculator but had been working on counting out mixed dollar amounts for several years without mastery of the skill. Since Tom was approaching high school, could use a calculator, and demonstrated the skill of using a credit card, Alicia asked Tom's parents if they would consider a declining balance credit card for Tom. Not only did this align better with Tom's strengths, but it also aligned better with his grade level standards for using numbers with decimals for addition and subtraction problems. Alicia quickly taught Tom to use the calculator to figure out the amount on his card, decide if he had enough money to make purchases, and use his communication skills to ask his parents for more money if he was running low. This is a true story of an experience by the author of this chapter.

In Figure 2, Tom had already shown Alicia the real-life event this standard could be addressed within, but Alicia knew there were many more opportunities as well. She decided to create video examples of different places Tom would go in the community to make purchases. She also provided Tom with varying quantities on his declining balance card when practicing this in her classroom and in his home. Finally, Alicia developed a routine in which Tom would check his balance before he left for an outing to decide if he had enough money, go into the community to make his purchase, and come home to calculate the remaining balance. In the contextualized math approach, students should accomplish multiple priorities using grade-level standards within real-world contexts. In Tom's vignette, the teacher was addressing academic, functional, self-determination, and communication skills.

Alignment

Alignment is a key factor to ensure students with ASD/IDD have access to the general curriculum and contextualized math. True alignment for students with disabilities occurs when the general curriculum or grade-aligned standards are used, instruction on these standards is done using sound, evidence-based and research-based practices, the student is being prepared for the general assessment or the alternate assessment, and the Individualized Education Program (IEP) addresses each of these three facets (see Figure 3; modified from Courtade & Browder, 2016).

Well-aligned IEPs have goals that are both meaningful to the student and promote access to the general curriculum. There are far too many standards in each grade level for an IEP to address each one, and the IEP is not designed to encompass everything that should be taught to a student. The IEP should target pivotal skills or concepts that are needed for the child to make progress in the general curriculum. Classroom instruction should be designed to target prioritized standards while addressing the IEP goals.

When the IEP aligns with the three sides of the triangle, the student's educational program is more cohesive, and the teacher's job is simplified to some degree because the targeted skills – the prioritized standards and the students' IEP goals—are working in unison. To illustrate, the left column of Table 1 provides a non-example of alignment with the IEP,

Figure 3
The Triangular Relationship between High Quality Instruction, Curriculum, and Assessment with the Standards-based IEP at the Core

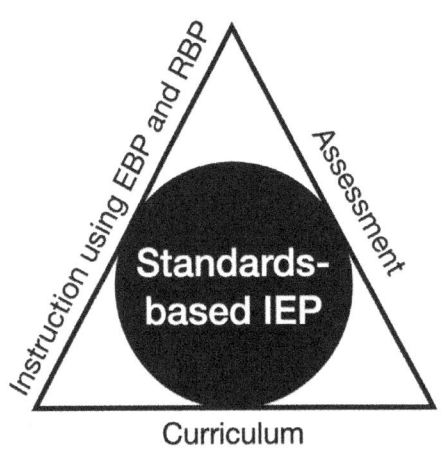

instruction, curriculum, and assessment. The IEP goal does not align with how the student will make progress towards the prioritized general curriculum standard that is also assessed on the alternate assessment. The right column provides an example of how to rectify the IEP goal to ensure better alignment by targeting a goal that with move the student towards being able to access the general education standard and perform the alternate assessment tasks (Courtade & Browder, 2016).

In the corrected example in Table 1, you can see the IEP goal is aligned with division, and the student is working on division using manipulatives. The teacher should use specially-designed instruction with research-based and evidence-based practices to teach the skill, and to make this contextualized, the teacher should design activities that are both meaningful and personally relevant applications of when this student may use this skill. For example, the teacher could use manipulatives and set makers (i.e., ovals drawn on an index card) to illustrate how to perform division tasks using a model-guided practice-independent practice approach (i.e., explicit instruction). First, they would model a few problems, with the student repeating the steps after her. Next, during guided practice, they would provide the student with an opportunity to try a problem and provide the system of least prompts to ensure the students performs the division task correctly, repeating for several trials until the student shows some proficiency. Finally, they

Table 1
Example and Non-Example for Alignment

Non-Example of Alignment	**Corrected Example of Alignment**
IEP goal & instruction: telling time to the quarter hour on an analog clock. *General curriculum standard:* division using equal shares. *Alternate assessment:* can students divide a group of objects into equal groups.	*IEP goal & instruction:* division of objects into equal groups using quantities of 15 or less. *General curriculum standard:* division using equal shares. *Alternate assessment:* can students divide a group of objects into equal groups.

would assess whether the student could do it on their own without help or feedback during independent practice. Figure 4 provides an example of alignment, as well as the teacher ensuring the student has conceptual understanding of division and practices division using a contextualized math approach.

How to Select What to Teach and Ensure Student Learning

The 3 P's Rule

The 3 P's Rule—'Prioritize, Pinpoint, and Progress Monitor"—should be used to make standards accessible for students with disabilities. One recommendation is to do this prior to the school year starting as a yearlong planning framework. The first step is to prioritize the

Figure 4
Illustration of the Model-Guided-Independent Practice Procedure for Division within Contextualized Math Instruction

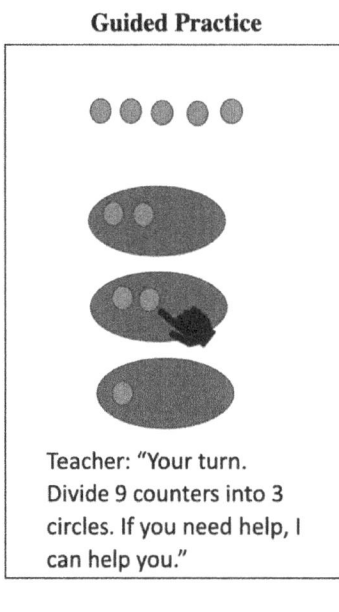
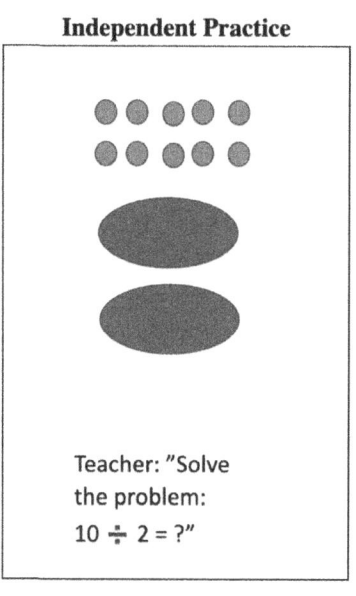

Beyond the use of manipulatives, the teacher incorporated opportunities for the student to practice the skill throughout the day during natural routines, such as passing out supplies in the classroom. In addition, the school was involved in a service-learning project packing backpacks with meals for families who did not have enough food on the weekend. The student was involved in dividing packages of food among backpacks. Here you can see alignment, as well as the teacher ensuring the student has conceptual understanding of division and practices division *using a contextualized math approach.*

standards. Standards progress, or build, over time. Figure 5 below shows a static version of the CCSSM Clickable Map 2.0 (Institute for Mathematics and Education, 2011)—a diagram of how domains in math are laid out over the K through 12th grade span. Educators need to determine which of these standards are pivotal skills for students to learn in order to progress in that domain and be prepared for what is to come. As most special education teachers are not experts in the field of mathematics, collaboration with a general education teacher is critical for this step. Special educators can begin the year by collaborating with a general education teacher to map out critical standards for their students' grade levels. Not only is this helpful in prioritizing standards, but the general education mathematics expert also may assist with understanding the standards. Furthermore, the general education teacher may be able to easily come up with ideas on how to contextualize the standards, providing examples of real-world applications. If collaboration is not an option, there are numerous resources for better understanding standards as well. At the time of this publication, North Carolina offered *Unpacking Documents* for math standards under the "Tools and Resources" tab found at https://sites.google.com/dpi.nc.gov/k-12-mathematics/resources?authuser=0.

Some states provide information on prioritized standards for students on the alternate assessment. These prioritized standards are often based on what is assessed and there may be information on the percentage of the alternate assessment that targets specific domains. For example, in Massachusetts, the standards assessed on the Massachusetts Comprehensive Assessment System-Alt are prioritized and diagrammed as a starting point for teachers to narrow down what to target within a grade level. If students with ASD/IDD are assessed using the general education assessment, it is critical to follow the general curriculum standards.

The second step is to pinpoint the standards selected. Standards are complex and encompass quite a bit of information. Sometimes an entire standard can be taught, but often, the standard needs to be narrowed down for students with ASD/IDD, such as this Common Core State Standards High School Functions standard:

CCSS.MATH.CONTENT.HSF.IF.B.4
For a function that models a relationship between two quantities, interpret key features of graphs and tables in terms of the quantities, and sketch graphs showing key features given a verbal description of the relationship. *Key features include: intercepts; intervals where the function is increasing, decreasing, positive, or negative; relative maximums and minimums; symmetries; end behavior; and periodicity.*
(Common Core State Standards Initiative, 2010)

A teacher of students with ASD/IDD may pinpoint the component on the objective that targets "the relationship between two quantities" and have students describe function graphs as increasing, decreasing, positive, or negative (see italicized component of standard).

Figure 5
A Static Picture of the Interactive Diagram of Mathematics Domains Across Grade Levels ([CCSSM Clickable Map 2.0](#))

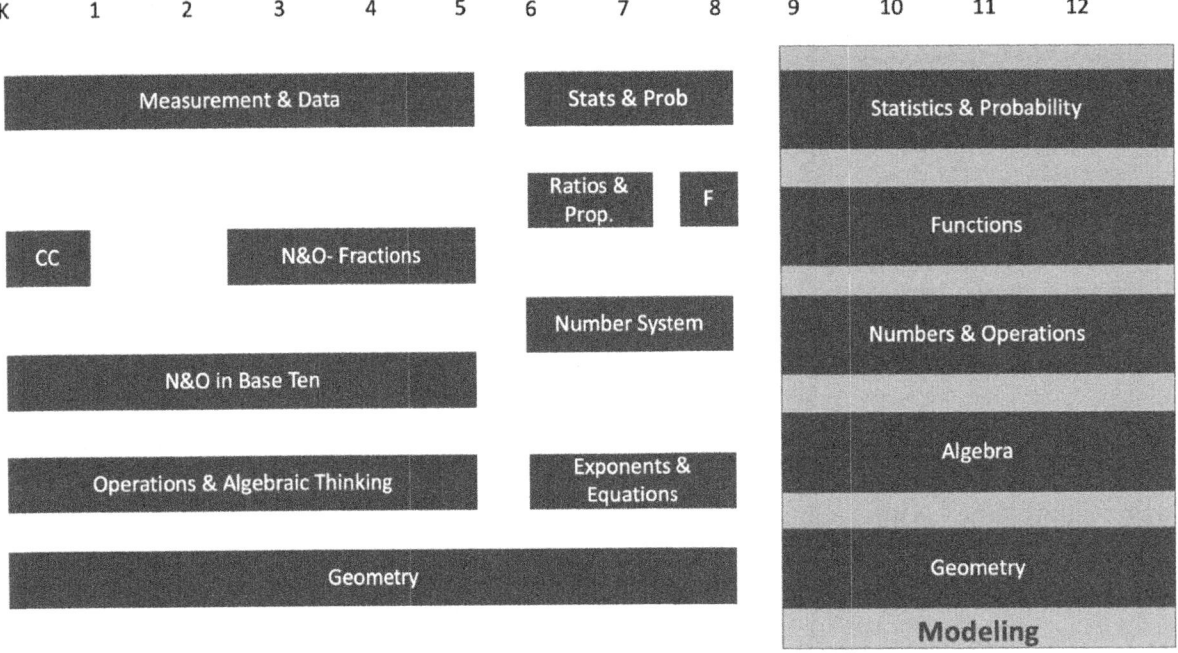

Notes. "Stat & Prob" = Statistics and Probability, "CC" = Counting and Cardinality, "N & O" = Numbers and Operations, "Ratios & Prop." = Ratios and Proportions, "F" = Functions

Another way to pinpoint the standard is to simplify the standard. Great caution should be taken when simplifying standards to ensure the standard has not been watered down too much and shifts too far from the grade-level standard to be considered aligned. Collaboration with a general education teacher is especially helpful for ensuring this does not occur. In addition, many states offer grade-aligned standards for students on the alternate assessment. Take a minute to research your state's education website to search for alternate achievement standards. If not, the National Center and State Collaborative Wiki website provides Core Content Connectors for students with disabilities at https://wiki.ncscpartners.org/index.php/Core_Content_Connectors. The Dynamic Learning Maps provides Essential Elements for students with disabilities at https://dynamiclearningmaps.org/sites/default/files/documents/Math_EEs/DLM_Essential_Elements_Math_(2013)_v4.pdf. It may be helpful to cross reference your state's alternate achievement standards with the two resources listed above to give you a better understanding of what to teach.

The third step is to progress monitor. Progress monitoring requires solid goal development, data sheet creation, data collection, and analyzing data to ensure student progress is being made. This chapter will target writing IEP goals and objectives and developing measurement systems. Progress monitoring will be discussed in greater length in Chapter 2.

Writing IEP Goals and Objectives

Guidelines for writing IEP goals and objectives may vary from state to state, or even district to district; however, the goals and objectives should be SMART. This acronym can be defined differently, but Jung (2007) defined this specific to IEP related goals as **S**pecific, **M**easurable, **A**ttainable or some texts say **A**ction Verbs, **R**ealistic and **R**elevant, and **T**ime Limited (Hedin & DeSpain, 2018). To be **S**pecific, the condition must specify the materials, accommodations, directions needed to accomplish the goal. The target behavior must be **M**easurable, which means it needs to be an observable, countable behavior. The goal must be **A**ttainable, meaning the student can achieve the goal in the timeframe. In addition, the goals must be **R**ealistic and **R**elevant, meaning the child should be working on something that is both meaningful and purposefully relevant for that learner. This emphasizes the need for using a contextualized approach. Furthermore, the student's strengths and needs must be considered when writing the goals. Finally, the goal must be **T**ime limited, meaning it is achievable within the IEP 12-month time frame and short term/benchmark objectives may be used to guide the timeline.

Constructing an IEP Goal

The IEP goals and objectives are constructed using five key parts: the condition(s), the target behavior, the mastery criteria, the measurement method, and the timeframe. All goals must include the first three components – condition(s), target behavior, and mastery criteria. Table 1 provides guidelines and specific math examples of the first three components of a SMART goal.

Depending on your district or states rules and IEP software program, the last two components of IEP goals and objectives—measurement method and timeframe—may appear in the IEP but not in the goal itself. For example, the measurement method might be a dropdown menu selection under each goal. The timeframe can appear in the broad IEP goal, or it can be dictated by short term/benchmark objectives that fall underneath the broad goal. The measurement method and timeframe should be goal dependent. In other words, the goal will drive the type of data collection recording method selected, as well as the timeframe. Chapter 2 discusses various types of data collection measures, many of which may be applicable for the IEP goals and objectives as well. It is very important to see if the student is making progress on a

Table 1

How to Construct an IEP Goal

Condition	Materials needed to perform target behavior/task	<ul><li>Manipulatives</li><li>Graphic organizers</li><li>Calculator or other assistive technology</li><li>Video models</li><li>Video simulation problems</li></ul>
	Assistance - quantity, type, and level of supports	<ul><li>Prompting specified</li><li>Student-friendly task analysis or self-monitoring checklist</li><li>Calculator</li><li>Mnemonics</li><li>Math fact tables</li></ul>
	Directions<ul><li>Specify how the student might complete the assessment/task</li><li>Specify type of intervention used</li></ul>	Examples:<ul><li>"Using your manipulatives…"</li><li>"Use the steps of the checklist and solve this problem."</li><li>"Using modified schema-based instruction"</li></ul>
Behavior	Behavior must be observable, measurable, and precise.	Define using *action verbs* you can see happen:<ul><li>Answer</li><li>Solve and write answer</li><li>Point to/select</li><li>Circle</li><li>Demonstrate an action that is specified</li></ul>Non-examples:<ul><li>Increase</li><li>Improve</li><li>Learn</li></ul>
Mastery Criteria	Mastery criteria must include both accuracy and maintenance over time (also called retention criteria) to reflect the stages of learning.	<ul><li>Example: 90% of problems for 3 consecutive sessions.</li><li>Nonexample: 90% of problems. [This student would master the IEP goal the first time they answered 90% of problems, but this student has not shown they can consistently do this over time, moving beyond acquisition.]</li></ul>Other common measures include trials and probes.
colspan="3" Example for Carlos from Figure 1 who was working on solving addition and subtraction word problems: *Given a graphic organizer, manipulatives, and a student friendly task analysis,* ← **condition** *Carlos will solve addition and subtraction word problems and write his answer* ← **behavior** *for 90% of word problems over 3 consecutive sessions.* ← **mastery, including accuracy and maintenance**.		

goal. For this reason, data collection using data recording sheets is recommended because these data can be graphed and visually analyzed to see if progress is being made. Remember, the behavior in IEP goals must be observable, measurable, and precise.

Often times on IEP menus for measurement methods, anecdotal records or permanent products are two options frequently selected. Teachers can write anecdotal notes to provide an objective narrative to record their observations of a student's behavior, skill or performance. Even if anecdotal records are being recorded, there should be a behavior observed that can be counted. For example, if Carlos from Figure 1 is solving word problems in his general education inclusion math class and the teacher records "Carlos is having great difficulty solving word problems. He is getting frustrated and shuts down." This information describes his attitude, but not where the skill breakdown is happening. However, if the teacher is using a task analytic data sheet for problem solving, and Carlos is clearly missing step 3 in every single problem presented, then the special education teacher, and general education teacher for that matter, have much more guidance on where the skill breakdown is happening and how to help Carlos solve the problems. Likewise, for permanent products, which typically would be worksheets or problems solved on some type of platform in math, there should be behaviors that can be counted, such as number of problems correct, or number of calculation errors made.

Measurement Method. A question teachers often have is how to select data sheets to measure the goals they have written. The type of skill and student's needs will determine the data sheet selected. Math involves both discrete skills and chained skills. Discrete skills require a single response (Collins, 2012). Chained skills require a number of individual behaviors that are sequenced together to make a more complex skill (Collins). See Table 2 for several math examples of discrete and chained skills.

Table 2
Sample Discrete and Chained Math Skills

Discrete Math Skills	Chained Math Skills
Number identification	Solving an equation or inequality
Shape identification	Finding the area of a 2-dimensional figure
Labeling quantities as "more" or "less"	Graphing data and analyzing

Trials, sessions, and probes can be confusing terms when writing goals. An instructional trial (see Figure 6) is defined as: (1) gaining the learner's attention; (2) delivering an antecedent stimulus, such as giving a task direction [e.g., "solve the problem"] and/or providing the student with materials [e.g., placing graphic organizer and manipulatives in front of the student], (3) the student responds; (4) a consequence occurs, such as the teacher scores the response as correct or incorrect, and provides either provides positive feedback [e.g.," Great job solving that problem. The answer is 4!"] or provides prompting until the student performs the correct response before moving on to the next trial (Collins, 2012).

A session is defined as a complete trial or set of trials (Collins, 2012). Sessions may occur multiple times within a day with breaks between, or they may occur daily or weekly. A probe is an assessment. These may occur daily, multiple times a week, weekly, or less frequently than that. Discrete skills often are measured in a multiple trial format, or multiple trials within a session. Chained tasks can be measured in multiple trial formats, such as presenting multiple word problems during one session, or they can be administered in a single trial format. Feedback is a powerful tool, especially when delivered in close proximity to the task or skill. Feedback should be specific and provide the learner with information on what needs to be fixed or explain the desired behavior observed. Reinforcement, when given, should be paired with specific feedback. For example, in shape identification, the teacher might say, "Great job! That is a quadrilateral," providing both verbal praise and specific feedback on what the student got

Figure 6
Diagram of an Instructional Trial

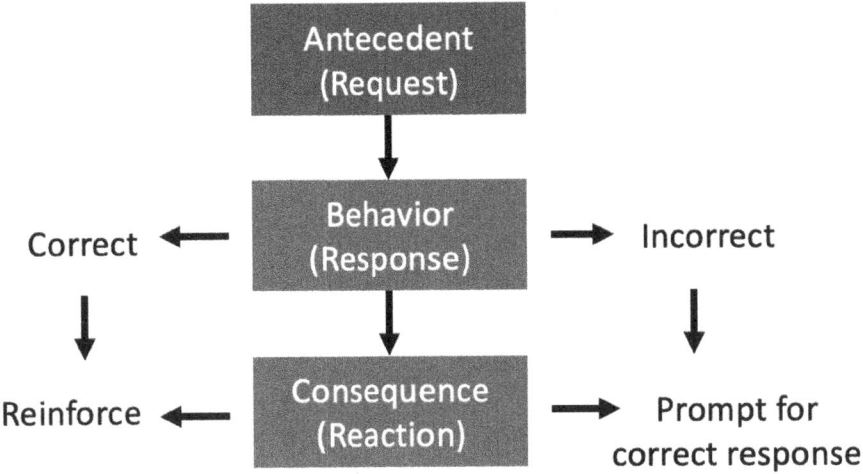

correct. The teacher may or may not provide reinforcement for each trial depending on the student's stage of learning and needs. If a student is just learning a new skill, it is important to deliver reinforcement each time. This can be faded as the student becomes more proficient in the skill. In probes, however, no error correction is provided, and the teacher may elect not to provide feedback or reinforcement for desired behaviors or responses (Collins, 2012).

The vignettes in Figures 7, 8, and 9 illustrate how to measure both discrete skills and chained tasks. With Jose (Figure 7), only one skill is being assessed—whether or not he can identify the concept of "more" using his head switch. Shaqwanna (Figure 8) is being assessed using multiple problems within a probe. Shaqwanna's example of two-digit subtraction with regrouping could easily be broken down step-by-step for a student in the acquisition phase, and thus would use the task analysis data sheet. Drew's vignette (Figure 9) provides an example of a task analytic data sheet for a chained skill—solving an algebraic equation. In this example, Drew is being taught to solve an algebraic equation using an 11-step task analysis with a graphic organizer and number line.

Figure 7
Example of Measuring Discrete and Chained Mathematics Tasks—Jose

Jose is an elementary student with cerebral palsy who uses a wheelchair. Jose is non-vocal and one of his communication goals is targeting using a head switch to respond to questions. In math, Jose is working on early numeracy concepts, such as the concepts of "more" and "less." The following data sheet shows Jose's responses to the concept of "more" using his AAC head switch.

Repeated Trial-One response Student: Jose				Goals: **Given two quantities of manipulatives placed in set makers side-by-side on a table, Jose will use a head switch to select the side that has "more" in 3 out of 5 trials across 3 consecutive sessions.**					
Dates:	10/8	10/8	10/8						
Target Response:	**more**	**more**	**more**						
Trial 1	+	-	+						
Trial 2	-	+	-						
Trial 3	+	+	+						
Trial 4	-	+	+						
Trial 5	-	-	+						
Total Independent Correct:	2	3	4						
Where:	C	CL	GC						
With:	PR	T	P						

Student Response Code:
I = Independent Correct
G = Gesture Prompt
V = Verbal Prompt
P = Physical Prompt
NR = No response

Where Code:
CL = Classroom
GC = General Ed. Classroom
C = Cafeteria
O = Other, *specify in notes

With Whom Code:
T = Teacher
PR = Paraprofessional
P = Peer

Repeated Trial- Single Response Data Sheet Analysis for Jose

- During the first session, the paraprofessional presents multiple trials of the skill in the cafeteria. Jose gets 2 correct.
- On the same day at a later time, thus a new "session," the special education teacher assesses the skill again in the classroom. Jose shows improvement and gets 3 correct.
- During the last session of the day, a peer tutor assesses the skill in the general education classroom. Jose shows improvement again and gets 4 correct during this session.
- Did Jose master his goal? No. This example shows why accuracy and maintenance over time are both important. If only accuracy was measured, Jose would have met his mastery criteria during the second session.
    - If Jose was assessed again the next morning and scored at least 3 or more trials correct, then he would meet mastery and a new goal would need to be written.
    - If Jose was assessed and scored lower than 3, then the consecutive sessions would restart and he would need at least 3 sessions scoring 3 or higher again.

Figure 8

Example of Measuring Discrete and Chained Mathematics Tasks—Shaqwanna

Shaqwanna is a fourth-grade student with mild intellectual disability who is well below grade level in computation. She receives intensive intervention in the resource classroom on two-digit subtraction. The following data sheet shows Shaqwanna's responses to her ongoing progress monitoring probes for two-digit subtraction. Each probe has 10 items.

Repeated Trial-Set of Responses Student: Shaqwanna					Task: Given two-digit subtraction problems requiring regrouping, Shaqwanna will solve 8 out of 10 problems correctly in 2 out of 3 probes						
Date:	11/6	11/8	11/13								
1.	+	+	+								
2.	+	-	+								
3.	+	+	+								
4.	+	+	+								
5.	+	+	+								
6.	+	+	+								
7.	+	+	+								
8.	-	+	+								
9.	+	+	+								
10.	+	+	+								
Total correct:	9	9	10								
Material Used:	VM	B10	PP								
Where:	R	T	GE								
With:	SET	MC	GET								

Materials Used:
PP = Pencil & paper only
B10 = Base 10 Blocks
VM = virtual manipulatives

Where:
GE = Gen Ed
R = Resource
T = Tutoring

With whom:
GET = Gen Ed Teacher
SET = Special Ed Teacher
MC = Math Coach

Repeated Trial- Set of Responses Data Sheet Analysis for Shaqwanna
- During the first probe, Shaqwanna got 9 out of 10 problems correct using virtual manipulatives in the resource classroom.
- Two days later, Shaqwanna got 9 out of 10 problems correct on the math probe using Base 10 blocks with the math coach.
- The following week, Shaqwanna got 10 out of 10 problems correct using paper and pencil only.
- Did Shaqwanna master her goal? Yes, she mastered her goal as written during the second probe. Shaqwanna not only mastered her goal, but she also displayed good conceptual understanding by demonstrating the skill using both virtual and concrete manipulatives, and can also solve with paper and pencil. How could this goal be modified?
- Shaqwanna seems to have a good understanding of this concept, but one missing piece is contextualized learning. She only appears to solve problems with numbers and no context. Perhaps to build generalization, her teachers could make a different goal adding in real-world problems for her to solve using two-digit addition with regrouping.

Figure 9

Example of Measuring Discrete and Chained Mathematics Tasks—Drew

Drew is an older student who spends part of his day at the high school and part at a job site working with a job coach. His IEP team uses a contextualized math approach to help him solve problems in his classroom, using video simulation problems, and at his job site to ensure he conceptually understands what he is doing and generalizes the skill to his everyday life.

Student Response Code: Where Code: With Whom Code: Material Used:

Student:	Task: Given an algebraic story problem, video simulation problem, or problem presented at work, Drew will use a graphic organizer with a number line and manipulatives to solve the problem and write his answer, performing 9 out of 11 steps correctly for 3 out of 4 consecutive problems.							
Date:	1-8	1-8	1-9					
1. Problem is read aloud	+	+	+					
2. Identifies first quantity in story problem	+	+	+					
3. Writes first quantity in "first fact" box	+	+	+					
4. Moves green chip to number on number line	P	+	+					
5. Finds last quantity in story problem	P	P	P					
6. Writes last quantity in "last fact" box	+	P	P					
7. Moves red chip to number on number line	P	P	P					
8. Identifies what is being solved for in story problem	P	P	P					
9. Writes "X" in "second fact box	P	P	P					
10. Determines if operation is addition or subtraction and circles "+/-" in "sign" box	-	+	-					
1. Counts number of jumps from chip to chip on number line to solve and writes answer	P	P	P					
Total Independent Correct:	4	5	4					
Materials	W	VS	VS					
With:	T	T	T					
Where:	CL	CL	CL					

(+) = Independent Correct CL= Classroom T = Teacher W = worksheet
(-) = Incorrect JS = job site PR= paraprofessional VS = video simulation
(P) = Prompt JC = job coach V = vocational materials

Task Analysis Data Sheet Analysis for Drew
- During the first session, Drew works with a story problem on a worksheet and only gets 4 steps independently correct. Most are prompted responses with one error. He added rather than subtracted. His teacher provided error correction for the missed step.
- During the second session, Drew works on a video simulation problem and gets 5 steps independently correct. The remaining steps are prompted.
- During the third session, Drew works on a video simulation problem again and gets 4 steps independently correct. He misses selecting the operation and receives error correction from his teacher.
- Did Drew master his goal? No. He is in the acquisition phase of learning, which is why his teacher decided to use the task analytic data sheet to break the skill down step-by-step. His IEP team decided to plan for generalization at his job site once he has mastered the skill as indicated on the data sheet, but he is not in that phase of learning quite yet.

Short Term/Benchmark Objectives. The decision factor on how to determine the short term/benchmark objective mastery criteria can vary. These may be determined by expected growth. For example, on a mathematics curriculum based measurement, this can be done by examining the rate on the prior year's CBMs, or by taking the median score of the initial three baseline measurements and adding it to the product of the weekly growth rate by number of weeks in term and across the year (Fuchs & Fuchs, n.d.; see Figure 10 for an example). Another method for determining benchmarks or short-term objectives with goals that require multiple operations or problem types may be to work on mastery of one operation or problem type for a set period of time. In addition, increasing the accuracy measure can be the stairstep for the benchmark, thus making it more difficult with each term until the IEP goal criteria is reached.

Figure 10
Sample IEP Goals and Short-Term Objectives for a CBM

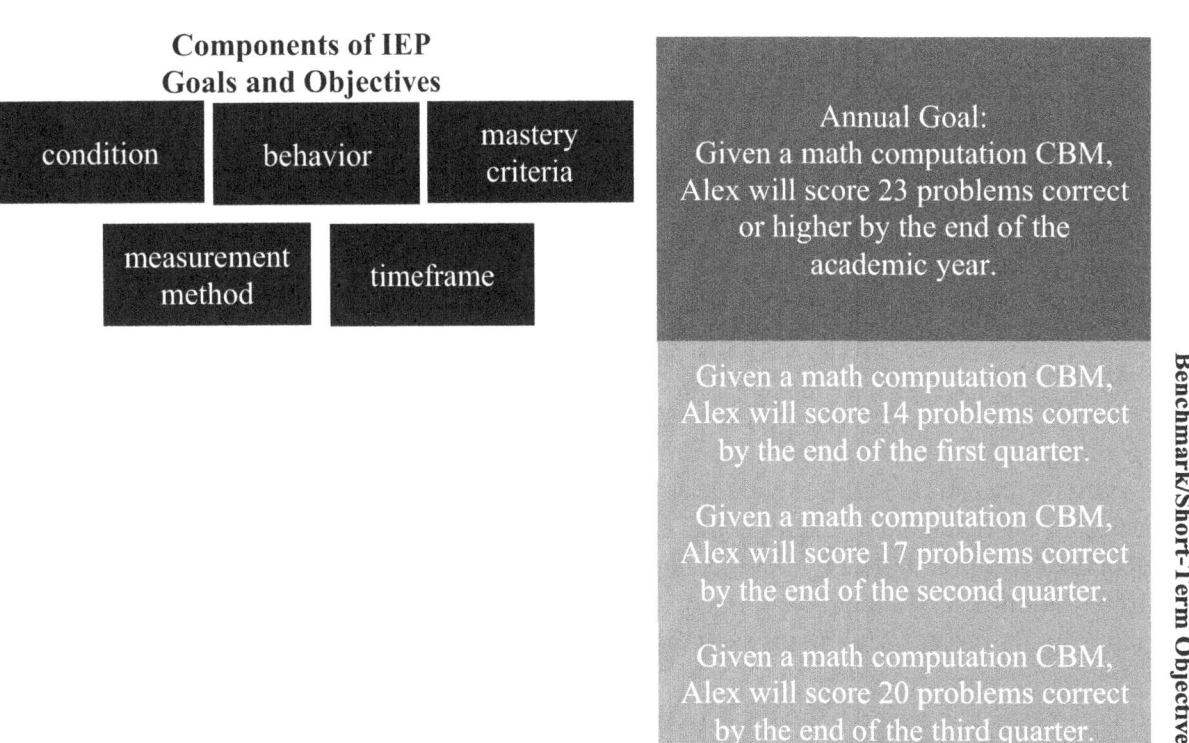

Putting it All Together

From a practical standpoint, the strategies in this chapter will be most useful if applied during the initial year planning to map out a year-long plan for instruction, and during each annual review for students' IEPs with goals in mind for both the current school year and the next academic year. To synthesize everything discussed, Table 3 provides a suggested step-by-step planning approach modified from Saunders et al. (2013). A blank copy of this planning approach is in the Appendices.

Table 3
Steps for Instructional Planning using Alignment and Contextualized Math

	Steps for Planning	**Activities/Examples**
1	Select, understand, and prioritize standards	<ul><li>Collaborate with general education teacher</li><li>Prioritize and pinpoint standards</li><li>Ensure alignment with IEP and assessment; this may require modifying IEP to create better alignment</li></ul>
2	Give standards a real-world context	<ul><li>Use contextualized math approach to build generalization of skills to everyday life</li><li>Use simulations, video models, or applications in context</li></ul>
3	Use evidence-based and research-based practices to teach	<ul><li>Explicit instruction</li><li>Systematic instruction</li><li>Task analytic instruction</li><li>Manipulatives</li><li>Graphic organizer</li><li>Technology-aided instruction</li><li>Embedded instruction</li></ul>
4	Select instructional supports	<ul><li>Self-monitoring checklist</li><li>Manipulatives</li><li>Graphic organizers</li></ul>
5	Monitor Progress	<ul><li>Create data sheet to match instructional activity and IEP goal</li><li>Collect data, review, and revise as needed</li></ul>

Table 4 provides an example of how a teacher might utilize the table during planning modified from Root et al. (2020). In this example, Root and colleagues built on a prior study (Root et al., 2018) to evaluate the effectiveness of using a contextualized approach for solving percent of change problems (grade-level standard) using modified schema-based instruction (instructional method). The students selected the location for shopping from a choice board, then watched a video scenario of the problem taking place in the community, before solving for the final price after a coupon was applied, and finally had to use the next dollar strategy to state how much money would be needed to make the purchase (contextualized math activity). A blank copy of this planning form is in the Appendices.

Table 4
Sample Planning Form using the Process in Table 3

Grade-aligned standard:	IEP Goal:	Contextualized Math Activity:	Instructional Methods:	Measurement Method:
Grade 7: Solving percent of change problems "Use proportional relationships to solve multistep ratio and percent problems. Examples: simple interest, tax, markups and markdowns, gratuities and commissions, fees, percent increase and decrease, percent error."	Given multiplicative word problems requiring percent of change and a self-monitoring checklist, Wes will solve at least two problems correctly, completing 20 out of 24 steps for 3 consecutive sessions.	• Using a coupon to find the final cost of an item • Use actual coupons and receipts to build generalization • Determine if the student has enough money using next dollar method • Plan for community applications when possible	Modified schema-based instruction using explicit instruction, a task analysis for self-monitoring, and a graphic organizer; system of least prompts delivered for each step of task analysis	Task analytic data sheet

Conclusion

It is important for teachers to use IEPs to drive instruction for students with ASD/IDD and to ensure alignment between their instruction, the assessment, and the general curriculum. Mathematics related IEP goals should align with grade-level standards but may include some foundational skills (often taught in earlier grade levels) as well that are critical for the student to master in order to make progress in more complex math. Teachers should plan instruction using sound evidence-based and research-based practices and ensure they are teaching conceptual understanding of skills. Implementing a contextualized approach, where the standards are taught in meaningful and relevant ways with clear applications to everyday life, will build generalization of the math skills so they are useful for students with ASD/IDD.

References

Collins, B. C. (2012). *Systematic instruction for students with moderate and severe disabilities.* Brookes.

Courtade, G., & Browder, D. (2016). *Aligning IEPs to state standards for students with moderate-to-severe disabilities.* Attainment.

Fuchs, L. S., & Fuchs, D. (n.d.) *Using curriculum based measurements in response to intervention framework: Introduction to using CBM for progress monitoring in math.* National Center on Response to Intervention: American Institutes for Research. https://rti4success.org/resource/using-cbm-determine-response-intervention

Hedin, L., & DeSpain, S. (2018). SMART or Not? Writing specific, measurable IEP goals. *TEACHING Exceptional Children, 51*(2), 100-110. https://doi.org/10.1177/0040059918802587

Institute for Mathematics and Education. (2011). *CCSSM Clickable Map 2.0.* Retrieved from http:/commoncoretools.me/wp-content/uploads/2011/11/ccssm-hyperlinked-map1.ppsx

Jung, L. A. (2007). Writing SMART objectives and strategies that fit the ROUTINE. *TEACHING Exceptional Children, 39*(4), 54-58. https://doi.org/10.1177/004005990703900406

Lee, A., Browder, D. M., Flowers, C., & Wakeman, S. (2016). Teacher evaluation of resources designed for adapting mathematics for students with significant cognitive disabilities. *Research and Practice for Persons with Severe Disabilities, 41,* 132-137. https://doi.org/10.1177/1540796916634099

National Governors Association Center for Best Practices & Council of Chief State School Officers. (2010). *Common Core State Standards for Mathematics (CCSSM).* Washington, DC: Author.

Root, J. R., Cox, S. K., Hammons, N., Saunders, A. F., & Gilley, D. (2018). Contextualizing mathematics: Teaching problem solving to secondary students with intellectual and developmental disabilities. *Intellectual and Developmental Disabilities*, *56*(6), 442-457. doi.org://10.1352/1934-9556-56.6.442

Root, J. R., Cox, S. C., Hammons, N., & Davis, K. (2020). Contextualizing mathematical problem solving instruction for secondary students with extensive support needs: A systematic replication. *Research and Practice for Persons with Severe Disabilities*. Advance online publication.

Saunders, A., Bethune, K. S., Spooner, F., & Browder, D. B. (2013). Solving the Common Core equation: Teaching Mathematics CCSS to students with moderate and severe disabilities. *Teaching Exceptional Children*, *45(3)*, 24-33.

Saunders, A. F., Root, J. R., & Jimenez, B. A. (2019). Recommendations for inclusive educational practices in mathematics for students with extensive support needs. *Inclusion*, *7*(2), 75-91. doi.org:// 10.1352/2326=6988-7.2.75

Trela, K., & Jimenez, B. A. (2013). From different to differentiated: Using "ecological framework" to support personally relevant access to general curriculum for students with significant intellectual disabilities. *Research and Practice for Persons with Severe Disabilities*, *38*(2), 117–119. https://doi.org/10.2511/027494813807714537

Chapter 2: Using Data to Design and Evaluate Math Instruction

Sarah Cox, Jenny Root, and Addie McConomy

Students with autism spectrum disorder and intellectual and developmental disabilities (ASD/IDD) can and do learn mathematics when provided high-quality instruction. Educational research helps identify interventions that are likely to be effective for students with specific characteristics. However, finding the best intervention or mix of interventions for specific students is a responsibility that rests on classroom teachers. Individualized education is the hallmark of special education. Teachers should draw from scientifically validated practices to create educational opportunities for students based on both their own pedagogical and content expertise and familiarity with an individual student's strengths and needs.

Supports for Mathematical Learning

Teachers should take student characteristics and learning history into account as they select and implement instructional practices and supports for individual students (Jimenez & Saunders, 2019). Students with ASD/IDD benefit from executive functioning supports. Executive functioning skills help students self-regulate and organize, which can be areas of need for individuals with ASD/IDD (Cragg & Gilmore, 2014; Hill, 2004). Students with ASD/IDD often have strengths in recognizing specific details, at the expense of realizing the larger concept formed from those details. These difficulties are known as weak central coherence (Frith & Happe, 1994), and can lead to strengths in routine procedures, but difficulties in connecting mathematical concepts. Mathematics education is no longer focused on rote procedures. As education has shifted away from the "Back to the Basics" movement and toward a more equitable mathematics education for all, teachers are encouraged to help students understand how and why procedures explain or solve mathematical phenomena (National Council for Teachers of Mathematics [NCTM], 2000).

Communication skills required to explain mathematical thinking may be a barrier to developing the robust understanding of mathematical concepts encouraged by mathematics education experts such as the National Council for Teachers of Mathematics (NCTM) as well as the Common Core State Standards (National Governor's Association, 2010). Further, students with ASD/IDD often experience a hard time understanding other people's perspectives (i.e., Theory of Mind). In mathematics, this can present challenges when students are asked to solve application-based problems that depict unfamiliar problems for unknown persons in unfamiliar contexts. For example, in the problem "An Olympic runner set a record for the 100m dash. The time was ten and sixty-two hundredths seconds. How would you write this as a number?" Students who are unfamiliar with the Olympics or track and field may not understand the premise of the question. These application-based problems are intended to help students use mathematics outside of the classroom, but also require perspective taking to unfamiliar contexts. Table 1 outlines examples of how these areas of need present in students' mathematical performance, and solutions teachers can consider to support these needs.

Students enter our classrooms with unique learning histories. These past experiences influence student preparedness to participate in mathematical learning opportunities as well as their individual expectations of what behavior is expected in a classroom. For some students with ASD/IDD, early grade instruction may have focused on behavioral or social goals, reducing the amount of time allocated for reading or mathematics instruction. Mathematics instruction that overemphasized functional skills such as time, money, and purchasing may also leave students without prerequisite or facilitating skills (e.g., estimation, number system knowledge; Cowan et al., 2014) to make progress in grade-aligned mathematics instruction. Alternatively, some students with ASD/IDD need additional time to develop these mathematics skills, and therefore may enter future grades needing supplementary instruction in foundational literacy or numeracy. These past learning experiences can create barriers for students with ASD/IDD if teachers do not provide adequate scaffolds or intensive instruction to reduce potential barriers. Table 1 contains examples of potential instructional solutions to minimize these barriers.

Table 1
Support Needs for Students with ASD/IDD Relative to Mathematics

Areas of Support	Elementary Example	Secondary Example	Potential Solutions
Student Level Characteristics			
Executive Functioning	When solving multi-step word problems, students may only complete the first procedure.	When learning to add, subtract, multiply, and divide fractions, students may overgeneralize procedures across operations	Incorporate self-monitoring strategies and visual supports to help students complete the task. Fade the supports as students move towards fluency.
Weak Central Coherence	When solving mathematical word problems, students may immediately add numerical quantities together rather than reading the full problem to understand the context and what operation is needed	Students may not generalize mathematical properties or procedures learned in school to another setting (e.g., community).	Intentionally plan for generalization by using multiple examples.
Communication /Reasoning	When asked to explain how they know their answer makes sense, the student may not be able to articulate their mathematical reasoning or may focus on the procedure rather than the justification.	During geometry lessons, students may have a difficult time explaining the geometric properties required to complete the proof process.	Use think alouds to model internal thought processes and allow students to practice sharing their thoughts in the student's preferred modality (e.g., written expression, verbal expression, pictorial representations through response items).
Theory of Mind	Students may have difficulty with cognitive flexibility, leading to not recognizing multiple strategies can be used to find the same solution.	When analyzing data, the student may not be able to make judgements and then express how the data informs their decision making.	Use explicit instruction to model, support, and give opportunities to practice cognitive flexibility and critical evaluation.

	Learning History		
Level of Literacy	Students may not exhibit fluent reading skills, and therefore are unable to access opportunities to engage in applied mathematical problems such as word problems.	During small group instruction, students may have a difficult time interpreting the mathematical vocabulary inherent in higher-level mathematical concepts (e.g., difference between numerator, denominator, mixed numbers and improper fractions).	Ensure students have meaningful opportunities to develop literacy skills while engaging in more abstract mathematics. Read alouds, text-to-speech assistive technology, and adapted text can all make text-based mathematics more accessible. Visual supports can also help students learn advanced mathematical vocabulary.
Level of Numeracy	Students may not enter school with the same numeracy skills as their typically developing peers. Therefore, they may not have important pre-requisite skills to draw on as they move forward in math (e.g., lack of one to one correspondence will make creating sets with manipulatives difficult)	Students may not be exposed to more complex or abstract mathematics until they reach mastery on what is seen as prerequisite skills (e.g., not exposed to multiplicative relationships because they haven't memorized addition or subtraction facts)	Expose students to grade-aligned complex mathematical concepts by using supports such as manipulatives or a calculator. Promote conceptual understanding while reducing the need for procedural skills.
Expectations	Students may exhibit behavioral challenges, and therefore the majority of instructional time is spent on pro-social behaviors expected to participate in classroom environments.	Early grade instruction often focuses on behavioral expectations and rote mathematical skills, leading to decreased expectations of the student's cognitive abilities.	Maintain high behavioral and academic expectations for students at all grade levels using positive behavioral supports and academic standards to guide instructional decisions.

This chapter is designed to help teachers make instructional decisions based on data and evidence-based practices to help reduce potential barriers for individual students, ensuring all students have adequate opportunities to learn mathematics. We will discuss the iterative (i.e., circular or repetitive) nature of instructional implementation, and provide examples of how this process can be used to improve mathematical outcomes for students with ASD/IDD.

Instructional Process

While instructional planning should begin with quality instructional practices effective for similar students with ASD/IDD, special education teachers must continuously monitor student progress and then adjust their instruction to include, add or remove supports based on what each individual student needs. Providing inadequate supports leads to insufficient opportunities to learn. On the other hand, providing too many supports can cause students to become unnecessarily reliant and limit independence and generalization. To balance this, teachers must engage in an iterative and ongoing planning process to assess the adequacy of instruction and make corresponding changes.

Teachers determine what to teach students based on a combination of IEP objectives, age-appropriate educational standards, and diagnostic assessment data identifying areas of need, as discussed in Chapter 1 of this book, which focuses on contextualizing mathematics standards. The iterative process outlined in this chapter (see Figure 1) occurs once these educational objectives (i.e., what to teach) have been identified. The process consists of (a) selecting and implementing a high-quality instructional strategy, (b) monitoring student progress, (c) making a decision regarding next instructional steps, (d) and then planning for additional adaptations or moving onto next steps in the learning progression. Figure 1 provides an outline of the intervention decision making flow chart and corresponds to the sections below. Although the process itself can be applied to multiple academic, behavioral, or social learning goals, for the purpose of this instructional text, we will focus on using this iterative decision-making process to teach mathematics to students with ASD/IDD. At the end of this chapter, we have provided two vignettes outlining how this iterative process can be used with different students.

Step 1: Select Instructional Strategy

The first step of the iterative decision-making process is selecting an effective instructional strategy to teach the specified mathematics goal (Cox & Root, 2020). This decision should be made after reviewing up-to-date evidence-based practices (EBP) for students with

Figure 1

Intervention Decision Making Flow Chart

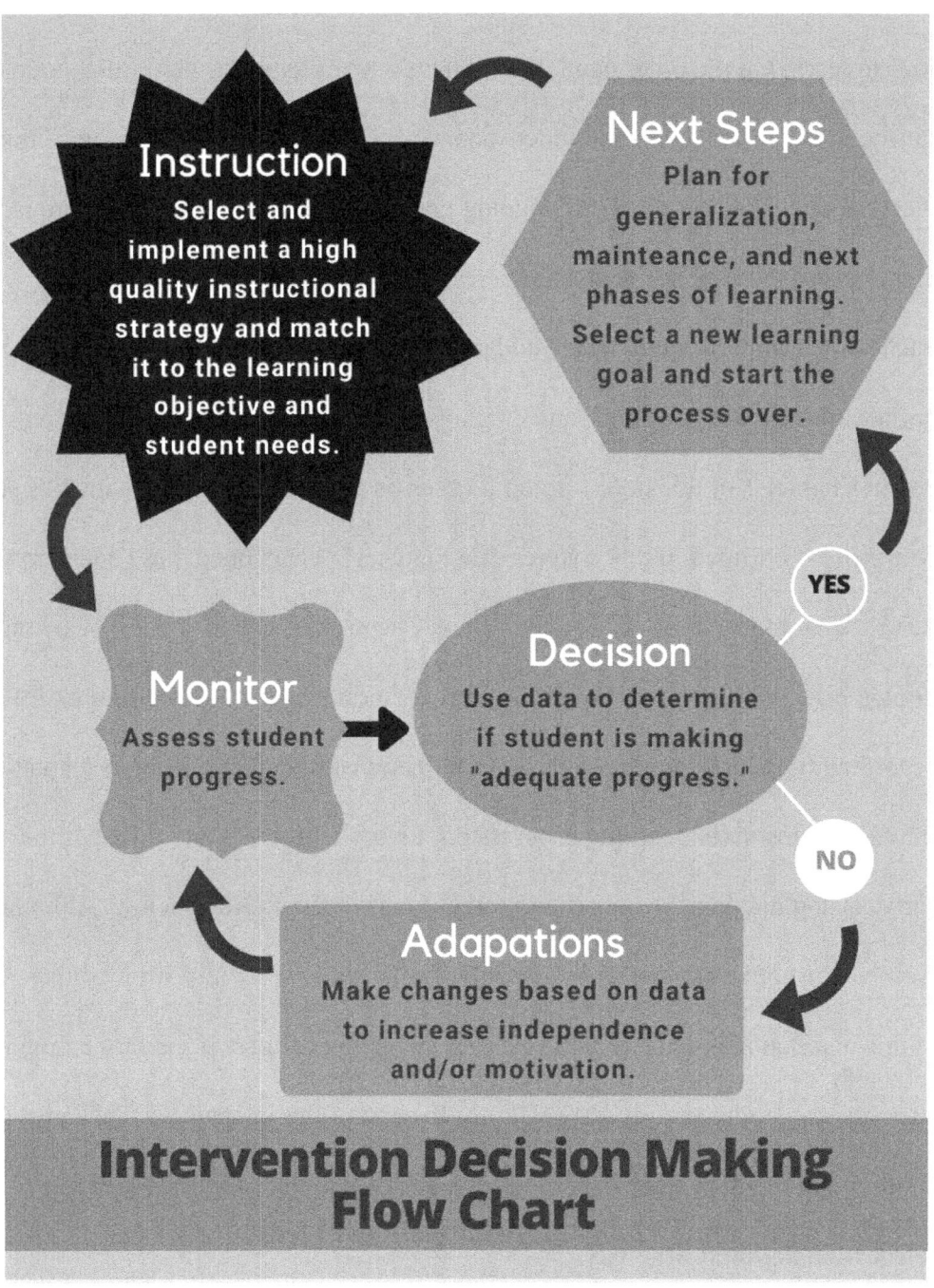

Note. Reprinted from *GCA Lab Blog,* Cox & Root (2020) thttps://gcalab.wixsite.com/gcalabfsu/post/intervention-decision-making-flow-chart

ASD/IDD. Ongoing research continuously adds to what we know works for which students under what conditions. Currently, researchers have identified systematic instruction, technology-aided instruction, graphic organizer/heuristic, manipulatives, and explicit instruction as evidence-based practice for teaching mathematics to students with ASD/IDD (Spooner et al., 2019). Matching the instructional strategy to the individual student and the targeted skill will increase the likelihood of effectiveness. By using an instructional strategy that is matched to the learner's needs and content to be taught, there is an increased likelihood that the instruction will be effective. Table 2 outlines the EBPs Spooner et al. identified for teaching students with ASD/IDD.

Step 2: Monitor

Monitoring student progress is the only way to determine effectiveness of instruction. Assessments play two main roles in mathematics instruction: summative and formative evaluations of student learning. Summative assessments occur at the end of a unit of learning or a specified amount of time and evaluate the overall progress students have made and typically include multiple skills (Root, Wood, et al. 2019). The intent of summative assessments is to measure individual student's mastery of the content. Formative assessments are often seen by the teacher and student as part of the learning or teaching process (Root, Wood, et al., 2019). In fact, federal legislation (e.g., Every Student Succeeds Act, 2015) emphasizes the importance of using formative assessment to deliver effective instruction.

Indirect Observation

One useful formative assessment measure is indirect observation, which occurs when teachers collect data from sources other than directly measuring the student's performance themselves (Root, Wood, et al., 2019). Reports from other professionals in the classroom (e.g.,

Table 2

Evidence-based Practices for Teaching Mathematics to Students with ASD/IDD

Instructional Strategy	Description	Examples
Systematic Instruction	Instruction based on the principles of Applied Behavior Analysis (ABA). Begins by defining the targeted skill(s), defining methods to use during instruction, directly teaching, and reviewing progress to modify instruction (Collins, 2012). Common methods in math instruction include task analytic instruction, system of least prompts, constant time delay, and simultaneous prompting.	System of least prompts is one systematic instruction technique that can be used to support independence by using only the necessary level of support. *To support independence in using a calculator, teacher could use a 3-level prompting hierarchy, such as: (1) verbal prompt (e.g., use your calculator to find 20% of $15 so you know how much your tip will be), (2) gesture (e.g., point to the percent button and then multiplication button), (3) model + retest (e.g., "Watch me, I'm going to type 20% x 15 = to find 20% of 15. Your turn.)*
Technology aided instruction (TAI)	Instruction or intervention in which technology is the central feature and the technology is specifically designed or employed to support learning or performance of a behavior or skill (Stenbrenner et al., 2020)	Video models are a form of TAI and can be used to teach students how to use math tools. *The teacher could create a video of herself using a protractor to measure an angle. The student would then watch the video before trying to measure an angle independently.*
Graphic organizer	Mathematics graphic organizers use visual representations (i.e., diagrams) to represent mathematical relationships to promote conceptual understanding.	Modified Schema-Based Instruction uses multiple forms of graphic organizers to teach mathematical problem-solving behaviors (Root & Browder, 2019). *A schema (diagram) can be used to map the mathematical quantities in a word problem onto a diagram. Problem-solving heuristics can also be used to guide students through a problem solving practice, reducing language requirements needed for traditional mnemonic strategies. For example, when a student is solving a multiplication word problem, they will need to write their equation with labels. A graphic organizer using different shapes for the referent, multiplier, and product will help learners organize the information in a uniform way.*
Manipulatives	The use of virtual or concrete objects to represent abstract mathematical procedures and concepts.	Manipulatives-based instructional sequences use concrete or virtual manipulatives to teach students the mathematical concept in addition to the procedure (see Chapter 4). *To teach multiplication, teacher can first use concrete or virtual manipulatives to make "copies" or sets of items, for example to represent*

		4x2 they would have four plates with two counters on each. Then moving to representation, students would learn to draw representations, such as four circles with two dots in each. If students are ready for abstract, they can memorize the algorithm or use a calculator to find 4x2.
Explicit instruction	The guided learning process supports students through a series of scaffolds and supports. Explicit instruction provides students a model and opportunities for practice opportunities (Archer & Hughes, 2011).	Model-lead-test or "I do, we do, you do" can be used to explicitly teach and then give scaffolded opportunities to practice a new skill. *When teaching students to find a common denominator, a teacher would first review previous related information (i.e., fractions have equal parts; what is a numerator, what is a denominator). Then the instructor would provide a reason the students might need to find a common denominator (e.g., sometimes we want to compare, add, or subtract fractions, but we can't do that unless we make sure they have the same denominator). Next, the teacher would model how to find a common denominator for two fractions (i.e., lead the class in completing the problem, demonstrating how to find common denominators while the class participates in errorless learning). After the model, the students would have an opportunity to complete a problem with immediate feedback (e.g., choral responding, group work). Finally, the students would have the opportunity to complete problems independently, to allow the teacher an opportunity to observe their current level of performance.*

paraprofessionals, general education teachers, therapists) can give helpful data. Families also provide useful information regarding student's progress. Teachers can talk with caregivers about how the student is doing at home when working on homework or when using the identified skills in a different setting. This information is highly valuable, as students with ASD/IDD often experience difficulties generalizing newly taught skills to unfamiliar settings.

Similarly, special education teachers can collect information from others who observe the students in different settings. For example, secondary students who are practicing job skills such as stocking shelves might need to utilize a specific mathematical skill such as patterning, computation, or spatial reasoning. The way skills are taught and practiced in the classroom setting will differ from a real-world setting. For example, a student working on making sets in the classroom may use mathematics manipulatives to represent quantities from an equation, but in a restaurant work environment this learner may be counting and placing silverware packets for patrons. While the application of the skill is different, errors made in the workplace could inform the classroom teacher of ways to modify the instruction to ensure that the discrete skill is generalizable. Teachers should check in with the job coach or employer to see if they are generalizing discretely taught skills from the classroom to their work environment.

Direct Observation

Perhaps the most common form of formative assessment is direct observation. During direct observation, teachers watch students as they perform mathematical tasks (Root, Wood, et al., 2019). These observations can occur as students complete independent work as the teacher walks around and observes student responses. It can also take place during guided practice activities, when students share their reasoning for selecting particular answers. Additionally, direct observation can occur through permanent products, allowing the teacher to analyze student's understanding in their written work. Table 3 provides four examples of direct observation that can be used within instruction on place value.

Math interviews. Math interviews are a method of direct assessment that allow students to explain their mathematical reasoning during a structured activity (Van de Walle et al., 2013). Understanding the reasoning and problem-solving strategies utilized by students with ASD/IDD can be simultaneously useful and also difficult to ascertain. Knowing the reasoning students employ when solving problems can help teachers address any misconceptions or incomplete conceptual understanding for students. However, not all formative assessments help teachers identify the "how" or "why" behind students' mathematical reasoning.

Task-based interviews are one version of math interviews that present problem-solving situations to students, asking students to make predictions, judgements, and comparisons during structured interviews (Goldin, 1997). Teachers can then further probe the student by asking specific follow-up questions contained in the task scripts. These structured problem-solving tasks are particularly useful after students have demonstrated acquisition and are working toward fluency or maintenance, as they provide useful information about where they are in their reasoning and learning process. For example, for students who are learning about fractions, a task-based interview can be used to identify how well they are able to describe their conceptual understanding of fractions separate from procedural tasks of solving computations with fractions. A teacher might give the student a pile of unifix cubes and says "I made 9 cookies for us to share. How many cookies should each of us take?". If the student takes the 9 cubes and splits them into 2 groups with one left over and answers 4, the teacher could follow up with "what if we wanted to eat all of the cookies?" If the student understands the concept of fractions, they would be able to answer 4 ½. Students who divide 9 by 2 and answer 4.5 might show they understand the procedure of division. The teacher could then follow up with "I am going to make thank you cards to send to my friends. Each friend is going to receive exactly 4 cards. I already made 10 cards. How many friends get a set of cards?" In this way, the teacher can observe if the student conceptually understands fractions, because the answer would be 2 friends rather than 2 ½ friends, because it wouldn't make sense to have half a friend.

Teachers can include additional supports or adaptations to conduct math interviews for students who use augmented or alternative communication (AAC) devices or students who are

Table 3

Examples of Direct Observation Used in Place Value Mathematics Instruction

Direct Observation Occurring	Form of Direct Observation	Examples for Place-Value instruction
Whole-Class Instruction	Choral Responding—Teacher uses a system with indicator to have students respond in unison to the posed question, either chorally (out loud), with hand signals (e.g., thumbs up, thumbs down) or by showing answers (e.g., response boards.)	When the teacher clicks her pen, the students respond in unison. The teacher asks "How many tens are in the number 31?" The teacher clicks her pen. The students respond "3" in unison, either vocally or by pressing the "3" on an AAC device. The teacher watches and listens for any students who do not respond with the expected answer.
Group or Partner Work	Teacher Questioning—The teacher asks intentional questions designed to evaluate students' current level of performance.	The students are working together to add double-digit numbers that require re-grouping. One of the posed questions was 26 + 17 = ?. The teacher walks around and watches how students add. Do they use 3 tens and 13 ones? Do they trade the 13 ones to create an additional ten and 3 ones? For groups who are counting by ones only (each individual base-ten block), the teacher might ask "Is there an easier way to count this number using your base-ten blocks?" If the students continue to count by ones, the teacher might model a different problem where she counted by tens, and then ask the group to solve a different problem.
Seat Work (Individual)	Permanent Product—With a permanent product, the students are asked to turn various types of evidence at the end of a session. Permanent products may include worksheets with example problems or a math journal entry.	The teacher asks the students to complete a worksheet with three questions similar to: "break apart one or both numbers to make them easier to add, then solve 27 + 12 = ___" Individual students then solve the equation. The teacher can use the worksheets to observe which students are using partial sums or adding by place value (e.g., 20 + 10 = 30, 7 + 2 = 9, 30 + 9 = 39), and observe students who are using alternative methods or making errors when solving.
Lesson wrap-up	Exit Tickets—A quick permanent product the students complete as they leave the classroom. This can be content-based (a question about what they have learned) or it can be a self-assessment of their learning.	The teacher hands out strips of paper with four emoji faces on them. The student is then asked to select which emoji best represents their learning progression. (1) I understand it well enough to teach it to someone else; (2) I can usually do this on my own, but sometimes I get stuck; (3) I am starting to understand, but I still need more practice; (4) I really don't understand this yet, HELP

minimally vocal. Before conducting a math interview with a student who uses AAC, teachers should program the device to ensure the student has adequate responses to the various questions. The teacher should conduct the same interview with peers and provide comparable options for the student programed into the device. Students with limited meaningful vocalizations, who do not use AAC consistently, can also participate in math interviews with appropriate supports. Teachers should provide an array of three choices for the student to select as responses. The array should contain one correct answer, one common error, and one distractor. For example, if the interview question was about patterning (two orange dots, one purple dot, two orange dots, one purple dot…what is the next dot) the array would include a picture of a purple dot, a picture of an orange dot, and a picture of a green dot. This allows the interviewer to observe if the student is in early acquisition and unaware of patterns (selects green dot), in acquisition phase and aware of patterning but unable to complete an AABAAB pattern (selects purple dot), or is building fluency and able to complete an AABAAB pattern (selects orange dot).

Checklists and task analysis. Checklists and task analysis are additional ways to provide meaningful assessment data to inform instructional decisions. Checklists are an informal method to assess skills across settings (Root, Wood, et al., 2019). In mathematics, the checklist may assess mastery of, for example, whole number identification, sign recognition, counting up procedure. An advantage of checklists is they do not need to be completed in one setting. The teacher can interview other providers working with the student, and complete observations over several days to collect data. Comprehensive checklists can be developed by all people who support the student in the area the checklist is being developed for. For example, if the mathematics skill being assessed is community purchasing, family members spending time in the community with the student should be involved in developing the checklist (see Figure 2 for an

Figure 2
Example of Checklist for Purchasing Skills

Checklist for community purchasing skills using cash Observer:					
Skill	Dates observed correctly				Notes on consistent errors
Identify value of coins					
Identify value of bills					
Uses dollar up when paying					
Uses estimation to check for expected total					
Uses receipt to count change					

example). Checklists may help with determining generalization, as they reveal areas of mastery in all settings and areas of need (Brown et al., 2020).

Task analysis is a valid and efficient tool because it supports instruction and assessment simultaneously. Task analyses can be used by teachers to collect data, but they can also be used by teachers to deliver instruction, as well as by the student to keep track of progress. This allows for frequent and efficient data collection that can be used by the teacher and the student to set goals (Brown et al., 2020). Task analysis is well suited for math instruction and assessment because it allows for measurement of each step in the desired skill. This step-by-step analysis creates an opportunity to identify specific areas of difficulty, which can then be addressed during instruction.

In order to develop a task analysis, the teacher should observe the student completing the task and complete the task personally. Each step should be recorded in a format that is easily understood by the learner. One way the task analysis can be used for assessment during instruction is to gather data on the level of prompt needed to support the learner in completing each step. Teachers may indicate the student completed the step independently correctly (IC), with a specific verbal prompt (SV), or a student may self-correct (SC) their initial error. This information can inform instructional decisions for fading or increasing supports (Courtade et al., 2010). In mathematics, task analysis can be used for any skill that requires a sequence of steps, such as finding a percent of change (Root, Cox, et al. 2020) and solving word problems (Browder et al., 2018).

As discussed in Chapter 1, data sheets should be developed that align to the instructional task. When using task analysis to break mathematics tasks into teachable components, the data sheet should facilitate documenting student performance on each step. One useful way to orient the data sheet is actually to list the steps in backwards chronological order and take data from the bottom up—known as an upside-down task analysis (Spooner & Test, 1996). The backward sequence allows for the creation of a graph right on the data sheet. Figure 3 provides an example of an upside-down task analysis. As the learner progresses through the steps, the teacher should use each box in the column that aligns to the session to collect data on the completion of the step. The teacher can use a slash mark to indicate the step was completed independently or use annotations to collect step level data. For example, a teacher may use a system of least prompts when fading supports. The teacher can code the level of prompt needed for each step of the task analysis using annotations linked to the prompt required. Figure 3 provides an example of an upside-down task analysis where the teacher collected data on the level of prompt needed as a student solved a percent of change word problem. The figure provides directions for how to create the graph with the data and an interpretation of the provided data. This intuitive process creates data easily and can be used to inform instructional decisions.

Curriculum-based monitoring. Curriculum based monitoring (CBM) allows teachers to use a standardized process to assess long-term goal progress in reading, spelling, written expression and math concepts (Hosp & Hosp, 2003). CBM is a simple way to measure a student's progress in the curriculum. It is reliable, valid, efficient, easily understood, and inexpensive (Deno, 1985). CBM provides a way to collect frequent, formative assessment data that aligns with student instruction. Data can be collected several times a week because the individual assessments require minimal materials and only take a few minutes. The frequent collection of data allows for timely adjustments in instruction.

Math CBMs should use probes of questions that are gathered from the curriculum that students are expected to make progress in during the school year. Students will be provided a specific number of minutes to complete the probe. The duration of the probe should be individualized for the student and used consistently throughout the school year (e.g., 2 minutes, 4 minutes, 6 minutes). When deciding how much time a student should be permitted, consider the individual student's processing time and current strategies for calculating. The goal of CBM is to assess the student's fluency, not to increase their anxiety over recalling math facts. Some students may feel anxious or pressured when they are aware of being timed or be upset that they didn't have the chance to "finish" if there are some problems left when the timer goes off. Timed CBM data is one piece of evidence that is crucial in determining which phase of learning the student is in. For a discussion on the impact of timed tests on student anxiety, along with alternative types of assessments, please consult work by Boaler (2014; 2019).

When a student indicates increased anxiety or fear about the narrow amount of time, teachers can allow the student the opportunity to complete all the problems while also making a note of which problems had been completed at the designated time point (e.g., 2 minutes, 4

Figure 3

Upside Down Task Analysis

Steps to solve a percent of change problem														
9. Sign your name on the receipt and return to the cashier	SV	IC	GV	IC	IC									
8. Write the total amount you want to leave on your receipt	EC	SV	IC	IC	IC									
7. Write the final cost in the purple oval	M	M	SV	SV	(IC)									
6. Add the original cost and the amount of change	SV	SV	GV	(IC)	IC									
5. Write the amount of change in the bottom triangle – this is your tip	EC	EC	M	EC	M									
4. Multiply 20% by the original amount to find your tip	EC	M	(SV)	SV	GV									
3. Write the percentage of tip you want to leave in the top red triangle	GV	(IC)	GV	IC	IC									
2. Write the subtotal in the blue square for original amount	(IC)	IC	IC	IC	IC									
1. Check if the receipt is correct	IC	IC	IC	IC	IC									
Session number	1	2	3	4	5	6	7	8	9	10	11	12	13	14
Session Date	2/18	2/19	2/22	2/23	2/25									
Prompting Key: IC = Independently Correct GV = General Verbal SV = Specific Verbal M = Model EC = Error Correction														
Directions: For each step of the task analysis, write the final level of prompt required before the student completed the step correctly. After all the steps are complete, count the number of independently correct (IC) steps for that day, and circle the corresponding number on the chart. Note, the number of steps IC in one day may not land on an IC for the specific step, circle based on the overall number of IC steps for that session. Draw a connecting line from the circle from the previous session to the completed session, this will form a graph of the student's independently correct steps over sessions.														

Notes: This upside-down task analysis provides two forms of evidence the student is improving in their ability to independently complete the math problem. First, the graph shows an increase in the number of independently solved steps from 2 correct in the first session steadily increasing to 7 steps in the fifth session. Secondly, the chart shows that the intensity of the prompts required is decreasing for most steps. When examining each step, the teacher can see the student is consistently completing steps one and two independently correct.

minutes) to assess fluency. Both of these data points might be informative (e.g., how many were finished correctly at 2 minutes, how many were finished correctly at the end, and how long it took to complete them all). This level of data may inform IEP teams as they make decisions regarding accommodations on high-stakes summative assessments like end of grade tests. The correct number of individual digits will be scored and graphed. Each CBM math probe should contain questions based on all problem types that will be taught throughout the year. No problems should be repeated but varying the numerals in the problems will allow an easy way to alter the problem and maintain the problem type. To establish a baseline score students should be administered three probes in one session or over consecutive days. The median number of correct digits should be used as the baseline and first data point graphed. (Hosp & Hosp, 2003). CBMs should be administered over the school year, ideally weekly. It is important that the IEP team determine a logical expected growth, students may be expected to show improvement of one additional correct digit bi-weekly or more or less frequently. Establishing the expected growth is an important component of instructional decision making and will need to be individually determined for students with ASD/IDD.

Step 3: Making Data-Based Decisions

The purpose of monitoring student progress is to use data to adjust instruction accordingly (i.e., data-based decision making; Jimenez et al., 2012). This process focuses on assessing the effectiveness of instruction and matching teaching methods to the needs of the student. As demonstrated in Figure 1, the instructional decision-making process is not linear, but rather iterative, and driven by analysis of student data. Multiple sources of data can and should be used to make these decisions, yet we caution teachers to compare "apples to apples". That is, directly comparing data from a CBM to a task analysis would not be appropriate. Rather, multiple sources can inform teachers of the conditions under which students are successful or demonstrate need for additional supports. For example, if a CBM indicates the student is able to fluently subtract (e.g., 10-3), but a task analysis for determining change when purchasing (e.g., change needed when $10 is given for $3 purchase) indicates the student is not able to complete all steps independently speaks more to generalization of the skill. Teachers can use data from error analysis, discrepancy analysis, and visual analysis to make instructional decisions.

Error Analysis

When teachers observe student behavior to watch for similar errors being made, it is called an error analysis (Peltier & Peltier, 2020). Error analysis is most beneficial when it uses a permanent product to evaluate student learning (Peltier & Peltier). Both task analysis and CBMs are good sources of data for error analysis. By analyzing the steps students take to solve problems rather than only the solution, teachers gain useful information to guide instructional decisions (Peltier & Peltier). Similar to math interviews, error analyses focus on student reasoning. However, in error analysis, teachers can observe student behavior and/or use permanent products rather than a structured interview. This allows teachers to compare student work samples, like completed task analysis or CBMs, making it easier to identify similar strengths or areas of need. After analyzing student errors, teachers can pin-point instruction that would be beneficial to the whole class, small-groups, or individual students based on observed patterns of performance. For example, during a unit on decimals, the teacher can use data from a CBM probe to analyze overall and individual performance. By conducting an error analysis of the students' responses to the CBM probe, the teacher can determine the current strengths and weaknesses related to the unit on decimals, and subsequently align instruction to address observed patterns of errors (National Center on Intensive Intervention, 2016). One error analysis method is to calculate the number of correct digits when students complete a computation CBM.

In a CBM computation error analysis, the teacher would administer the CBM probe to all students in the class and then create a table to compare responses. Table 4 below provides an outline of this table. To complete the table, the teacher would first write the correct problem with the correct answer in the second column. The teacher would then add two columns for each student, one column for the student's response (or answer) and a second column to calculate the number of correct digits contained in the student's response. The teacher would then compare each student's response to the correct answer to calculate the number of correct digits. The teacher would compare the digit in each place value from the correct answer to the student's response. For every correct digit (in the correct place value), the student would score one point. For example, if the answer was 123 and the student answered 12, the student would receive 0 correct points, because the correct answer has 1 hundred, 2 tens, and 3 ones while the student's response was 1 ten and 2 ones. The teacher can then use the error analysis chart to make instructional decisions.

Discrepancy Analysis

Discrepancy analysis is a way to identify and prioritize skills to target as well as determine what supports a student may need to be successful (Root, Wood, et al., 2019). Whereas error analysis focuses on the pattern of errors a student makes, discrepancy analysis compares performance to typically developing same-age peers in order to identify discrepancies between current and desired skill level. According to Root, Wood, et al. this process can be guided by three questions: (1) What would a same-age peer without disabilities do in this situation?, (2) What can the student with ASD/IDD do now?, and (3) What skills does the student with ASD/IDD need to participate more like same-age peers? Teachers can consider rate, duration, accuracy, and qualities of responses when comparing performance between students.

Visual Analysis of Graphed Data

Graphing data allows teachers to make ongoing assessments about the fit or quality of instruction itself (Jimenez et al., 2012). For ongoing skills, teachers can create a line graph and

Table 4

Computation Error Analysis Example

Item	Completed Problem	Raj's Response	Raj's Correct Digits	Hannah's Response	Hannah's Correct Digits	Yan's Response	Yan's Correct Digits
1	40.23 + 3.14 43.37	4337	0	43.37	4	43.37	4
2	72.46 + 32.50 104.96	10496	0	104.96	5	104.96	5
3	29.47 + 36.23 65.70	6570	0	6.57	0	65.7	3
4	88.42 + 65.04 153.46	15346	0	153.46	5	143.46	4
5	26.74 + 3.1 29.84	2984	0	27.05	1	29.84	4
	Analysis	Raj scored 0 out of 21 digits correct on this CBM. Analyzing the number of digits correct, Raj is not successfully adding decimals to the hundredths. Closely analyzing Raj's answers, however, indicate he is calculating each place value correctly, but not attending to the decimal.		Hannah scored 15 out of 21 digits correct on her CBM, which suggests Hannah is able to answer some types of addition problems into the hundredths. Using error analysis, the teacher is able to identify Hannah's errors are with problem 3 and 5 that did not contain numerical quantities in both the tenths and hundreds place for all values.		Yan answered 20 out of 21 digits correct. The overall digits correct suggest that Yan is able to accurately add values in the hundredths place. Further analysis suggests the digit Yan missed was likely related to not carrying an extra set of ten ones into the tens place.	
	Next Steps	The teacher would provide instruction on the place value system to highlight the different values attributed to tens, ones, tenths, and hundredths. Raj would then practice solving more problems containing decimals up to the hundredths.		The teacher would provide Hannah with instruction on the place value system to highlight the importance of lining up the decimal when adding. This instruction would also include examples with products ending with zero tenths or hundredths to explicitly demonstrate not all products will have values with two numbers in the hundredths place.		The teacher would remind Yan to show her work and then check that her answer is correct. Checking her work might help Yan correct this error in the future, since there is evidence that she understands how to carry values in the number system.	

add data from each session either using electronic spreadsheet tools (e.g., Excel, Google Sheets) or on paper by hand. The Y-axis should represent the quantity of correct responses (e.g., number or percent) and the X-axis represents teaching sessions. Table 5 explains the steps and procedures to create a data-based decision graph, and Figure 4 provides an example graph. There are five possible conclusions that can be drawn once teachers have analyzed the relationship between the aim line and trend line (Jimenez et al., 2012). Teachers should observe the graphed data to determine if individual students have (a) mastered the learning objective, (b) are making

Table 5
Steps and procedures for graphing data to make data-based decisions

Step	Procedure
1. Graph data	1. Put a dot on the graph to indicate number of unprompted correct responses in each session 2. Connect dots across sessions
2. Draw aim line (progress needed to meet goal)	1. Find median by putting first three data points in order from least to greatest and identify the number in the middle 2. Draw median dot by marking a dot on the graph at the intersection of the median score of first three sessions and the second session 3. Draw aim star by marking a star at the criterion from the lesson objective 4. Draw straight aim line by connecting median dot and aim star
3. Draw trend line (student progress)	1. Find median of last three data points by putting them in order from least to greatest and identifying the middle score 2. Draw median dot by marking a dot on the graph at the intersection of the median score of the last three sessions and the next to last session on the x-axis 3. Draw trend line by connecting median dots of first three and last three sessions
4. Analyze relationship between aim line and trend line	1. Determine direction of the trend line - it can be flat (horizontal), accelerating (going up from left to right) or decelerating (going down from left to right) 2. Determine position of the trend line in relation to the aim line - above or below

adequate progress, (c) are making slow or inadequate progress, (d) are not making progress, or if (e) there is potentially a motivation issue. Table 6 provides details for how to interpret graphed data as well as instructional decisions based on that interpretation.

Data-based decision: Shift to next phase of learning. Once student data indicates the student met the learning goal (indicated by goal line; e.g., at least 6/7 steps independently correct for 3 consecutive sessions), instruction and learning goals should be shifted to support the next phase of learning (i.e., acquisition, fluency, generalization, and maintenance) rather than just moving on to another skill entirely (Shurr et al., 2019). Teachers should determine the ideal rate and accuracy for a skill (perhaps using discrepancy analysis) to set fluency goals. Students will need frequent opportunities to practice the new skill to develop automaticity (automatic retrieval) and fluency (accurate and efficient retrieval). Root, Wood et al. (2019) argued students can quickly and accurately use new math skills they may have more working memory to apply to complex tasks (e.g., reasoning and communicating strategies) rather than foundational skills (e.g., accurately writing an equation). Mathematics skills must be maintained over time in order for students to make progress, especially given the way many are interrelated and dependent (Shurr et al., 2019). Teachers can promote maintenance of previously mastered skills by periodically reviewing and reusing content. Finally, mathematical learning will have the most value if students are able to generalize content and skills across contexts (Shurr et al., 2019). Table 7 demonstrates an example of how learning goals can be scaffolded to support student progression across the four phases of learning; for a more detailed description of the four phases of learning please see Shurr et al. (2019).

Data-based decision: Make adaptations and monitor. As shown in Table 6, data-based decision making goes beyond simply determining whether or not a student is making adequate

Figure 4
Example of graphed data used to make a data-based decision

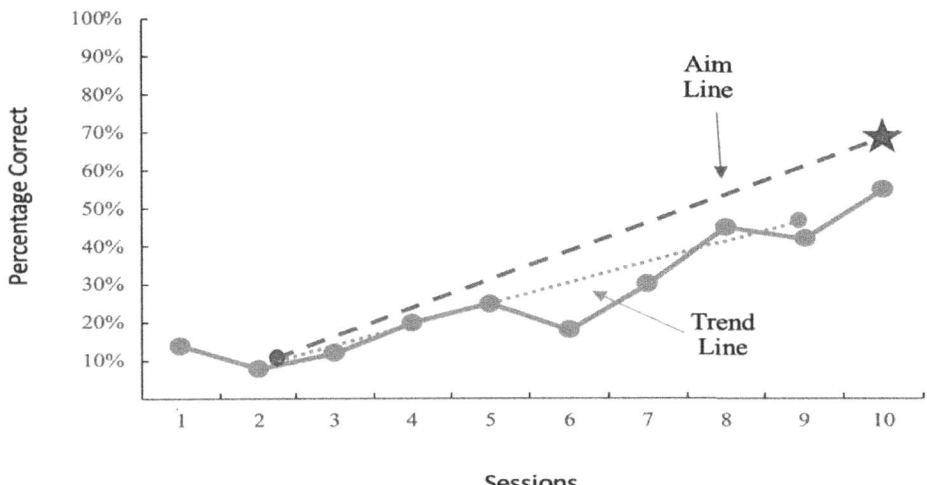

Note. In this example, the student is making slow progress. See Table 6 for more information.

Table 6
Conclusions from Data and Corresponding Instructional Decisions

Data	Adequate Progress?	Instructional Decision
Mastery Trend line is on or above aim line and visual inspection of the raw data indicates criterion has been met for the specified number of lessons	Yes	Shift focus to next phase of learning
Adequate Progress Trend is accelerating and is above or on the aim line, but specific criteria across lessons has not yet been met	Yes	Continue with instruction - student will likely continue to improve and meet mastery given more time
Slow or inadequate Progress Trend is accelerating only slightly but below aim line	No	Make adaptations and monitor: Intensify dosage or instruction to increase independent responses
No Progress Flat trend line that is well below the aim line	No	Make adaptations and monitor: Consider simplifying the task and/or intensifying instruction complexity
Motivation Issue Decelerating trend line with variable raw data	No	Improve motivation: deceleration indicates student was able to perform skill but lost interest over time

Note. Based on Jimenez et al. (2012)

Table 7

Example of Math Goals Across Phases of Learning

Acquisition	Fluency	Maintenance	Generalization
Given 10 or more objects, student will make sets of 2-5 objects with verbal prompting on 6/10 attempts.	Given 10 or more objects, Student will make sets of 2-5 objects independently within 1 minute on 8/10 attempts.	Given 10 or more objects, student will make sets of 2-5 objects independently within 1 minute on 9/10 attempts on bi-weekly maintenance probes.	Given 10 or more classroom supplies, student will gather supplies for 2-5 classmates within 1 minute.

progress. Analysis of the relationship between the aim line (progress needed to meet goal) and trend line (student performance) is used to determine if or which elements of instruction need to be changed to support student success (Jimenez et al., 2012). Students making slow or no progress will need instruction to intensify in order for their data to change. Identifying specific components of the task or instruction that students are struggling with can help teachers make a corresponding instructional change. Taking data using an upside-down task analysis (as shown in Figure 3) facilitates this fine-grained attention to student performance (Test & Spooner, 1996). Instruction can be intensified by making changes to materials, instructional methods, and/or the task.

Changing Materials. Data may indicate students need additional or modified materials. For example, task analyses may need to be tailored to individual students with ASD/IDD. They can be made more explicit by breaking steps into component steps/behaviors adding or changing picture supports or modifying wording of the step (see Figure 5).

Visual supports such as graphic organizers, number lines, or equation templates are common components of research-based strategies for teaching math to students with ASD/IDD (Spooner et al., 2019). Yet, limited fine motor skills and difficulty with motor planning are common barriers for students with ASD/IDD that teachers should consider when selecting and designing visual supports. Technology can be used to create and display accessible electronic graphic organizers using apps such as GoWorksheet, SmartNotebook, SnapType, Kidspiration Maps, or ActivInsire (see Table 8).

Providing students with an equation template gives a structure and a visual prompt for each component of an equation or number sentence can help students both who have difficulty

Figure 5
Example of Making Original Task Analysis (left) more Explicit (right)

1.		Talk about the problem out loud ❑ What do we know about the problem? ❑ What do we want to find out? ❑ What kind of problem is it?
2.		Mark and label original cost
3.		Mark and label percent of change
4.		Calculate amount of change
5.		+ or -
6.		Calculate final cost

1.		Underline the question
2.		This is a _____ problem
3.		The final cost is _____
4.		The discount is for _____ off
5.		Mark and label original cost
6.		Mark and label percent of change
7.		Calculate the amount of change
8.		Because this is a _____ problem I need to _____ . + or -
9.		Calculate the final cost
10.		Write down the final cost
11.		Show how to pay for the total

Note. Adapted from Root et al., 2020

Table 8
Technology Resources for Electronic Graphic Organizers

Resource	Website address
ActivInsire	https://www.prometheanworld.com/products/lesson-delivery-software/activinspire/
GoWorksheet	https://www.attainmentcompany.com/goworksheet-maker
Kidspiration Maps	https://apps.apple.com/us/app/kidspiration-maps/id1492319524
SmartNotebook	https://www.smarttech.com/en/products/education-software/notebook
SnapType	http://www.snaptypeapp.com/

regulating the size of their writing and remembering all of the necessary components (Root & Browder, 2019; see Figure 6). Other examples of changes to visual supports include adding Velcro with response options (in place of requiring students to write), increasing their size, and enhancing salient features, such as by highlighting or color coding.

Figure 6
Equation Template

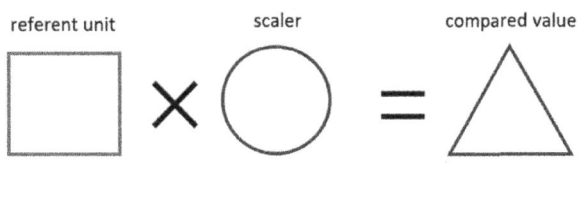

Teachers can consider fading these added or enhanced supports once data indicate students with ASD/IDD have mastered the learning goal. Supports can be faded once students have moved past the initial acquisition phase of learning (Root et al., 2020). Students may be more likely to maintain skills if supports are gradually faded rather than abruptly removed (Cooper et al., 2020). This can be done by removing supports one at a time, changing their features, or teaching students to draw them for themselves. However, not all supports can or should be removed for all students. Instructional efficiency is key, meaning the absence of a support should not substantially decrease the students' opportunities to respond because the task now takes the student much longer to complete. For example, if in a 10-minute independent practice segment of a lesson a student accurately and independently solves three problems when provided with the visual support of a graphic organizer and equation template, but only one problem when the visual supports are removed (despite practice and reinforcement), total removal of visual supports would not be efficient, and therefore not recommended. Rather, a teacher could gradually alter the presentation of visual supports (e.g., remove color coding, remove one box of the equation template at a time, use faint dotted lines that are gradually removed). This would support the student to build fluency without supports.

Changes to instructional methods. Intensifying instruction can take place prior to, alongside, or after making modifications to materials. When deciding how to intensify instruction, teachers should tighten their prompting method and corresponding reinforcement by making sure it is being consistently delivered. If multiple personnel are responsible for instruction (e.g., teachers, paraprofessionals, and peers), ensure everyone is following the same instructional procedure. For example, is everyone consistently using the same hierarchy of prompting in a system of least prompts? Does the student receive the same number of opportunities to respond in each session? Is language used to explain concepts and procedures consistent? One common error observed is teachers using questioning techniques rather than explicit or systematic instruction (see Table 9 for examples). When students with ASD/IDD make errors, they need an efficient error correction that maximizes success and minimizes repeated errors (Root, Wood et al., 2019). If the student is in the early acquisition phase of learning, a model-retest is recommended (Root, Wood et al., 2019). In this case, the teacher models the correct behavior and then gives the student an opportunity to repeat it. If the student is in a later phase of learning (i.e., fluency, maintenance, or generalization), teachers can use a system of least prompts (Root, Wood et al., 2019). Table 9 contrasts what repeatedly questioning students (i.e., asking the same question in a different way) looks like as compared to a model-retest procedure or a system of least prompts.

Table 9

Example of Error Correction Procedures

Fernando is using manipulatives and a graphic organizer to find the solution to the equation "5 + 3". He put four manipulatives in the first group (error in making sets).

Error Correction Technique	**Appropriate Phase of Learning**	**Example**
Model-Retest	Acquisition	*Teacher removes the 4 manipulatives from the first group and immediately gives a <u>model prompt</u>* "The number sentence says 5 + 3. You need to make a set of 5 in your first group. Watch me." *Teacher puts 5 manipulatives into the first group, counting aloud.* "1, 2, 3, 4, 5". *Teacher removes the 5 manipulatives from the first group and gives the student a chance to perform the behavior using a <u>retest</u>* "Your turn. Now you make a set of 5 in the first group."
System of Least Prompts	Fluency, Maintenance, Generalization	*Teacher removes the 4 manipulatives from the first group and gives a <u>verbal prompt</u>.* "The number sentence says 5 + 3" *If the student does not correctly make a set of 5 in the first group, the teacher gives a <u>specific verbal prompt.</u>* "Make a set of 5 in the first group". *If the student still does not correctly make a set of 5 in the first group, the teacher gives a <u>model prompt</u>.* "Watch me. I am going to make a set of 5 in the first group. 1, 2, 3, 4, 5. Your turn. Now you make a set of 5 in the first group"
Repeated Questioning	Not recommended	*Teacher leaves 4 manipulatives in the first group and uses a series of questions in an attempt to guide the student to realize they made an error and correct the behavior, such as:* "Did you put enough in your first group?" "What does the number sentence say?" "How many did you put in your first group?" "How many should you have put in the first group?" "Can you try again?"

Spooner et al. (2017) recommended combining systematic and explicit instruction by using a system of least prompts when students engage in guided practice. Chapter 5, within this book, on problem solving provides specific information on designing prompting hierarchies and those most frequently used in research. They generally consist of three levels that gradually provide increasing assistance to students, with the final prompt serving as a controlling prompt, which results in the student performing the skill correctly. This is usually a full model, with an opportunity for the student to repeat the behavior (re-test). Teachers can also consider using an errorless learning method, such as constant time delay or simultaneous prompting (Collins, 2012). These errorless learning procedures intend to prevent mistakes so that students do not have to unlearn practiced errors. They are appropriate when students are in the acquisition phase of learning and are unlikely to acquire the skill without many trials supported by prompts. They are not appropriate when the student is working toward fluency. The goal is to use the least amount of prompting necessary to get the student to respond correctly.

Changes to the task. Students may not be making adequate progress because the task requires skills that the student does not have, making the task too difficult (Jimenez et al., 2012). We suggest teachers can consider two categories of skills existing: prerequisite and facilitating. Prerequisite skills are those necessary to independently complete the task. For example, counting with 1:1 correspondence is a prerequisite skill for making sets with manipulatives. Facilitating skills are those that may increase efficiency or decrease cognitive load. Subitizing, or recognizing familiar sets, is a facilitating skill for making sets with manipulatives (Jimenez & Saunders, 2019). Teachers should carefully consider and identify true prerequisite skills and determine whether they should teach them prior to or alongside the targeted grade-level skills. Another option is to provide accommodations such as calculators or support partial participation, so that the student with ASD/IDD is working on a smaller number of targeted math skills within a more advanced math task, as discussed in Chapter 6 within this book on embedded instruction. Making decisions about instructional priorities is crucial and should be done in concert with the instructional team (i.e., special educator, general educator and paraprofessionals), as discussed in Chapter 1 within this book on contextualizing math standards.

Math tasks can be simplified by decreasing how many skills are targeted within an instructional session or manipulating the difficulty of the skills or task. Data may indicate students are experiencing difficulty with specific steps or skills. This is particularly problematic for chained tasks (i.e., steps are sequenced together to form a more complex skill; Collins et al., 2012) when independence or accuracy on one step directly influences subsequent steps. In this situation, the specific step or skill should be pulled out of the chain, taught in isolation to mastery, and then reintroduced within the chain (Bellamy et al., 1979). For example, in the example from Table 9, the student struggled to make a set accurately; therefore, to solve the addition problem multiple skills are performed in sequence (i.e., task analysis). The student may have accurately identified the numerals and recognized the two sets of objects are combined together (i.e., the concept of addition), but need additional practice on the targeted skill of making sets.

Data-based decision: Improve motivation. When presented without the concern of medical issues, variable data indicate a possible motivation problem or data collection issue (Jimenez et al., 2012). Teachers should use a positive behavioral intervention and supports (PBIS) framework to provide positive reinforcement and clear expectations (Office of Special Education Programs [OSEP] Technical Assistance Center on Positive Behavioral Interventions and Supports, 2019). When students know what is expected of them, they are more likely to meet the expectation. Similarly, when reinforcement is specific and frequent it increases the likelihood that the learner will apply the feedback and the skill will be repeated. Positive reinforcement increases the likelihood of the behavior occurring again (Cooper et al., 2019). Common examples include praise and tokens which can be exchanged for a reinforcer from a reward menu (Cooper et al., 2019). Highly motivating reinforcements, like a preferred food or activity, can be used but must include a plan to fade the reinforcement. Negative reinforcement includes the removal of non-preferred stimuli (Cooper et al., 2019). For example, a teacher may provide reinforcement for students by removing a homework requirement for those students who independently completed their classwork with more than 80% accuracy. Teachers can also adjust the frequency of feedback to adapt instruction, keep students interested, and promote independence. When initially learning a new skill, students should be provided with frequent reinforcement, perhaps for each correct response, which should then be faded to facilitate moving past acquisition into fluency and maintenance (Shurr et al., 2019).

Motivation can also be improved by communicating clear expectations. Before asking students to complete independent work it is helpful to have students ask themselves questions to gain their understanding of the task and success criteria expected (see Figure 7 for examples).

Step 4: Continue Monitoring Student Progress

After using data to make adaptions to instructional strategy, it is essential to continue to monitor student progress. In order to make direct comparisons, teachers should continue to use the same measurement method used after the first intervention. This way any improvement can be attributed reasonably to the adaptations made to instruction. After three-to-five additional sessions, teachers analyze data to decide if the student is making adequate progress. If the student has reached mastery for the targeted learning goal, it is time to plan for the next phases of

Figure 7
Example of Self-Questioning Visual Support

I am ready to work when I know the answers to these questions;	
What is the task or activity?	 📄
How long will I be working on it?	 🕐
What type of work will I need to do?	 ✏️
How will I know when I am done?	 ★
What happens next?	 ⏭

learning (i.e., fluency, maintenance, and generalization). On occasions when the student does not make adequate progress, consideration of what aspect the student is still experiencing difficulties with is important to make further adaptations.

For students who are not making adequate progress, educators should assess if the student is demonstrating a performance deficit or skill deficit (Brown et al., 2020). Performance deficits occur when students are capable of completing the task independently, but they are not doing so consistently. These performance deficits may be related to a lack of motivation (e.g., interest in topic, relevance), unclear expectations, or inadequate reinforcement. Students who exhibit attention-seeking behaviors during math lessons may benefit from further adaptations to support performance during these lessons. Teachers can use elements of positive behavior supports to increase student engagement during math lessons. Specifically, teachers can make behavioral expectations clear, help students use self-monitoring tools (see Figure 8), and provide positive reinforcement. Levels of support should be determined based on student needs, and should be faded when possible, to increase student independence (Shurr et al., 2019).

For students who are not making adequate progress as a result of a skill deficit, teachers should select an instructional strategy to target the specific deficit exhibited by the student (Brown et al., 2020). For example, in the self-management tool in Figure 7, if the student continues to need help during step five (check your work), the teacher could provide students with massed trials targeting that specific skill by giving multiple work-samples and practicing checking it. Teachers should continue to adapt and monitor until the student has reached the desired levels of achievement.

Conclusion

This chapter discussed the iterative nature of using data to design and evaluate mathematics instruction for students with ASD/IDD. Quality mathematics instruction involves using scientifically validated instructional practices, but to ensure individual students are making adequate progress, teachers must use data to evaluate student performance to make instructional decisions. The steps outlined in the chapter are reflective of the possible steps in the iterative process outlined in Figure 1, but we caution readers to not think of these steps as being complete after number four, but rather an ongoing process to ensure students are making progress through as many instructional goals (including generalization, maintenance, and fluency) as possible. To highlight the circular nature of the process, we have included two student vignettes below (see Figures 9 and 10), which demonstrate how this process can be used to make instructional decisions for students.

Figure 8
Comparing Fractions Worksheet with Self-Graphing Option

Example Problems:

Directions: For each set of fractions, compare the value to decide which fraction is smaller, larger, or if the values are equivalent. Write <, >, or = in the box for each set of fractions.

1. $\frac{1}{2}\ =\ \frac{2}{4}$

5. $\frac{3}{4}\ >\ \frac{1}{4}$

2. $\frac{4}{5}\ <\ \frac{5}{6}$

$$\frac{5 \times 5}{6 \times 5} = \frac{25}{30}$$

$$\frac{4 \times 6}{5 \times 6} = \frac{24}{30}$$

3. $\frac{2}{2}\ >\ \frac{2}{3}$

$$\frac{2}{2} = 1$$

$$\frac{2}{3} < 1$$

Student Name: Priya Comparing Fractions Date: 9/6

		Question 1		Question 2		Question 3		Question 4	
Steps	Ask yourself	Myself	With help	Myself	With help	Myself	With help	Myself	With help
1. Read the directions	How do I know what to do?		✓	✓		✓		✓	
2. Underline what you need to do	What do I need to do?		✓	✓		✓		✓	
3. Choose a strategy (draw a picture, find a common denominator, use reasoning)	Can I compare these fractions as they are? Or do I need to do something to help me make a comparison?	✓		✓		✓		✓	
4. Mark your answer	Are the fractions equal? If not, which one is larger?		✓	✓		✓		✓	
5. Check your work	Does my answer make sense? Can I use another strategy to check my work?	✓		✓		✓		✓	

20						
19						
18						
17						
16						
15						
14						
13						
12				X		
11				X		
10			X	X		
9			X	X		
8			X	X		
7		X	X	X		
6		X	X	X		
5		X	X	X		
4		X	X	X		
3		X	X	X		
2	X	X	X	X		
1	X	X	X	X		
date	9/1	9/3	9/5	9/6		

To earn my break, I will complete at least _____ steps correctly, by myself.

Note. The teacher would fill in how many steps Priya must answer independently to earn the preferred task or item.

Figure 9

Vignette 1: Keshanna

Keshanna is a 13-year-old female student with a moderate intellectual disability. Keshanna enjoys school and is motivated to learn. She prefers to work on a device like an iPad because technology is highly motivating to her. She can set goals for her academic skills and uses feedback. When Keshanna has a question or needs help she uses appropriate social skills to communicate, although her volume and cadence of speech is hard to understand for unfamiliar listeners. Keshanna can use a calculator independently to complete mathematical equations although she does not have math facts memorized. She can decode and comprehend texts written at a 3rd grade level. Keshanna has opportunities to participate in the community with her family but has limited experience making purchases independently in the community. She has only used her math skills in classroom settings. Keshanna also has weak central coherence and will focus attention on individual mathematical procedures rather than the relationships between mathematical concepts. Previous mathematical interventions have focused on single step computation with a model, guided practice and independent practice instructional format. Keshanna's teacher has decided the next best focus for her mathematics instruction is to learn how to set up and solve multi step equations that can be generalized to a community setting. The table below transitions through the steps of the iterative data-based decision making process, describing the teacher's actions as well as the student's response.

Step	Teacher Behavior	Student Behavior
Instruction	Mr. Patel observed Keshanna and noted her accuracy in math computation is consistent and correct. He is ready to provide more mathematics instruction to Keshanna and would like to build on her math computation skills that can be applied in community settings. Mr. Patel developed the following goal for Keshanna's mathematics instruction; When given a graphic organizer, Keshanna will be able to set up and solve equations with one variable based on real-world percent of change word problems. The student will also solve real-world, multi-step problems using positive and negative rational numbers Mr. Patel used MSBI in previous lessons with Keshanna and knows that it is a successful instructional strategy for her (see Chapter 5 on modified schema-based instruction for details). The goal for Keshanna's instruction is to be able to generalize the mathematical problem solving to the community. As a result, Mr. Patel decides to orient each lesson to a community location. All of the percent of change word problems will be based on a local business that Keshanna could visit and leave a tip. Keshanna is provided with a task analysis to help her complete each step and not overlook any parts of the problem. Mr. Patel uses MSBI to teach Keshanna how to complete each step of the problem and how to use the information from the receipt to set up the problem. In order to show mastery of the learning objective, Keshanna will need to complete 6 of the 8 steps in the equation independently correct.	Keshanna enjoys working with Mr. Patel and is looking forward to learning more about using mathematics in her community based instruction trips. Keshanna is able to read the receipts and the word problems and relate the question to the 30 second video that introduces the community location. Keshanna is able to complete each step of the problem with a specific verbal prompt from Mr. Patel. She is not able to label the final response, which shows that she has a limited understanding of how the individual steps of the problem are related to the math concept of a percent of change problem.
Monitor	After lessons with modeling and guided practice, Keshanna begins completing percent of change word problems on her own. Although she is able to complete each step, she asks Mr. Patel "what's next" after each step is completed. Mr. Patel provides specific verbal prompts for each step of the mathematical problem. While Keshanna is working, Mr. Patel collects data through direct observation. Mr. Patel looks at the data graph and notes that there is no consistent trend in independently correct responses for Keshanna.	Keshanna has never completed multi-step problems before and she anticipates receiving a prompt before each step of the problem. She can complete each computation independently with her calculator, but she pauses after each step to ask Mr. Patel what to do next. She is not using the task analysis.
Decision	Mr. Patel decides that Keshanna needs more support to complete multi-step problems. Keshanna was provided with a task analysis during independent practice and Mr. Patel used the same task analysis during MSBI; however, Keshanna does not use the task analysis on her own. Because Keshanna is highly motivated by technology, Mr. Patel decides to transfer the paper task analysis to an electronic task analysis. To do this, Mr. Patel uses a presentation software that allows him to record his voice on each slide. He types the task analysis step onto the slide, adds a recording of himself reading the slide and uses a large green "done" circle to advance the screen to the next slide and step in the task analysis.	Keshanna is excited to use an electronic task analysis to complete math problems. With the electronic task analysis, Keshanna is able to complete each step independently with limited prompts for correction. Her independently correct responses are consistently at mastery level (6 or more independently correct responses) and she is able to label her final response correctly indicating an understanding of the whole problem.

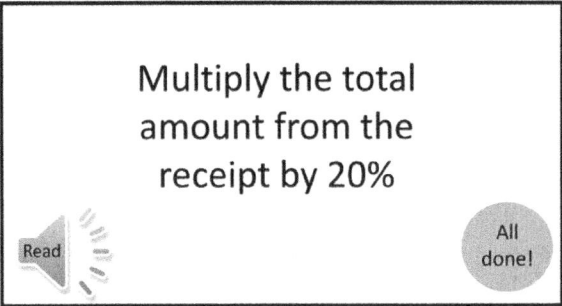

Adaptations	Because the electronic task analysis was an effective intervention for Keshanna and mastery was achieved Mr. Patel begins to plan for generalization to faded supports. The first step is to reduce Keshanna's dependency on the task analysis. To fade this support Mr. Patel combines some of the steps on the task analysis. Now, instead of 8 prompts the task analysis uses 5 prompts.	Keshanna learns how the new task analysis is similar to the original task analysis and is engaged when Mr. Patel models how to use it.

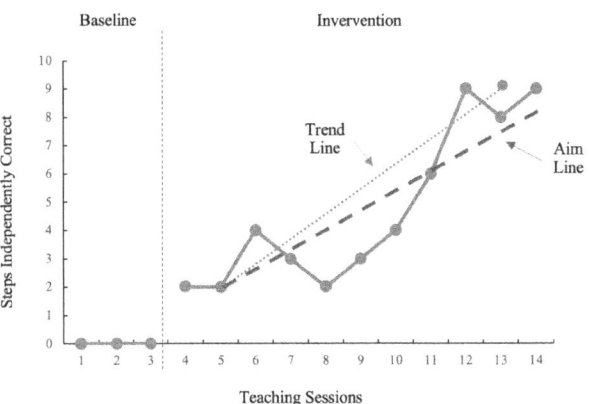

Monitor	With the new task analysis Keshanna needs to complete 4 out of 5 steps independently correct. This represents an increase in mastery level (75% - 80%) and also more independent problem solving because the supports have been faded. Keshanna is able to complete all of the mathematics and is successful completing the grouped steps in the task analysis.	Keshanna understands that the problem depends on each step being completed correctly. She is able to complete each step and also checks her work before moving to the next step.
Decision	Mr. Patel now has data that supports the decision to move Keshanna's mathematics instruction into a generalized setting. Although Keshanna will continue to work on the skill in the classroom setting she is able to begin generalization simultaneously. Providing instruction in the classroom and the novel setting will support Keshanna's mastery. Mr. Patel would like Keshanna to make purchases at a local restaurant and leave a 20% tip independently. Keshanna will still need the support of a task analysis, although she does have a conceptualized understanding of the mathematic word problem her weak	Keshanna enjoys community settings and is looking forward to the purchasing trips. She requests specific restaurants to visit. She is concerned about ordering for herself because she has not done this in the past and unfamiliar communication partners often do not understand her. Keshanna has used money in the past and is looking forward to paying.

	central coherence limits her ability to complete all the steps in a logical order without support.	
Adaptations	In order to provide Keshanna task analytic support in an unobtrusive, socially accepted manner Mr. Patel creates abbreviated task analytic steps and displays them on a small iPhone. This pocket-sized guide will support Keshanna as she leaves an appropriate tip in the community.	Keshanna is able to read the short task analysis and practices with it in the classroom setting several times.

> **Leaving a tip**
> 1. Circle total on receipt
> 2. Multiply by 20% with calculator
> 3. Write tip amount <u>on line</u>
> 4. Add tip to total
> 5. Sign receipt and return to employee

Monitor	Mr. Patel completes a model lesson with the tip card short task analysis in the classroom setting. Although Keshanna is able to complete all the steps the reduced support is making it difficult for her to remember if she completed the previous step before moving to the next step. However, she consistently gets 4 out of 5 steps independently correct. It takes her more time than Mr. Patel anticipated.	Keshanna is able to read the tip card short task analysis and practices with it in the classroom setting several times. She is able to meet mastery level with the faded supports, but the duration of the task would not be socially appropriate, it takes her more than 5 minutes to complete the tip leaving mathematical process.
Decision	Mr. Patel decides that Keshanna needs more supported opportunities to practice before using the tip card in the community. However, he also wants to begin the process of generalizing the mathematical skill. As a result, Mr. Patel has decided to ask members of the school community to allow Keshanna to make mock purchases and leave a tip in a sheltered setting.	Keshanna will use her task analysis pocket card to solve for a 20% tip in the school lunchroom and at the concession stand during a basketball game.
Next Steps	Once Keshanna is able to complete the mathematical problem solving for leaving a tip with the faded supports at mastery level in 2 minutes or less, Keshanna will begin making purchases and leaving a tip on community-based instruction trips and with her family.	

Figure 10

Vignette 1: Geoff

Geoff is an 8-year-old male student with ASD/IDD. He attends his local public school and the third-grade class is about to plant an organic garden. Geoff enjoys spending time with other children and is looking forward to being outside for this task. He is working toward becoming more independent in his work and increasing the intervals of time he spends completing non-preferred tasks. Currently, Geoff will work independently for three minutes before getting out of his chair or talking to a friend. Geoff is able to use diagrams or counters with one to one correspondence to calculate addition and subtraction problems with sums up to 40. Geoff knows some of his addition and multiplication facts, although he struggles to apply mathematical procedures to solve word problems. Previous interventions have been most successful when presented systematically and allow Geoff to follow a specific routine. Geoff's teachers have decided the next goal for Geoff is going to be to learn to find the perimeter and area of quadrilaterals with equations. They will use the community garden as an opportunity to expose Geoff to real-world geometric concepts. As participation with other children in the community garden is a preferred task for Geoff, they will also use this opportunity to increase Geoff's independence by working to reduce the number of prompts required for Geoff to complete his work. The table below walks through the steps in the iterative process to describe the teacher's actions. how Geoff responds, and then the decision and next steps the teacher makes based on Geoff's behavior.

Step	Teacher Behavior	Student Behavior
Instruction	Mr. Dietz examines Geoff's current levels of performance and determines Geometry is an area of mathematics that Geoff has not been adequately exposed to in previous lessons. Mrs. Dietz decides to build on Geoff's understanding of addition and multiplication by introducing algebraic expressions to represent the formulas for perimeter and area of rectangles. Geoff enjoys watching videos on the computer, so Mrs. Dietz decides to use a video model to introduce Geoff to the new concept. Mrs. Dietz creates a series of three video models that demonstrate the concept of perimeter and area using the community garden. She uses point-of-view video modeling to capture her hands drawing out rectangles on graph paper and then counting out the number of centimeter lines for perimeter and the number of shaded squares for area. She then writes an equation for each shape on the graph paper to represent the perimeter and area. The perimeter of each shape is always traced with a blue marker, while the area of the rectangle is always shaded with a red marker, and the equations always match the visual representation of each measurement. The video pauses instruction and asks Geoff to use his graph paper to make the same shapes and algebraic equations that he sees on the screen.	Geoff will watch each video in a series. First, he will watch the first video and copy the first example onto his graph paper. When he is finished, he will check his work against the hard-copy of Mrs. Dietz's version, and then turn in his copy to Mrs. Dietz to be checked. If Geoff has correctly drawn the modeled rectangle and accurately labeled the perimeter and area for the first rectangle, he will watch the second video the next day. If his work is incorrect, Mrs. Dietz will provide corrective feedback and have Geoff re-watch the first video until he completes the work independently. This pattern will continue until Geoff has drawn three rectangles and labeled their perimeter and area.

Objective: Given a set of three rectangles on graph paper, Geoff will accurately represent the perimeter and area on the graph paper and then solve for the perimeter and area (by counting) of all three shapes with three or fewer prompts for three consecutive sessions.

CCSS.MATH.CONTENT.3.MD.D.8: Solve real world and mathematical problems involving perimeters of polygons, including finding the perimeter given the side lengths…

CCSS.MATH.CONTENT.3.MD.C.6: Measure areas by counting unit squares

Monitor	Geoff's learning objective states he will accurately draw the rectangles and then solve for the perimeter and area for three problems, while receiving fewer than three prompts. Therefore, Mrs. Dietz has drawn several sets of three rectangles, and after the three model days, begins collecting data on how many prompts Geoff needs to write his algebraic equations and solve for the perimeter and area of all three problems. She is going to graph this data on the chart below.	Geoff requires numerous prompts over seven sessions to complete the task. The first two days, Mrs. Dietz prompts him to remember to add the lines for perimeter and shade the squares for area. By the third day, Mrs. Dietz has to prompt Geoff to remain seated and complete his assignments. Mrs. Dietz prompts him 11 to 15 times to complete his work, but does not give him any more than one academic prompt related to solving the problems.
Decision	Mrs. Dietz views Geoff's graph and determines he is making inadequate progress. She also considers the types of prompts she has delivered over the past five days. Her prompts have focused on Geoff's performance (i.e., remaining in his seat) rather than the skill (i.e. finding the perimeter and area of the rectangles). Therefore, Mrs. Dietz decides she needs to provide additional accommodations to increase Geoff's performance during the math problems.	

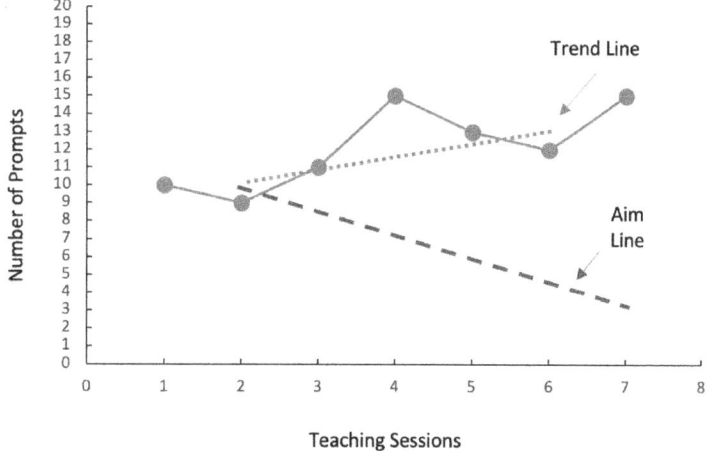

Number of prompts required for Geoff to complete three perimeter/area problems after the first intervention.

Adaptations	After reviewing possible EBPs to support Geoff's task completion, Mrs. Dietz decides to add a token economy to reinforce Geoff's independent completion of the problems without prompts. She talks with Geoff about what activity he would like to earn for completing his work without reminders, and together they decided on visiting the community garden with other third-grade students.	Mrs. Dietz provides Geoff with ten tickets at the beginning of each session. Each time she has to prompt him to return to his seat or continue his work, she takes one of his tickets. If he has any tickets remaining after he solved all three problems, he gets to visit the community garden. After each successful session, Mrs. Dietz provides one less ticket at the beginning of the following session to fade prompting supports.
Monitor	Mrs. Dietz continues to collect data on how many prompts Geoff requires during each session. She graphs her data onto the same chart, after inserting a line indicating the start of an additional accommodation.	Geoff begins to complete the geometric problems more independently, with fewer prompts from Mrs. Dietz. After 7 additional sessions with the reinforcement intervention added, Geoff completes all problems with 3 or less prompts three days in a row.

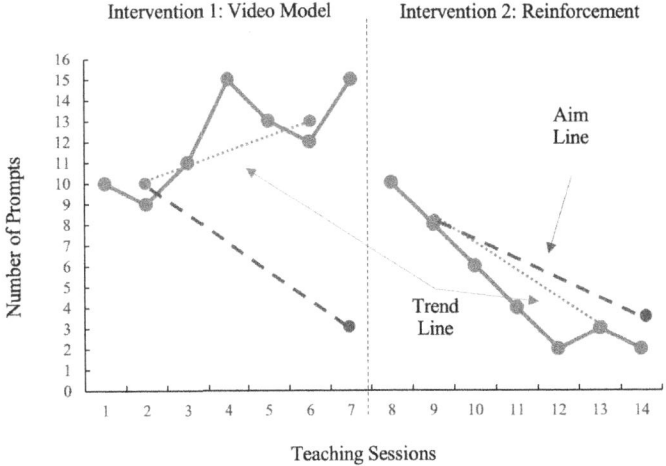

Number of prompts required for Geoff to complete three perimeter/area problems after the second intervention.

Decision	Using the graph, Mrs. Dietz determines Geoff made adequate progress and met the learning objective, with three consecutive days needing three or fewer prompts to complete the problem.	
Next Steps	Mrs. Dietz develops a plan for generalization of the skills to solve problems about perimeter and area within a new setting (in the garden with the general education classroom). Currently, Geoff is able to solve the perimeter and area problems with visual and behavioral supports one-on-one with his special education teacher. Mrs. Dietz faded the behavioral	After an initial drop in performance, Mrs. Dietz and the General education teacher implement a similar reward structure in the new environment. With the increased behavioral supports, Geoff is able to maintain his performance in the community garden with his peers. He

	supports and the number of prompts required, and Geoff maintained performance. Mrs. Dietz is now going to work with the general education teacher to ensure Geoff generalizes his skills to a new environment. If Geoff's performance drops, Mrs. Dietz will choose another EBP to explicitly train for generalization in the community garden. draws the rectangles for the community garden on graph paper and calculates the perimeter and area of all three rectangles independently. Geoff also continues to need fewer than three prompts to complete the questions, even after reinforcement is eliminated.
Instruction	After Geoff mastered the previous learning goal and generalized his performance to a new environment, Mrs. Dietz will now select a new learning objective and begin the cycle over again. She will continue to monitor Geoff's maintenance of the perimeter and area skills.

References

Archer, A., & Hughes, C. A. (2011). *Explicit instruction: Effective and efficient teaching.* Guilford Press.

Bellamy, G. T., Horner, R. H., & Inman, D. P. (1979). *Vocational habilitation of severely retarded adults: A direct service technology.* University Park Press.

Boaler, J. (2014). Research suggests timed tests cause math anxiety. *Teaching Children Mathematics, 20*(8), 469-474. https://www.jstor.org/stable/10.5951/teacchilmath.20.issue-8

Boaler, J. (2019). *Limitless mind: Learn, lead, and live without barriers.* HarperOne.

Bogin, J., Sullivan, L., & Rogers, S. (2011). *Discrete trial training (DTT): Online training module.* (Sacramento, CA: National Professional Development Center on Autism Spectrum Disorders, M.I.N.D. Institute, University of California at Davis Medical School). In Ohio Center for Autism and Low Incidence (OCALI), Autism Internet Modules, www.autisminternetmodules.org. OCALI.

Browder, D. M., Spooner, F., Lo, Y-y., Saunders, A. F., Root, J. R., Ley Davis, L., & Brosh, C. (2017). *Project solutions implementation manual.* https://access.uncc.edu/sites/access.uncc.edu/files/media/solutions/TheSolutionsProject_Manual%20For%20Dissemination.pdf

Brown, F., McDonnell, J., Snell, M. (2020). *Instruction of students with severe disabilities* (9th ed.). Pearson Education Inc.

Cragg, L., & Gilmore, C. (2014). Skills underlying mathematics: The role of executive function in the development of mathematical proficiency. *Trends in Neuroscience and Education, 3*(2), 63-68. https://doi.org/10.1016/j.tine.2013.12.001

Collins, B. C. (2012). *Systematic instruction for students with moderate and severe disabilities.* Brookes.

Cooper, J. O., Heron, T. E., & Heward, W. L. (2019). *Applied behavior analysis* (3rd ed). Pearson.

Courtade, G. R., Browder, D. M., Spooner, F., & DiBiase, W. (2010). Training teachers to use an inquiry-based task analysis to teach science to students with moderate and severe disabilities. *Education and Training in Autism and Developmental Disabilities*, 45(3), 378-399. https://www.jstor.org/stable/23880112

Cowan, R., & Powell, D.(2014). The contributions of domain-general and numerical factors to third-grade arithmetic skills and mathematical learning disability. *Journal of Educational Psychology, 106*(1), 214-229. https://doi.org/10.1037/a0034097

Cox, S. C., & Root, J. R. (2020). Intervention decision making framework. Retrieved from https://gcalab.wixsite.com/gcalabfsu/post/intervention-decision-making-flow-chart

Deno, S. L. (1985). Curriculum-based measurement: The emerging alternative. *Exceptional children*, 52(3), 219-232. https://doi.org/10.1177/001440298505200303

Doabler, C. T., Cary, M. S., Jungjohann, K., Clarke, B., Fien, H., Baker, S., Smolkowski, K., & Chard, D. (2012). Enhancing core mathematics instruction for students at risk for mathematics disabilities. *Teaching Exceptional Children*, 44(4), 48-57. https://doi.org/10.1177/004005991204400405

Every Student Succeeds Act, 20 U.S.C. § 6301 (2015). https://www.congress.gov/bill/114th-congress/senate-bill/1177

Fraser, D. W., Marder, T. J., deBettencourt, L. U., Myers, L. A., Kalymon, K. M., & Harrell, R.

M. (2020). Using a mixed-reality environment to train special educators working with students with autism spectrum disorder to implement discrete trial teaching. *Focus on Autism and Other Developmental Disabilities, 35*(1), 3-14. https://doi.org/10.1177/1088357619844696

Frith, U., & Happé, F. (1994). Language and communication in autistic disorders. *Philosophical Transactions of the Royal Society of London. Series B: Biological Sciences, 346*(1315), 97-104. https://doi.org/10.1098/rstb.1994.0133

Fuchs, L. S., & Fuchs, D. (1991). Curriculum-based measurements: Current applications and future directions. Preventing School Failure: *Alternative Education for Children and Youth, 35*(3), 6-11. https://doi.org/10.1080/1045988X.1991.10871068

Gilley, D. P., Root, J. R., & Cox, S. K. (2020). Development of mathematics and self-determination skills for young adults with extensive support needs. *The Journal of Special Education.* Advance online publication. https://doi.org/10.1177/0022466920902768

Goldin, G. A. (1997). Observing mathematical problem solving through task-based interviews. *Journal for Research in Mathematics Education. Monograph, 9,* 40-62. https://www.jstor.org/stable/749946

Hill, E. L. (2004). Executive dysfunction in autism. *TRENDS in Cognitive Sciences, 8*(1), 26-32. https://doi.org/10.1016/j.tics.2003.11.003

Horner, R. H., Kincaid, D., Sugai, G., Lewis, T., Eber, L., Barrett, S., Dickey, C. R., Richter, M., Sullivan, E., Boezio, C., Algozzine, B., Reynolds, H., & Johnson, N. (2014). Scaling up school-wide positive behavioral interventions and supports: Experiences of seven states with documented success. *Journal of Positive Behavior Interventions, 16*(4), 197-208. https://doi.org/10.1177/1098300713503685

Hosp, M. K., & Hosp, J. L. (2003). Curriculum-based measurement for reading, spelling, and math: How to do it and why. *Preventing School Failure, 48*(1), 10-17. https://doi.org/10.1080/1045988X.2003.10871074

Hughes, C. A., Morris, J. R., Therrien, W. J., & Benson, S. K. (2017). Explicit instruction: Historical and contemporary contexts. *Learning Disabilities Research & Practice, 32*(3), 140-148. https://doi.org/10.1111/ldrp.12142

Jimenez, B. A., Mims, P. J., & Browder, D. M. (2012). Data-based decisions guidelines for teachers of students with severe intellectual and developmental disabilities. *Education and Training in Autism and Developmental Disabilities, 47*(4), 407-413. https://www.jstor.org/stable/23879634

McDonnell, J., Snell, M. E., Brown, F., Coleman, O., & Eichelberger, C. (2020). Individualized instructional strategies. In F. Brown, J. McDonnell, M.E. Snell (Eds.), *Instruction of students with severe disabilities* (9th ed., pp. 156-206). Pearson.

National Governor's Association Center for Best Practices, & Council of Chief State School Officers. (2010). Common Core State Standards for Mathematics. http://www.corestandards.org/Math/

National Council of Teachers of Mathematics. (2000). *Principles and standards for school mathematics.* NCTM

Office of Special Education Programs (OSEP) Technical Assistance Center on Positive Behavioral Interventions and Supports (2020, July 1). *Positive Behavioral Interventions & Supports.* www.pbis.org.

Peltier, C., & Peltier, T. (2020). Mining instruction from student mistakes: Conducting an error analysis for mathematical problem solving. *Beyond Behavior.* Advance online publication. https://doi.org/10.1177/1074295620903050

Root, J. R., & Browder, D. M. (2019). Algebraic Problem Solving for Middle School Students with Autism and Intellectual Disability. *Exceptionality, 27*(2), 118 – 132. https://doi.org/10.1080/09362835.2017.1394304

Root, J. R., Cox, S. K., Saunders, A., & Gilley, D. (2020). Applying the universal design for learning framework to mathematics instruction for learners with extensive support needs. *Remedial and Special Education, 41*(4), 194-206. Doi:10.1177/0741932519887235

Root, J. R., Henning, B., & Boccumini, E. (2018). Teaching students with autism and intellectual disability to solve algebraic word problems. *Education and Training in Autism and Developmental Disabilities, 53*(3), 325-338.

Root, J., Henning, B., & Cox, S. K. (2020). *Evidence-based practices for teaching mathematical word problem solving to students with autism* [Manuscript submitted for publication].

Root, J. R., Wood, L., & Browder, D. (2019). Assessment and planning. In F. Brown, J. McDonnell, & M. Snell (Eds.). *Instruction of Students with Severe Disabilities (9th ed)*. Routledge.

Steinbrenner, J. R., Hume, K., Odom, S. L., Morin, K. L., Nowell, S. W., Tomaszewski, B., Szendrey, S., McIntyre, N. S., Yücesoy-Özkan, S., & Savage, M. N. (2020). *Evidence-based practices for children, youth, and young adults with Autism.* The University of North Carolina at Chapel Hill, Frank Porter Graham Child Development Institute, National Clearinghouse on Autism Evidence and Practice Review Team.

Spooner, F., Saunders, A., Root, J. R., & Brosh, C. (2017). Promoting access to common core mathematics for students with severe disabilities through mathematical problem solving. *Research & Practice for Persons with Severe Disability, 42*(3), 171-186. https://doi.org/10.1177/1540796917697119

Spooner, F., Root, J. R., Saunders, A. F., & Browder, D. M. (2019). An updated evidence-based practice review on teaching mathematics to students with moderate and severe disabilities. *Remedial and Special Education, 40*(3), 150-165. https://doi.org/10.1177/0741932517751055

Test, D. W., & Spooner, F. (1996). *Innovations: community-based instructional support.* American Association on Mental Retardation.

Van de Walle, K., & Karp, K. S. Bay-Williams (2013). *Elementary and middle school mathematics: Teaching developmentally* (8th ed). Pearson.

Wheeler, J. J., & Richey, D. D. (2019). *Behavior management: Principles and practices of positive behavior supports.* Pearson.

Wong, C., Odom, S. L., Hume, K. A., Cox, A. W., Fettig, A., Kucharczyk, S., Brock, M. E., Plavnick, J. B., Fleury, V. P., Schultz, T. R. (2015). Evidence-based practices for children, youth, and young adults with autism spectrum disorder: A comprehensive review. *Journal of Autism and Developmental Disorders, 45*(7), 1951-1966. https://doi.org/10.1007/s10803-014-2351-z

Chapter 3: Multi-Tiered System of Supports in Mathematics

Jessica A Bowman & Gail Ghere

Planning high-quality instruction and support for students with autism, intellectual disability, and other developmental disabilities (ASD/IDD) in the area of mathematics has the potential to ensure that these students have full access and make progress in the general education curriculum. Through the use of universally designed instruction and high-leverage practices, teachers can create environments where mathematics is accessible to each learner, including learners with ASD/IDD. However, it can be difficult for some to envision how students with ASD/IDD fit in the grand scheme of academics in K-12 schools, especially given the persistently low expectations of students with disabilities (Cameron & Cook, 2013; Roberts et al., 2018). One possible way to conceptualize mathematics instruction for students with ASD/IDD is through a lens of multi-tiered systems of support (MTSS), a system that many school districts utilize to ensure appropriate support for students (Choi et al., 2017; Sailor et al., 2018). This chapter will describe what MTSS is, how the MTSS model is supported in the research, how the model can be applied to teach mathematics to students with ASD/IDD, and how students with ASD/IDD can be fully included in each Tier of MTSS, as needed.

What is MTSS?

MTSS is an organizational framework for providing increasing intensive and individualized supports to any student regardless of needs or label (Lane et al., 2015). In the areas of academics, this is commonly referred to as Response to Intervention (RTI), and for behavior it is commonly referred to as Positive Behavioral Interventions and Supports (PBIS; IRIS Center, 2019: Lane et al., 2015). Both RTI and PBIS are frameworks designed to prevent referrals for special education evaluations by providing effective and intensive instruction and intervention within general education, with a focus on students with learning disabilities (Torgeson, 2009; Wanzek & Vaughn, 2010). As the potential of MTSS evolved and researchers conducted more research, the benefits of MTSS was evident for more students and the walls between and within how general education and special education services might be provided became less distinct and more collaborative (Sailor, 2015).

More recently, scholars considered MTSS a framework for effectively supporting the learning of *all* students—including students with ASD/IDD—through integrating a continuum of evidence-based practices into a cohesive system and increase teacher effectiveness (Every Student Succeeds Act, 2015; Thurlow et al., 2020). This includes the integration of specially-designed instruction, where the content, methodology, or delivery of instruction is adapted, as appropriate, to meet the needs of students with disabilities. Intensive instruction, a high leverage practice and a form of specially designed instruction, also has a place within MTSS, when data demonstrate a need for increased instructional intensity (Riccomini et al., 2017). This shift in how MTSS is framed and its wider impact "...places special education within, rather than appended to, general education" (Horner et al., 2020, p. 75). Within MTSS, special education becomes a continuum of *supports* integrated with general education rather than a continuum of *placements*, where only one of which is general education. Thurlow et al. (2020) proposed a framework for providing access to MTSS for students with ASD/IDD (see Table 1). This chapter will describe each element of this MTSS framework in terms of how it can be used to provide full and authentic access to the general education curriculum in mathematics for students with ASD/IDD.

To fully understand MTSS and its power as an organizing framework for effective instruction and inclusive practices, it is best to consider the framework from a school-wide

Table 1
MTSS Supports for All Students

Tiers	For all students/ School-wide focus	Aligned supplementary strategies for students with ASD/IDD
Tier 1—Standards-based curriculum and instruction	• Priority learning targets identified and taught • Effective, research-based teaching practices in place • Universal Design for Learning implemented	• Focus on high priority learning targets • Differentiate how students express what they learn • Integrate concepts and vocabulary with Augmentative and Alternative Communication (AAC) system
Tier 2—Targeted instruction	• Use of flexible grouping within class focused on priority learning targets • School-wide supports (e.g., additional content area blocks or flex periods)	• Pre-teach to build prior knowledge • Re-teach to reinforce priority learning • Build conceptual understanding
Tier 3—Individualized instruction	• Intensive instruction to eliminate/ minimize gaps	• Focus on skill gaps related to prioritized learning targets and additional academic goals (e.g., reading skills)

Note: Adapted from Thurlow et al., 2020

perspective as well as an individual student perspective. A school-wide model of MTSS (see Figure 1) typically has three tiers (National Center on Response to Intervention, 2020). The tiers are additive. All students receive Tier 1 instruction, some students receive Tier 2 instruction, and an even more limited number of students receive Tier 3 interventions. Students should continue to receive Tier 1 supports whether they are receiving Tier 2 and/or Tier 3 interventions.

Consider the metaphor of a triple-scoop ice cream cone to picture the additive nature of MTSS. A triple-scoop cone has three scoops stacked atop the cone. The first scoop is placed on the cone. It is the foundation for all of the other ice cream scoops. When the second scoop is added, the first scoop remains on the cone. When the third scoop is added, the first and second scoops are not removed, they remain in place. MTSS is organized in the exact same way. Tier 1 is the "first scoop," the base level of instruction for all students. In terms of academics, this means that all students access grade-level general education curriculum through lessons designed using Universal Design for Learning (UDL) and that include the use of evidence-based practices (McIntosh & Goodman, 2016). Lessons designed using UDL consider how learners will engage with the lesson, how information is presented to learners, and how learners express themselves (CAST, 2020). Tier 2, the "second scoop" of instruction, is for students who would benefit from additional instruction on focused skills in order to successfully access and make progress in the general education curriculum. Tier 2 instruction can be provided through flexible small group instruction that is embedded into a class or through additional instruction for any student who would benefit. Tier 3 is the most intensive level of support. It is a "third scoop" of instruction for

Figure 1

The MTSS Triangle that Integrates Academic and Behavioral Tiers of Supports

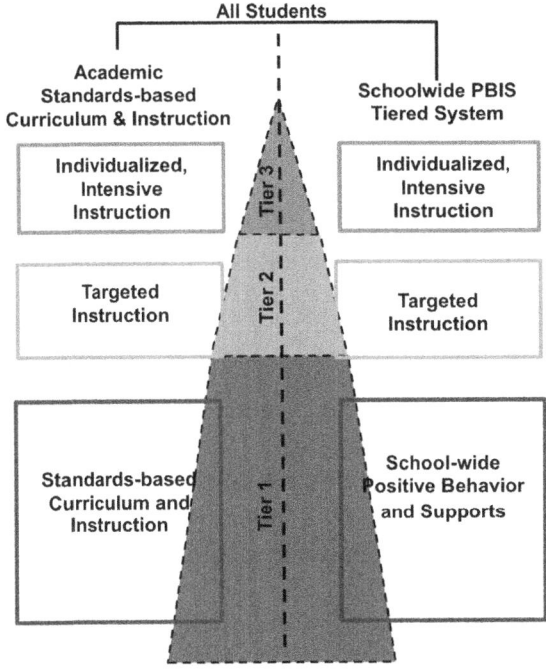

Note: Adapted from Thurlow et al. (2020)

students who require intensive interventions. Tier 3 instruction is very individualized and often focused on reducing or eliminating skill gaps, such as increasing reading proficiency or basic mathematics skills (Wanzek & Vaughn, 2011; Wisconsin Response to Intervention Center, 2020). Please see Figure 2, or an example of tiered supports for a student with ASD/IDD.

The MTSS framework is a collaborative system. Systems are composed of multiple elements, including the people (such as, administrators, general educators, special educators, related service providers, and paraprofessionals), structures (for example, a master schedule that is built for common planning time, professional learning communities [PLC], co-teaching teams), and processes (such as, how schoolwide positive behavior expectations will be taught to every student, data analysis protocols for PLCs, co-planning supports). Collaboration within and across tiers is a significant feature of a MTSS system. Effective and efficient MTSS that benefit student learning happens when these elements fit together in a tiered system and are continually assessed and nurtured.

Figure 2
Example of Tiered Supports for a Student with ASD/IDD

Hayden is a student with ASD/IDD and is in a 6th grade mathematics class. The general education teacher and special education teacher work together to support Hayden during lessons, and prioritize content for him to learn, based on the current unit. Hayden knows that content will be presented in multiple ways, and that he and his classmates can often choose how to complete assignments, whether they draw, use manipulatives, online tools and supports, or work with a partner. Once a week or so, one of the teachers will work with Hayden and others in the class to either go over the content they learned in class in more depth, or review content that they'll be learning during the next class. Because of Hayden's disability, he is missing some key prerequisite skills in mathematics that limit his ability to fully participate in the mathematics curriculum. Each day, Hayden is provided opportunities within the general education classroom and curriculum to focus on those skills (e.g., problem solving, fluency with basic operations). In addition, Hayden has a period every day with his special education teacher where he receives additional and highly contextualized instruction on these skill gap areas

Data are a key component of an MTSS framework (National Center on Response to Intervention, 2010). Data inform both the development and effectiveness of the system, as well as the growth or lack of growth of individual students (see Chapter 2). To look at both system-level impact and individual student needs, schools employ screening, progress monitoring and summative assessment measures. In a robust schoolwide system, screening measures are in place for all students for reading, mathematics, and social-emotional learning (Center on Multi-Tiered System of Support, 2020). These data are used to identify students who need additional support so teams can proactively implement supports before students become too discrepant from their peers. Data also inform school leaders about how well the tiered system is working and provide guidance about where further system development is needed. Data about the tiered system includes information about what is happening in classrooms, and whether teachers are using scientifically validated instruction across each tier. In MTSS, collective expertise that considers data is a strength. The value of having multiple perspectives from general educators, special educators, English Learner teachers, and other colleagues to analyze data and propose next steps opens the door for new ways of meeting student needs. It also builds stronger relationships where adults support each other as they support all students.

At the instructional level, ongoing formative assessments that are part of effective instruction provide immediate information about what each student is learning and what areas need greater instruction (Van de Walle et al., 2016). Individual student data are used to guide decisions about whether a student needs additional support beyond Tier 1 to meet their needs (McIntosh & Goodman, 2016). It helps to assures all students are learning in the academic curriculum and that their social-emotional needs are being met.

MTSS provides a continuum of support that can meet the academic and behavioral needs of all students, including students with ASD/IDD (Thurlow et al., 2020). MTSS is also a framework for effective inclusion for all students. "Schoolwide inclusion asks not, "What is the least restrictive place to instruct this student?" but asks, "What is the best instructional situation for this student to successfully engage the general education curriculum?" (Sailor, 2015, p. 94). The key is building multi-tiered systems that take both a top-down perspective to construct collaborative systems that meet the needs of all students and a ground-up perspective that provides effective instructional tiers of support for all students.

Research on MTSS

Research on MTSS models demonstrates their efficacy for students in the area of mathematics, including for students who are at-risk and those with disabilities (e.g., Choi et al., 2017; Fuchs et al., 2008). However, there are no known studies that specifically studied the impact of MTSS for students with ASD/IDD. Anecdotal evidence from inclusive schools where students with significant needs for support are included in all parts of the school day indicates MTSS holds potential as a unifying structure that promotes inclusion (Shogren et al., 2015). Additionally, UDL—what should be a key component of Tier 1 instruction—reduces the need for individualized accommodations (Morningstar et al., 2015). However, the reality is that most practitioners are not aware of how to create MTSS structures that are accessible to students with ASD/IDD (Taub et al., 2017; Walker et al., 2018).

Inclusion of Students with ASD/IDD in MTSS

While schools have historically excluded students with ASD/IDD from MTSS structures, we believe inclusion in MTSS promotes the provision of appropriate supports for all students to engage in the general education curriculum, taught by a general education teacher, alongside grade-level peers. For inclusion in MTSS structures to occur, education teams must find consensus around the basic ideas presented in Table 2.

Focusing on finding consensus on these ideas can ensure students with disabilities, including students with ASD/IDD, are a part of the tiered supports that schools are already implementing and that special education services are in addition to, and not in place of, the same instruction, settings, and activities available to all students. To promote equitable and inclusive schools, it is essential that school staff—including principals and educators—presume students with ASD/IDD can benefit from school wide initiatives, including MTSS. Further, for students with ASD/IDD to benefit from MTSS, they need the same access as any other student to all three Tiers of support, as appropriate. The following section will describe considerations that must be taken into account to fully include students with ASD/IDD in each tier of MTSS, including the role of special education services and supports among the tiers.

Table 2
Indicators of Inclusive MTSS

Indicators of Inclusive MTSS
• MTSS is about meeting students' needs through a continuum of *services*, not a continuum of *placements*. When a student demonstrates an increased need for services, this should not lead to a more restrictive placement, rather, it should lead to more intensive instruction and data-based problem solving.
• MTSS assumes high-quality instruction in Tier 1, with avenues for more intensive instruction in Tiers 2 and 3. For students with disabilities, including students with ASD/IDD, special education supports and specially designed instruction must be integrated at each tier of instruction.
• MTSS calls for a focus on high-quality and accessible instruction for each learner in Tier 1, and interventions in Tiers 2 and 3 when needed. For students with ASD/IDD, Tier 1 instruction would include access to grade-aligned standards-based instruction and prioritized learning targets. When needed, Tier 2 instruction can provide the pre-teaching and re-teaching that is needed to build background knowledge and reinforce new learning, and Tier 3 instruction can provide the intensive and individualized instruction in skill gap areas.
• This emphasis on high-quality and accessible instruction requires general and special educator collaboration at each tier (Thurlow et al., 2020).

Special Education Services and Supports

The Individuals with Disabilities Education Act (IDEA, 2004) stated an IEP must include

> "...special education and related services and supplementary aids and services, based on peer-reviewed research to the extent practicable, to be provided to the child, or on behalf of the child, and a statement of the program modifications or supports for school personnel that will be provided to enable the child— (i) To advance appropriately toward attaining the annual goals; (ii) To be involved in and make progress in the general education curriculum...and to participate in extracurricular and other nonacademic activities; and (iii) To be educated and participate with other children with disabilities and nondisabled children (IDEA, 2004, Section 300.320)."

In many ways, when a student's IEP team establishes special education and related services and supplementary aids and services in a student's IEP, that is a Tier 3 support. A Tier 3 support does not dictate instruction in a separate location. The team is making educated decisions on how to support an *individual* student, based on *individual* data. Further, these supports are designed to allow the student "to be involved in and make progress in the general education curriculum" (IDEA, 2004, Section 300.320). Given this requirement, these supports must be provided any time a student is engaged in the general education curriculum regardless of placement. Thurlow and colleagues (2020) stated MTSS frameworks "...include aligned general education and special education delivery systems where supplemental special education supports simplify, magnify, and possibly modify what is taught in general education (p. 5)." When students with ASD/IDD receive instruction at any time and in any Tier, it is essential they receive the support necessary for them to be successful (e.g., communication support, prompting, modified work, visual supports). Aligned supplementary strategies for students with ASD/IDD should be available in each Tier of instruction that a student is receiving (Thurlow et al., 2020). Given some thought and planning, as well as flexible delivery of instruction, supports identified as essential for students with ASD/IDD can easily be embedded into all tiers of instruction to ensure accessibility across all three Tiers, as needed. Table 3 is an example of a student's special education and related services and supplementary aids and services identified by their IEP team. Once special education and related services and supplementary aids and services are determined, instructional teams must ensure these are available to the student across all tiers of instruction that they receive. In the following sections, Tiers 1, 2, and 3 will be defined, with examples of how two students' (one elementary and one secondary) special education services and supports are provided within each Tier.

Table 3
Example of Special Education and Related Services and Supplementary Aids and Services to Ensure Access to Mathematics

Gabe is a 6th grade student at Lakeside Middle School. His class schedule includes five periods in general education classes and one period in a special education class. Gabe communicates using three-to-four word phrases and is working on increasing his vocabulary using low-tech picture supports throughout the school day. His school recently transitioned to using MTSS as a problem-solving model to ensure that all students have access to timely and focused intervention when they demonstrate a need. Gabe, a student with IDD, requires extensive support to learn and generalize new information. His IEP team identified that he could benefit from the following special education and related services and supplementary aids and services related to mathematics:

Special Education and Related Services	Supplementary Aids and Services

• Co-planned lessons in all core content areas,
• Three co-taught lessons per week (one in each core content area),
• 30 minutes of intensive instruction daily from a special education teacher,
• 60 minutes weekly with speech language pathologist support in general education classes,
• 60 minutes weekly with occupational therapist support in general education classes.
	• Curricular accommodations, including use of
	  ○ manipulatives,
	  ○ scribe,
	  ○ prompts and cues, and
	  ○ visual supports
	• Collaborative supports, including:
	  ○ Collaborative planning,
	  ○ Training for all staff on use of assistive technology

Tier 1

Grade-aligned standards-based curriculum and instruction, often delivered by a general education teacher to all students, is considered Tier 1 (McIntosh & Goodman, 2016). Instruction in this Tier should be high-quality, engaging, and accessible to all learners. Accessibility for students with ASD/IDD can be accomplished through general education and special education collaboration by designing lessons that are rigorous, contextualized (see Chapter 1), and designed using UDL guidelines. When all students are able to access and participate in engaging instruction, the need for more restrictive placements and more intensive classroom supports and interventions is lessened (Center on Multi-Tiered System of Supports, 2020). Accessible and universally designed instruction allows students with ASD/IDD to remain in a less restrictive environment for core instruction, hence ensuring adequate time spent accessing the general education curriculum from a content expert and having opportunities to engage with peers without disabilities (Lowrey et al., 2017).

Given the complexity of state core content standards in all subject areas, especially in secondary grade bands, an instructional team will need to identify ways to ensure accessibility and alignment to a student's IEP. One way to do this is by utilizing the 3 P's Rule ("Prioritize, Pinpoint, and Progress Monitor") presented in Chapter 2. Special education services and supports for students with ASD/IDD in Tier 1 could include a focus on high priority targets, alternative ways for them to express what they know, and integration of all concepts and vocabulary with their communication system. Identifying high priority targets can help a team to narrow their focus to ensure that a student learns the most important or relevant content in a unit. For example, if a first-grade class is learning about composing two-dimensional shapes, including rectangles, squares, trapezoids, triangles, half-circles, and quarter-circles, a student with

ASD/IDD who had difficulty with this may focus on composing a square and triangle. If a seventh-grade math class is learning about using proportional relationships to solve real-world problems, a lesson may be focusing on filling out a graphic organizer for a proportional relationship of number of hours worked to the amount of dollars earned (dollars earned = number of hours worked x hourly rate; see Figure 3). For most students, the goal will be to express that proportion in a graph, a function table, and an equation. However, a student with ASD/IDD might focus on expressing the proportion using a visual function table and identifying an equation and summary description to match (see Figure 3). One tool that can be used to identify high priority targets are a state's alternate achievement standards (Sabia et al., 2020).

In addition to a focus on priority learning targets, students with ASD/IDD also benefit from having flexible ways to participate and show what they know during lessons and activities. In Figure 3, a student with IDD will have accessible options to express what they know about proportional relationships. These options include being able to place ten-dollar bills into the function table, and the ability to choose from a field of three for the equation and the descriptive summary. Other strategies to ensure students with ASD/IDD can show what they know is to have all mathematics vocabulary available in either high (e.g., AAC) or low tech (e.g., picture supports) options for students to use during lessons. If a student relies on a core vocabulary board, this could include having fringe vocabulary boards also available for each content area.

Collaborative planning. Making specialized adaptations and modifications for students with ASD/IDD within Tier 1 instruction relies primarily on focused, collaborative planning between a general and special education teacher, and related service providers, as appropriate. Given that this planning time is not often provided on a regular basis, it could also occur asynchronously, using e-mail, and/or online document collaboration tools (e.g., Google Docs,

Figure 3

Class Graphic Organizer and Adapted Graphic Organizer

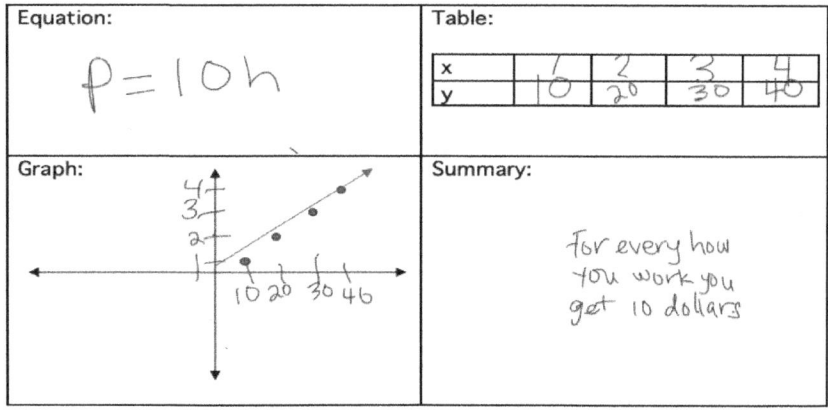

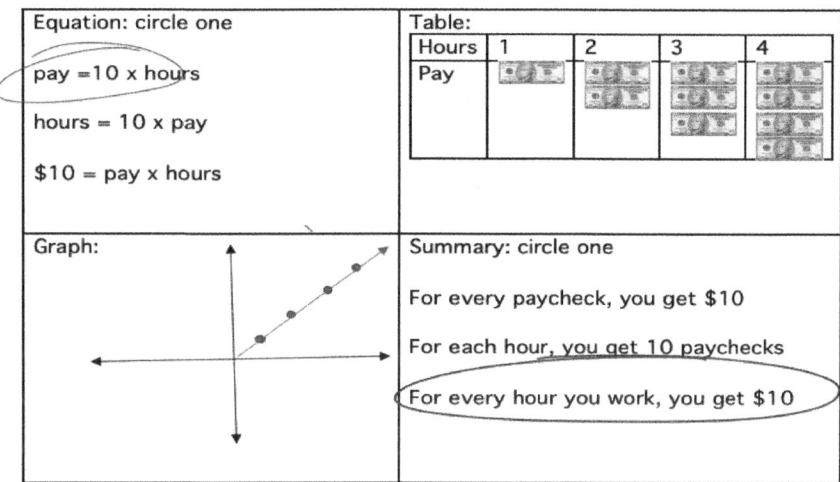

Box). Collaborative meetings focused on Tier 1 instruction should start at the beginning of the school year with a discussion of:

- context (routines and expectations in the general education classroom),
- content (what will be taught and using which instructional strategies),
- strategies and supports for students with ASD/IDD (including meeting their cognitive, behavioral, and communication needs), and
- evaluation and grading.

While an initial meeting could be lengthy, it sets the stage for a successful school year of meaningful inclusion in Tier 1 instruction for a student with ASD/IDD. General education teachers can share information about how their class runs, what key content they will cover over the course of the school year, and common instructional strategies used. The special education teacher should spend time discussing students with ASD/IDD, their strengths and needs, what worked well during the previous year, and how to best support them in academic, behavioral, and communicative development. As the school year progresses, the general education teacher and special education teacher will need to meet to continue to identify priority learning targets (as the content shifts from unit to unit) and discuss how to ensure that all instructional strategies and activities are accessible to students with ASD/IDD.

Universal Design for Learning. During collaborative planning, teams may discuss how to make daily instruction accessible to all students, including any students with ASD/IDD. Universal Design for Learning (UDL) is one framework educators can use to proactively design lessons where all students are able to actively engage in the content and activities (CAST, 2018; Saunders et al., 2019). Designing lessons using UDL requires educators to proactively consider the barriers that might exist within a lesson and build in flexibility in the way that students engage with, access, and demonstrate mastery of the content. In the UDL framework, educators consider how flexibility can be embedded in a lesson in the areas of representation of content, student engagement, and student action or expression.

Representation. By providing multiple means of representation, the goal is to create learners who are resourceful and knowledgeable (CAST, 2018). While all students may have preferences regarding how content is presented, other learners will rely heavily on a small number of representation options. For example, some students with ASD/IDD may prefer content presented in graphic format (i.e., visuals, diagrams, multimedia), while other learners will not be able to access information in this way without accommodations (e.g., students who are blind). Student preference of course should not be confused with learning styles, which have been deemed to be an educational myth (http://www.danielwillingham.com/learning-styles-faq.html). By ensuring content is perceptible for all students, vocabulary and/or symbols are clarified, and students are supported in making meaning of the content, educators create equitable classrooms where all students have authentic access to the mathematics curriculum (see Table 4). Questions to consider when making adjustments for content representation for students with ASD/IDD include:

1. How can content and information be presented in multiple ways (audio, visual, tactile)?
2. What vocabulary or symbols will be used in a lesson and how can those be clarified so that all students understand?
3. How can we support students who may not have the necessary skills and prior knowledge to make meaning of the content and information in this lesson? (CAST, 2018)

When all learners can access and connect new math learning to their everyday environments, they gain skills necessary for making progress in the curriculum and for interpreting their everyday experiences through the lens of mathematics. In addition, when students are given multiple means of accessing information, they can begin to make connections with those avenues in which they experience the most success and become more self-directed in their own learning.

Engagement. The goal of increasing flexibility around student engagement is to create learners who are purposeful and motivated (CAST, 2018). Purposeful and motivated learners are especially important in the area of mathematics, as the direct application of some mathematics

Table 4

Examples and Nonexamples of UDL

	Representation	**Engagement**	**Expression**
Examples	During a mathematics lesson, the teacher uses verbal think alouds alongside mathematical symbols and manipulatives for all to see.	Given the barriers with group work that some may experience, the teacher explicitly teaches students how to engage in group work, including roles and responsibilities, alongside modeling and role play. Group and independent work are strategically varied across the week to allow for opportunities for both.	Given a class assignment that includes one story-based problem, the teacher allows students flexibility in how they respond. They can respond using (1) paper and pencil with drawings or symbols, or (2) by using a tablet with manipulatives (virtual or photos of physical manipulatives) alongside a recorded explanation.
Nonexamples	During a mathematics lesson, the teacher uses verbal think alouds alongside mathematical symbols and the paraprofessional models the instruction using manipulatives with one student with ASD/IDD.	Because one student with ASD/IDD has difficulty with participating in group work, they are allowed to work independently if they choose.	In an assignment that includes five multiple choice questions and one short answer, one student who experiences barriers with writing is allowed to complete their assessment by using a tablet and recording their response verbally.

content can easily become unclear to learners. For all students, including those with ASD/IDD, there are some initial questions that teachers can work through to improve engagement. These questions include:

1. What environmental barriers in the math classroom may need remediation (e.g., routines, pace, social demands)?

2. How can student choice be used in this lesson?

3. How is this lesson or content relevant to students?

4. What supports could help students struggling to sustain effort and motivation? (CAST, 2018)

Creating a mathematics classroom where all learners are supported to engage in classroom activities and routines is essential for producing students who are purposeful in their learning and motivated to persist in the demands of a lesson, even when the content becomes more complex or abstract.

Action and Expression. The last element of the UDL framework is that students have multiple means of action and expression so that they can be strategic and goal-directed (CAST, 2018). This element can be especially important to consider for students who may have difficulty interacting with materials or communicating their learning through common avenues (e.g., writing, verbal communication). Mathematics is unique because of the various options that exist for learning. Through the use of concrete materials and hands-on, problem-based activities, textbook and worksheet-based lessons can transform into accessible and engaging lessons for every student (Van de Walle et al., 2016). Questions for educators to consider when ensuring that all students have a way to interact with lesson materials and successfully demonstrate their learning could include:

1. How can we address barriers to students' physical interaction with the lesson materials?
2. How can we provide multiple ways for students to express themselves during this lesson (e.g., text, speech, drawing, comics, film, music, sculpture, video, physical/virtual manipulatives)?
3. In what ways do students need support using metacognitive strategies in this lesson?

4. How might assistive technology (high or low tech) support student access to materials (e.g., use of virtual manipulatives instead of physical) or expression (e.g., use of picture symbols to use for answer selection)? (CAST, 2018)

Planning a lesson with a focus on successful student action and expression can allow for all students to actively engage in their learning and more clearly demonstrate what they know. By providing flexible options for action and expression, educators can not only make their lessons accessible to students with ASD/IDD but improve the learning experience for every student in their classroom.

In Figures 4 and 5, classroom examples are presented of general education teachers and special education teachers planning for including students with ASD/IDD in a general education mathematics lesson, using the UDL framework to identify barriers, supporting all students at the Tier 1 level. By identifying barriers for students with ASD/IDD, teachers have an opportunity to reach all learners.

Tier 2. Tier 2 includes supplemental instruction that some students in the class may receive related to targeted skills that need to be strengthened. This instruction will be more intense (focused on specific learning goals) with more opportunities for students to receive feedback compared to Tier 1 instruction. In the area of mathematics, this supplemental instruction could be provided in a wide range of skills related to reteaching or pre-teaching what is being taught in the classroom, often using explicit instruction, think-alouds, and modeling (Van de Walle et al., 2016). For example, in Figure 6, within a mathematics unit on multiplying and dividing fractions, the general education teacher organizes a small group activity on the conceptual understanding of fractions and how to check whether an answer makes sense. Embedded instruction is another strategy that could be used to provide Tier 2 supports to a group

Figure 4
Example of example of collaborative planning Tier 1 instruction using the UDL framework

Ms. Martinez is a fifth-grade general education teacher and is planning for the next mathematics unit on multiplying fractions that is set to begin in two weeks. Ms. Martinez knows she needs to plan for how to meet the needs of Chandra, a student in her class who has an IDD. She sees Mr. Backman, the special education teacher, in the hallway, and tells him she'd like to meet to discuss supporting Chandra in this next unit. They aren't able to find a common time to plan extensively, so Mr. Backman agrees to have a quick 15-minute planning session the next morning before school.

During their 15-minute meeting, Ms. Martinez goes over
- the focus standards of the unit
- instructional strategies that she will use

Once these are established, Ms. Martinez and Mr. Backman will identify:
- one to two priority learning targets for Chandra
- barrier(s) Chandra might experience
- how to remove that barrier

Focus standards:
CCSS.MATH.5.NF.B.4 - Apply and extend previous understandings of multiplication to multiply a fraction or whole number by a fraction.

CCSS.MATH.5.NF.B.5
Interpret multiplication as scaling (resizing), by:
- Comparing the size of a product to the size of one factor on the basis of the size of the other factor, without performing the indicated multiplication.
- Explaining why multiplying a given number by a fraction greater than 1 results in a product greater than the given number (recognizing multiplication by whole numbers greater than 1 as a familiar case).

CCSS.MATH.5.NF.B.6 - Solve real-world problems involving multiplication of fractions and mixed numbers, e.g., by using visual fraction models or equations to represent the problem.

Instructional strategies: Classroom discussion, use of concrete (fraction manipulatives), representational (fraction drawings, including area models), and abstract (symbols to represent fractions and use of numerical strategies) representations, explicit instruction, and small group and partner work.

Priority learning: Both teachers are already aware that Chandra is a student who is working on several foundational math skills, including identifying numbers over 20 and doing basic addition and subtraction. Given this, they are going to identify priority content for Chandra to learn. An alternative achievement standard in their state is related to identifying fractional parts (½, ⅓, and ¼) and demonstrating the concept of multiplication. Ms. Martinez and Mr. Backman agreed these seemed like great entry points for Chandra and agreed to prioritize them as Chandra engages in this unit.

Barriers:
Engagement
- *Barrier:* Chandra may struggle to maintain attention to the lesson.
- *Solution:* Real-world problems will be presented keeping Chandra's interests in mind.

Representation
- *Barrier:* Difficulty with comprehending mathematics symbols shown in equations.
- *Solution:* All mathematical symbols will be represented using concrete manipulatives, drawings, and symbols (see Chapter 4 for more information on manipulative-based instructional sequences).
- *Barrier:* No mastery of multiplication, even for whole numbers (an important prerequisite skill for this lesson).
- *Solution:* Chandra will receive additional instruction in multiplication with the special education teacher.

Action/Expression
- *Barrier:* Chandra is not able to reliably write or draw.
- *Solution:* All students will be able to choose to demonstrate their learning through drawing, writing, use of concrete models and sentence starters with picture-supported word banks.

Reflection: After the lesson, Ms. Martinez reflected with Mr. Backman that she noticed that one student, Jack, who is typically difficult to engage in mathematics content, was especially engaged in use of concrete models and manipulatives.

Figure 5
Secondary example of collaborative planning Tier 1 instruction using the UDL framework

Mr. Zartman is an eighth-grade general education mathematics teacher and is planning for the next mathematics unit on geometry. Mr. Zartman knows he needs to plan for how to meet the needs of Aaron, a student in his class who has ASD. Mr. Zartman sends an email to Ms. Olson, the special education teacher, and asks if they can plan remotely for how to support Aaron in this next unit.

Mr. Zartman uploads a planning template they use into their online folder. It covers:
- the focus standards of the unit
- instructional strategies that will be used
- one to two priority learning targets for Aaron
- one barrier(s) Aaron might experience
- how to remove that barrier

Focus standards:
CCSS.MATH.8.G.A.3
Describe the effect of dilations, translations, rotations, and reflections on two-dimensional figures using coordinates.

CCSS.MATH.8.G.A.4
Understand that a two-dimensional figure is similar to another if the second can be obtained from the first by a sequence of rotations, reflections, translations, and dilations; given two similar two-dimensional figures, describe a sequence that exhibits the similarity between them.

Instructional strategies: Classroom discussion, use of concrete (tangrams), representational (pictures, figures on a grid), and abstract (symbols to represent congruence and motions of translations and rotations) representations, explicit instruction, and small group and partner work.

Priority learning: Mr. Zartman and Ms. Olson take time to think about the standards in relation to where Aaron is performing. Aaron is able to do many math tasks with accommodations (use of visuals, manipulatives, and technology), so his priority content will not change.

Barriers:
Engagement
- *Barrier:* Aaron may struggle to persist when work is challenging.
- *Solution:* Choice will be provided to all students throughout assignments (do a problem/cross one out, choice of application problems to solve).

Representation
- *Barrier:* Difficulty with processing translation/reflection/rotation/dilation sequences when represented as symbols.
- *Solution:* All sequences will be represented alongside visual and verbal examples and information [e.g., (-3, 2) - *"three to the left and up two"*)].

Action/Expression
- *Barrier:* Aaron experiences frustration with drawing, which will occur when students draw figures on coordinate planes.
- *Solution:* All students will be able to choose to conduct sequences on an online coordinate plane or a geoboard with rubber bands.

Reflection: After the lesson, Mr. Zartman was reviewing student work and noticed that a few students who frequently turn in incomplete assignments did not skip any questions at all. By allowing students to choose which problems to solve, these students were more motivated to complete the assignment in full.

Note: Planning format adapted from the TIES Center's 5-15-45 tool at tiescenter.org

Figure 6
Example of elementary teacher providing Tier 2 instruction

Based on some of the exit slips completed by the class, Ms. Martinez is aware that there are several students in her class who are having difficulty with the content on multiplying fractions. The day before, students were to answer the following word problem in an exit slip.

> Julie made five loaves of bread that had 1/4 cup of flour in each loaf. How many cups of flour were used in all?

Ms. Martinez identified one main issue with the students who incorrectly answered: difficulties with conceptual understandings of fraction multiplication. Ms. Martinez knows students should be able to answer this question in their heads without relying on an algorithm. One fourth multiplied by five is one whole and one fourth more. However, some students responded with $\frac{1}{20}$ due to multiplying $\frac{1}{4 \times 5}$. Because of this, she will have a Tier 2 small group on fractional concepts, focusing on solving fraction multiplication problems using concrete and virtual manipulatives (as shown below). She will have students work through the following guiding questions:
- How did you solve the problem?
- Show me how to solve this problem using manipulatives.
- How can we use repeated addition to solve this problem?
- How can we solve this problem using our algorithm? How can we know if our answer makes sense?

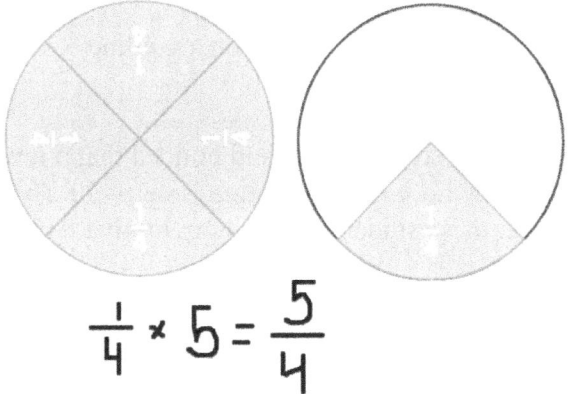

(from https://app.brainingcamp.com/manipulatives/fraction-circles/)

Because Chandra also demonstrates difficulties with fractional concepts, she will participate while also being provided with her normal special education supplementary aids and services, which include visual supports for vocabulary and use of concrete mathematics manipulatives. In this lesson, Chandra utilized all of these supports to remain engaged and communicative throughout the lesson. The teacher made sure to also have Chandra identify the fractional part that represented ¼ from a field of 4 and give her a chance to multiply using repeated addition, putting the counters together until she made a whole and identifying her solution using her fringe vocabulary.

of students (see Chapter 6). Within Tier 2, progress monitoring occurs regularly, at least monthly, to determine whether students are making progress, if intervention is having an impact, and which students continue to require Tier 2 interventions (McIntosh & Goodman, 2016). In the example in Figure 7, Ms. Martinez and Mr. Zartman identify students who may need additional instruction related to their unit.

Tier 3. Tier 3 instruction provides even more intensive instruction to the fewer students who may continue to struggle, even when Tier 2 interventions are provided (McIntosh & Goodman, 2016). While Tier 2 instruction is often delivered to groups of students, Tier 3 is delivered based upon individual student's skill gaps (Thurlow et al., 2020). Instructional teams design intensive and individualized instruction in Tier 3 to eliminate or minimize most prominent student skill gaps. This instruction should be highly contextualized and provided in a one-on-one format or in very small groups, in addition to, not in place of, Tier 1 and 2 instruction (Batsche, 2014). For students with ASD/IDD, the skill gaps addressed in Tier 3 may include prerequisite skill needs for priority learning targets or could focus on student IEP goals, developed by their educational team as required for making progress in the general education curriculum. Progress monitoring in Tier 3 occurs frequently and will align with the guidelines set forth in Chapter 2.

To ensure students with ASD/IDD receive plentiful opportunities for Tier 3 instruction while still also receiving Tiers 1 and 2 support, general and special educators should work together to develop flexible roles and routines that allow multiple staff and/or peers to provide this intensive instruction. There are several options for providing Tier 3 supports. First, a school may build in a skills block into its schedule, allowing all students to work on focused skills at the same time. In elementary schools, you may see this as a secondary literacy or mathematics block

Figure 7

Example of elementary teacher providing Tier 2 instruction

Secondary Tier 2 Vignette: Mr. Zartman gives a weekly math quiz. During the first week of the unit, he noticed several students making the same error on one of the questions.

What single transformation was applied to triangle A to get triangle B?

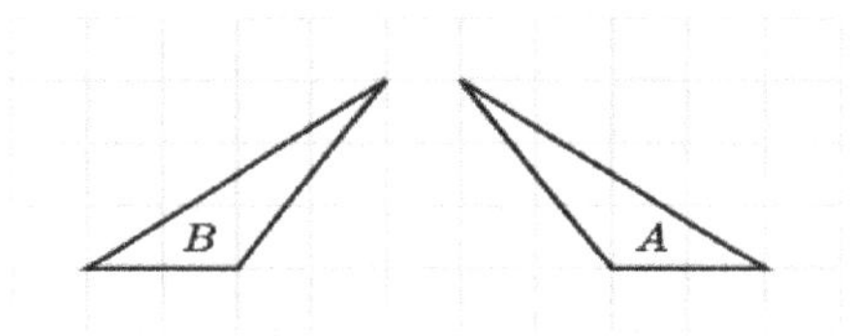

Choose 1 answer:

- INCORRECT Translation
- INCORRECT Rotation
- CORRECT (SELECTED) Reflection
- INCORRECT Dilation

(Geometric transformations: Quiz 1, n.d.)

Given the confusion of several students between rotations and reflections, Mr. Zartman will work with Ms. Olson during co-teaching to do some embedded instructional trials to reteach some of the vocabulary concepts (especially targeting rotations and reflections) with the targeted group of students during individual work time.

in a grade level schedule where students focus on accelerating, reinforcing or developing their skills. In secondary schools, a student may be scheduled to have a companion literacy or mathematics course that reinforces (Tier 2) key concepts that were taught in the core course (Tier 1) and provides individual instruction to minimize or eliminate skill gaps (Tier 3). In both situations, special education teachers could provide this additional support through co-teaching, pulling small groups, or leading centers or rotations. A second method identified in the literature for providing students with ASD/IDD instruction in individualized content without being removed from a general education setting is embedded instruction (see Chapter 6). This strategy allows for flexible responsibility, and can be delivered by a special education teacher, general education teacher, a paraprofessional, or peer during any natural opportunity in a general education classroom. Read the examples in Figure 8 and 9 to see how the elementary and secondary teacher teams plan for Tier 3 supports for Chandra and Aaron.

Conclusion

MTSS are an effective way to ensure all students receive the support necessary to access and make progress in the general education mathematics curriculum. Given teacher collaboration, UDL, and the provision of special education services and supports at each Tier, the needs of students with ASD/IDD can be met within the structures of MTSS. This deeper focus on accessible instruction and student learning has the potential to improve the outcomes of students with disabilities, including students with ASD/IDD in the area of mathematics.

Figure 8
Elementary Example of Tier 3 Instruction

Chandra is a student with significant skill gaps in all core content areas. Due to her disability and low expectations set for her early on, she was not provided instruction in mathematics outside of number identification and counting until 5th grade. Due to her skill gaps, her instructional team has decided to continue Tier 3 instruction in early numeracy skills, including her ability to make sets and compose and decompose numbers in the context of problem-solving, using modified schema-based instruction (see Chapter 5). This instruction occurs daily, when she receives embedded instruction on at least two-word problems per day in her mathematics class. Mr. Backman and Ms. Martinez developed a schedule to ensure that Chandra received instruction on her individualized goals daily, and that data collection occurred weekly.

Monday	Tuesday	Wednesday	Thursday	Friday
Word Problems (WP) 1 & 2 Mr. Backman	WP 3 & 4 Ms. Snodgress (paraprofessional)	WP 1 & 3 Ms. Martinez	WP 2 & 4 Mr. Thomas (student teacher)	WP 5 & 6 data collection probe* Mr. Backman

Figure 9
Secondary Example of Tier 3 Instruction

Aaron's IEP goal in the area of mathematics is the following:
> Given a mathematics discussion in a small group, Aaron will increasingly participate in sharing his own reasoning and critiquing the reasoning of others by offering 4 on topic comments per day for 7 consecutive days.

Mr. Zartman and Ms. Olson have worked together to support Aaron in reaching this goal. To further his progress, Aaron has been given sentence starters in a laminated sheet in his desk to prompt his contributions during discussion. In addition, both teachers provide additional prompting during discussion to ensure that Aaron stays on topic and uses his supports as necessary.

Math Discussion Participation

★ I solved the problem by…
★ I solved it this way because…
★ One question I have about the problem is…
★ I'm curious why you solved the problem that way because…

Data are collected twice a week on Aaron's participation during small group discussion in his math class. Mr. Zartman and Ms. Olson share responsibility for the data collection by marking the frequency of Aaron's on topic contributions related to problem solving.

References

Batsche, G. (2014). MTSS for inclusive schools. In McLeskey, Waldron, Spooner, & Algozzine (Eds). *Handbook of Effective Inclusive Schools* (pp. 183-196). Routledge.

Cameron, D. L., & Cook, B. G. (2013). General education teachers' goals and expectations for their included students with mild and severe disabilities. *Education and training in autism and developmental disabilities, 48*(1), 18-30.

CAST (2020). *Key questions to consider when planning lessons.* Author. (Reprinted from *Universal design for learning: theory and practice*, by Meyer, A., Rose, D.H., & Gordon, D., 2014, Author). Retrieved from http://www.cast.org/our-work/publications/2020/udl-guidelines-key-questions-planning-lessons.html

CAST (2018). Universal Design for Learning Guidelines version 2.2. http://udlguidelines.cast.org

Center on Multi-Tiered System of Support (2020). Multi-level prevention system. Retrieved at: https://mtss4success.org/essential-components/multi-level-prevention-system

Choi, J. H., McCart, A. B., & Sailor, W. (2020). Achievement of Students With IEPs and Associated Relationships With an Inclusive MTSS Framework. *The Journal of Special Education.* (Advance Online Publication). https://doi.org/10.1177/0022466919897408

Choi, J. H., Meisenheimer, J. M., McCart, A. B., & Sailor, W. (2017). Improving learning for all students through equity-based inclusive reform practices: Effectiveness of a fully integrated schoolwide model on student reading and math achievement. *Remedial and Special Education, 38*(1), 28-41. https://doi.org/10.1177/0741932516644054

Dymond, S. K., Renzaglia, A., Rosenstein, A., Chun, E. J., Banks, R. A., Niswander, V., & Gilson, C. L. (2006). Using a participatory action research approach to create a universally designed inclusive high school science course: A case study. *Research and Practice for Persons with Severe Disabilities, 31*(4), 293-308.

Every Student Succeeds Act of 2015, Pub. L. No. 114-95 § 114 Stat. 1177 (2015–2016).

Fuchs, L. S., Fuchs, D., Craddock, C., Hollenbeck, K. N., Hamlett, C. L., & Schatschneider, C. (2008). Effects of small-group tutoring with and without validated classroom instruction on at-risk students' math problem solving: Are two tiers of prevention better than one? *Journal of Educational Psychology, 100*, 491–509.

Geometric transformations: Quiz 1. (n.d.). *Khan Academy*. Retrieved from: https://www.khanacademy.org/math/cc-eighth-grade-math/geometric-transformations

Horner, R. H., & Halle, J. W. (2019). Implications of emerging educational reforms for individuals with severe disabilities. *Research and Practice for Persons with Severe Disabilities.* [Advance Online Publication]. https://doi.org/10.1177/1540796919872210

Individuals with Disabilities Education Improvement Act of 2004, 20 U. S. C. §1414. (2004).

IRIS Center. (2019). Definition: Multi-tiered system of support. https://iris.peabody.vanderbilt.edu/module/rti-math/cresource/q1/p01/multi-tiered-system-of-support-mtss/#content

Lane, K. L., Carter, E. W., Jenkins, A., Dwiggins, L., & Germer, K. (2015). Supporting comprehensive, integrated, three–tiered models of prevention in schools: Administrator's perspectives. *Journal of Positive Behavior Interventions, 17*, 209–222. DOI: 10.1177/1098300715578916

Lee, S., Wehmeyer, M. L., Soukup, J. H., Palmer, S. B. (2010). Impact of curriculum modifications on access to the general education curriculum for students with disabilities. *Exceptional Children, 76*(2), 213–233.

Lowrey, K. A., Hollingshead, A., Howery, K., & Bishop, J. B. (2017). More than one way: Stories of UDL and inclusive classrooms. *Research and Practice for Persons with Severe Disabilities, 42*(4), 225-242. https://doi.org/10.1177/1540796917711668

McIntosh, K., & Goodman, S. (2016). *Integrated multi-tiered systems of support: Blending RTI and PBIS*. Guilford Publications.

McLeskey, J., Maheady, L., Billingsley, B., Brownell, M.T., & Lewis, T. (2019). *High leverage practices for inclusive classrooms*. Routledge.

Morningstar, M. E., Shogren, K. A., Lee, H., & Born, K. (2015). Preliminary lessons about supporting participation and learning in inclusive classrooms. *Research and Practice for Persons with Severe Disabilities, 40*(3), 192-210.

Riccomini, P. J., Morano, S., & Hughes, C. A. (2017). Big ideas in special education: Specially designed instruction, high-leverage practices, explicit instruction, and intensive instruction. *Teaching Exceptional Children, 50*(1), 20-27.

Roberts, C. A., Ruppar, A. L., & Olson, A. J. (2018). Perceptions matter: Administrators' vision of instruction for students with severe disabilities. *Research and Practice for Persons with Severe Disabilities, 43*(1), 3-19. https://doi.org/10.1177/1540796917743931

Sabia, R., Bowman, J., Thurlow, M. L., & Lazarus, S. S. (2020, April). *Providing meaningful general education curriculum access to students with significant cognitive disabilities* (Brief #4). TIES Center. https://tiescenter.org/resource/ties-brief-4-providing-meaningful-general-education-curriculum-access-to-students-with-significant-cognitive-disabilities

Sailor, W. (2015). Advances in schoolwide inclusive school reform. *Remedial and Special Education, 36*(2), 94-99. https://doi.org/10.1177/0741932514555021

Sailor, W., McCart, A., Choi, J. (2018). Reconceptualizing inclusive education through multi-tiered systems of support. *Inclusion, 6*(1), 3-18. https://doi.org/10.1352/2326-6988-6.1.3

Saunders, A. F., Root, J. R., & Jimenez, B. A. (2019). Recommendations for inclusive educational practices in mathematics for students with extensive support needs. *Inclusion, 7*(2), 75-91. https://doi.org/10.1352/2326-6988-7.2.75

Saunders, A. F., Wakemen, S., Reyes, E., Thurlow, M., and Vandercook, T. (2020). *Instructional practices for students with the most significant disabilities in inclusive settings: A review of the literature* (TIES Center Report 104). The TIES Center.

Shogren, K. A., McCart, A. B., Lyon, K. J., & Sailor, W. S. (2015). All means all: Building knowledge for inclusive schoolwide transformation. *Research and Practice for Persons with Severe Disabilities, 40*(3), 173–191. https://doi.org/10.1177/1540796915586191

Taub, D. A., McCord, J. A., & Ryndak, D. L. (2017). Opportunities to learn for students with extensive support needs: A context of research-supported practices for all in general education classes. *The Journal of Special Education, 51*(3), 127–137. https://doi.org/10.1177/0022466917696263

Thurlow, M. L., Ghere, G., Lazarus, S. S., & Liu, K. K. (2020). *MTSS for all: Including students with the most significant cognitive disabilities.* National Center on Educational Outcomes. TIES Center.

Torgesen, J. K. (2009). The response to intervention instructional model: Some outcomes from a large-scale implementation in Reading First schools. *Child Development Perspectives, 3*(1), 38-40.

Van de Walle, J., Karp, K., & Bay-Williams, J. (2019). *Elementary and middle school mathematics: Teaching developmentally* (10th ed.). Pearson.

Walker, V. L., Loman, S. L., Hara, M., Park, K. L., & Strickland-Cohen, M. K. (2018). Examining the inclusion of students with severe disabilities in school-wide positive behavioral interventions and supports. *Research and Practice for Persons with Severe Disabilities, 43*(4), 223-238. https://doi.org/10.1177/1540796918779370

Wanzek, J., & Vaughn, S. (2010). Is a three-tier reading intervention model associated with reduced placement in special education? *Remedial and Special Education, 32*(2), 167–175. https://doi.org/10.1177/0741932510361267

Wisconsin Response to Intervention Center (2020). Continuum of supports. Retrieved at: https://www.wisconsinrticenter.org/key-system-feature/continuum-of-supports/

Chapter 4: Manipulatives and Manipulative-Based Instructional Sequences

Emily C. Bouck & Holly Long

Manipulatives

Manipulatives are tools to support students in mathematics, particularly as students develop conceptual understanding of how to approach and solve different types of mathematics (Carbonneau et al., 2013; Uribe-Flórez & Wilkins, 2010). When one references manipulatives, historically one is referring to concrete manipulatives. Concrete manipulatives are physical objects students interact with to approach mathematics (Bouck & Flanagan, 2010; see Table 1 for examples of manipulatives). However, another type of manipulative also exists – virtual manipulatives. Virtual manipulatives are digital versions of manipulatives for use on a computer online or through an app for mobile devices (see Table 2 for examples of virtual manipulative websites and apps; Bouck, Working, & Bone, 2018; Bouck & Flanagan, 2010; Moyer et al., 2002).

Table 1
Examples of Manipulatives for Different Mathematics

Mathematics Skills and Domains	Manipulatives
Place value	Base 10 Blocks
Addition and subtraction (with and without regrouping)	Base 10 Blocks
Single-digit multiplication and division	Color tiles
Algebra	Algebra Tiles
Fractions (identifying, equivalent, adding and subtracting)	Fraction tiles, tower, or pieces
Division with remainders	Cuisenaire rods
Double-digit addition	Factor track, Base 10 Blocks

Table 2

Example of App-Based and Online Virtual Manipulatives

Virtual Manipulative	Description
Brainingcamp https://www.brainingcamp.com/	• Apps for use on iPad, Chromebooks, or website for use on computer • Multiple different apps, based on concrete manipulatives (e.g., algebra tiles, fraction pieces, base 10 blocks, • Can purchase all apps as a bundle or individually purchase each one. 30-day free trial for web-based apps
National Library of Virtual Manipulatives (NLVM) http://nlvm.usu.edu/en/nav/vlibrary.html	• Online manipulatives designed to enhance K-12 math instruction through interaction • Needs flash; does not work with iPads or Chromebooks • Entire resource is free, with multiple manipulatives that range across different grade levels and the five mathematic areas identified by the National Council of Teachers of Mathematics
The Math Learning Center https://www.mathlearningcenter.org/resources/apps	• Apps for the computer (web-based) as well as downloadable for an iPad • Free resource • Multiple different tools available (e.g., number line, money, ten-frame, fractions)

All students, but particularly elementary students, are likely to use manipulatives in their mathematics classroom (Bouck & Park, 2018; Uribe-Florez & Wilkins, 2017). The use of manipulatives in mathematics teaching and learning is endorsed by the National Council of Teachers of Mathematics (NCTM; National Council of Teachers of Mathematics, 2000). Further, many mathematics curricula encourage or reference the use of manipulatives for mathematics (Bouck & Park, 2018). While most of the aforementioned endorsements and supported use focus on concrete manipulatives, as educators increasingly use technology for teaching and learning access to and use of virtual manipulatives also increases (Cambridge Assessment International Education, 2018).

Increased attention to and use of virtual manipulatives is likely the result of both advancing technology as well as research finding virtual manipulatives offer additional benefits to concrete manipulatives (i.e., built-in supports [such as labels, mats, and constraints that prevent students from making common errors]) yet equivalent levels of effectiveness (Bouck, Mathews, & Peltier, 2020; Peltier et al., 2019; Sarama & Clements, 2016). Virtual manipulatives are suggested to be more age-appropriate for older students, as often concrete manipulatives are associated with and more commonly used by elementary students (Satsangi & Miller, 2017). Virtual manipulatives can also offer portability (i.e., can be transported across multiple classrooms via a mobile device and/or access at home if families have technology) solutions as well as potentially lower costs associated with using virtual manipulatives (Bouck et al., 2012).

Researchers also found students experience greater independence when using virtual manipulatives, due to built-in supports that reduce errors not inherent in concrete manipulatives, which would likely require an adult or peer to replicate with concrete manipulatives (Bouck, Chamberlain, & Park, 2017; Bouck, Mathews, & Peltier, 2020). For example, with the Base 10 Blocks by Brainingcamp (2020), the app does not allow students to ungroup from the subtrahend. The app also only allows students to regroup exactly 10 ones into a ten block and ungroup exactly 10 ones from one ten block. These built-in supports can be beneficial to scaffold learning when students are first introduced to a skill. Options without supports or where supports can be faded can be used when the student becomes more independent with the manipulatives as well as the mathematics to not promote dependence on the supports. Further, across the studies comparing concrete and virtual manipulatives, the majority of students with disabilities report a preference for the virtual manipulatives (e.g., Bouck, Chamberlain, & Park, 2017; Bouck, Mathews, & Peltier, 2020; Satsangi et al., 2016).

Research on Manipulatives and Students with ASD/IDD

Researchers suggest positive results for use of manipulatives for students with disabilities, even if manipulatives cannot be classified as an evidence-based practice due to additional studies needed (Bouck & Park, 2018; Peltier et al., 2019). For students with autism spectrum disorders (ASD) and intellectual and developmental disabilities (IDD; ASD/IDD) in particular, the research is also positive (e.g., Bouck, Park, Levy, et al., 2019; Yakubova et al., 2016). Researchers explored manipulative use by students with ASD/IDD generally across three different approaches: (a) use of manipulatives as part of a manipulative-based sequence of instruction, which will be discussed subsequently in the chapter; (b) comparing concrete manipulatives and virtual manipulatives; and (c) use of manipulatives as a tool for teaching and learning.

Within the literature on use of manipulatives for mathematics teaching and learning, researchers primarily explored the use of manipulatives taught by explicit instruction (i.e., teachers modeling two problems, guiding students as they attempted two problems, and then allowing students to solve five to 10 problems independently) to middle school students with ASD/IDD. Bouck, Park, Levy, et al. (2019) taught middle school students with ASD/IDD to use virtual Cuisenaire® rods to solve division with remainder problems. Delivered by explicit instruction, three students all acquired the skills, although not all students successfully generalized to solving when the virtual-manipulative was not present. Bouck and colleagues (Bouck & Park, 2020; Bouck, Long, & Park, 2020) also examined the use of virtual manipulatives (two-color counters and number line, respectively) to support addition of positive and negative integers by middle school students with ASD/IDD. Also, utilizing explicit instruction, researchers found students acquired the skill of adding integers in both studies, with success in terms of maintenance and generalization.

The existing research base on comparing concrete and virtual manipulatives for students with ASD/IDD supports both types of manipulatives for elementary and middle school students.

Students were successful in learning the mathematics (e.g., subtraction with regrouping, comparison problems, fractions, algebra) with both types, although in some studies students were more successful and/or more independent (i.e., needing fewer prompts) in solving the problems with virtual manipulatives (Bouck, Chamberlain, & Park, 2017; Long et al., 2020; Bouck et al., 2014; Bouck, Shurr, et al., 2018; Jimenez & Besaw, 2020; Root et al., 2017). The similar levels of success between concrete and virtual manipulatives provides support for virtual manipulatives as an option to complement or be used in place of concrete manipulatives under the right conditions.

Implementation of Manipulatives

For students with disabilities, in general, manipulatives serve a variety of roles in mathematics teaching and learning. Of course, these same roles can be used for students with ASD/IDD (see Figures 1 and 2). Manipulatives are often listed as a common accommodation on student's Individualized Education Program (IEP; Maccini & Gagnon, 2000). Second, manipulatives can be used as a means for teachers to support Universal Design for Learning (UDL; Bouck, Mathews, & Peltier, 2020; see Figure 3 for a discussion of manipulatives and UDL), with manipulatives available in the mathematics classroom for anyone to use to engage with the teaching and learning. Jimenez and Besaw (2020) found students were more engaged with the lessons and materials when virtual manipulatives were introduced. Manipulatives can be used for students to engage in independent work within the classroom after instruction or as part of center or station-based activities. Finally, manipulatives can be used to develop conceptual understanding as instruction is being delivered, both stand-alone and as part of a graduated sequence of instruction (Bouck, Mathews, Peltier, 2020).

Figure 1
Example of a Secondary Teacher Using Manipulatives

At Morrice Middle School, Ms. Nowak teaches a self-contained mathematics class, which consists primarily of students identified with ASD/IDD. Ms. Nowak's students demonstrate a range of mathematical strengths and challenges. She uses an alternative mathematics curriculum, in addition to independent activities to meet students' IEP goals relative to basic operations and application of operations to real-life situations. Ms. Nowak notes that some of her students still struggle with addition and subtraction with regrouping yet also refuse to use the concrete Base 10 blocks available within her room. However, Ms. Nowak does have a few Chromebooks and iPads and is interested in how she might be able to put them to use with her mathematics teaching and learning. After exploring, Ms. Nowak decides to purchase a few Brainingcamp licenses for the Base 10 Blocks, although acknowledges she could also use the similar free Math Learning Center app for the iPad or computer (not Chromebook). To teach addition and subtraction with regrouping and virtual base 10 blocks, Ms. Nowak elects to use explicit instruction paired with the system of least prompts as she knows both are considered evidence-based practices for students with disabilities. Rather than a calculator, Ms. Nowak decides to use manipulatives to continue to build her students' conceptual understanding of how to solve the problems. Ms. Nowak works with her students in math in small groups and decides to start with the small group struggling with addition and subtraction with regrouping and will deliver the explicit instruction to use the virtual Base 10 Blocks in this small group setting. With her use of explicit instruction, Ms. Nowak provides the system of least prompts (SLP) during the independent portion for the first few lessons she delivers and then fades the prompting. Ms. Nowak begins with the first session using virtual manipulatives. She models how to solve the two problems using the virtual manipulatives and explains each step with verbal narration as she is solving. Ms. Nowak then instructs her students to complete two problems on their own using the virtual manipulatives. If the students make an error or forget the next step, she uses the SLP to guide them. Finally, Ms. Nowak provides her students with five problems to complete independently and uses the system of least prompts if her students make an error or need guidance on what to do next. Her SLP involves (a) gestures, such as pointing to the app; (b) indirect verbal, such as asking what should be done next; (c) direct verbal, such as asking if students remember to ungroup from the tens place; and (d) modeling, such as demonstrating how to use the virtual manipulative on the particular step of the problem the student is stuck or solving incorrectly. Ms. Nowak collects data on the number of problems her students answer correctly (accuracy) and the kind of prompts she provided (independence) to track her students' progress. As the students make progress and require less prompts, Ms. Nowak fades the SLP until the students are completing the problems on their own.

When teaching students with disabilities to use manipulatives to understand and solve different mathematics problems, teachers can use task analytic instruction. Task analytic instruction utilizes a task analysis—a series of sequential steps to complete a task—to teach the

Figure 2
Elementary school Example of Teacher Planning to Use Manipulatives

Mr. Yadav teaches and supports fourth and fifth-grade students with ASD/IDD. Part of the time the students receive instruction in his classroom and part of the time they push into general education classes. Mr. Yadav works with his students' general education teachers to create manipulative support for all students in the classes, following the principles of UDL. To do so, Mr. Yadav and the general education teachers place concrete manipulatives related to the current math topic they are learning as well as others they have recently learned in a math area of each classroom. They also install the free Math Learning Center apps on the iPads in each classroom. They make sure all students in the classroom know how to use both the virtual manipulative apps as well as the concrete manipulatives and encourage students to use either the concrete manipulatives or the virtual manipulatives, as needed when working on mathematics.

Figure 3
Manipulatives and UDL

First, manipulatives can support UDL through multiple means of engagement. When student preference is considered in choosing a manipulative to work with (e.g., concrete or virtual or even unifix cubes vs. base 10 blocks), this engages the students' interest and promotes choice and autonomy. In addition to student preference, it is important to consider the demands associated with different manipulatives. For students with ASD/IDD who may struggle with motor skills, using small concrete manipulatives or controlling manipulatives on a small tablet screen could be difficult. It is important to choose an option that presents a lower demand for the student to facilitate engagement with the mathematics skill. Second, manipulatives can support UDL through multiple means of representation. As discussed previously (see Table 1 for examples of manipulatives), there are many different manipulatives to target similar mathematics content (i.e. fraction tiles, fraction towers, fraction pieces to use with fraction problems). In addition, students and teachers can choose between how they prefer to display these manipulatives, including concrete manipulatives, virtual manipulatives on a website through the computer, or virtual manipulatives available through an application on a tablet or mobile device. Students can also choose when they may want to use a manipulative—whatever type—and when they may want to draw (i.e., use pictorial representation) or solve just with numerical strategies. This choice also supports students' multiple means of expression.

skill (Shurr et al., 2019). To engage in task analytic instruction, teachers develop a task analysis

and then teach students to complete the task (i.e., solve problems) in this particular way.

Teachers can also use task analyses to assess for accuracy as well as independence as students work on the mathematics. See Table 3 for examples of task analyses relative to using manipulatives and mathematics.

Manipulative-Based Instructional Sequences

Manipulative-based sequences provide instruction in a manner that gradually shifts students from learning with a manipulative (e.g., concrete or virtual) to representations (i.e., drawing), to abstract or numerical strategies (Agrawal & Morin, 2016). Manipulative-based instructional sequences exist as the concrete-representational-abstract (CRA) instructional sequence, the virtual-representational-abstract (VRA) instructional sequence, the virtual-abstract (VA) instructional sequence, and the virtual-representational (VR) instructional sequence (see

Table 3
Examples of Task Analyses for Mathematics

Algebra	Division	Double-digit addition word problems
Concrete or Virtual Algebra Tiles	Virtual Color Tiles	Base 10 Blocks
1. Represent x 2. Represent the constant (if applicable) 3. Represent the sum/difference/product 4. Bring out the inverse of the constant (get x by itself) 5. Apply inverse to the other side of the equation 6. Simply 7. FOR 2-STEP: Evenly distribute across the x-tiles 8. Write down the answer 9. Clear tiles	1. State the problem, putting into mathematical terms (e.g., 16 ÷ 4 is that I have 16 objects and want to evenly divide them among 4 groups) 2. Pull out the number of tiles needed for the dividend (e.g., 16) 3. Draw the number of groups (e.g., circle) to divided into (e.g., divisor; 4 4. Equally distribute the tiles into each group (i.e., circle) – putting one in each group before putting multiple in any one group 5. Check that there are no leftover tiles and there are tiles in each group/circle 6. Count the number of tiles/objects in one group 7. Write down answer 8. Clear	1. Read the word problem 2. Write down the first tens of the addition problem 3. Write down the first ones of the addition problem 4. Write down the second tens of the addition problem 5. Write down the second ones of the addition problem 6. Write down the sign (+) 7. Set up the tens blocks for the first number of the problem 8. Set up the ones blocks for the first number of the problem 9. Set up the tens blocks for the second number of the problem 10. Set up the ones blocks for the second number of the problem 11. Regroup ones to solve the problem (exchange 10 ones for 1 ten) 12. Count the number of ones 13. Write answer for ones 14. Count the number of tens 15. Write answer for tens

Table 4 for visual and textual representations of the manipulative-based instructional sequences). These sequences are similarly structured, although the initial type of manipulative can vary (i.e., concrete or virtual) as well as the need for a representational phase in which students draw pictures (Bouck & Sprick, 2019). The sequences all rely on explicit instruction as the means to deliver the instruction (i.e., teach each phase of the graduated sequence of instruction; Agrawal & Morin, 2016). The CRA, VRA, VA, and VR instructional sequences can be used across a variety of mathematical domains—basically any mathematics in which manipulatives can be used to support understanding.

As said, the CRA, VRA, VA, and VR instructional sequences each involve students first learning to solve mathematical problems with a manipulative – either concrete (CRA) or virtual (VRA, VA, or VR). When students demonstrate mastery with the first phase of concrete manipulatives or virtual manipulatives, students transition to the next phase – either representational or abstract. Teachers can set mastery criteria for transitioning between phases, such as three sessions with 80% accuracy, two sessions with 100% accuracy, or five session with 90% accuracy. Accuracy can refer to the correct answer or correct digits and a mastery criterion need not be accuracy alone; a teacher could set mastery criteria based on independence. It is important to think about these instructional sequences as a framework through which teachers can guide student at an individual pace. While there is a sequence, if a student is struggling in the representational phase, they can return to the concrete. Manipulative-based sequences need not be so rigid, but teachers can make data-based decision-making based on student performance and permit flexibility or fluidity as appropriate.

In the representational phase, students draw pictures (or glue or Velcro images) to visually represent the mathematical problems, often similar to the concrete manipulative. When

Table 4

Visual and Textual Representation of Manipulative-Based Graduated Sequences

Instructional Sequence	Manipulative	Representational/ Pictorial	Abstract/ Numerical Strategy
CRA (with money; making change)	Concrete:		If Olivia pays $1 and the ice cream costs $0.94, I need to add up from $0.94 to $1. $0.94 plus 1 penny is $0.95, two pennies $0.96," and so on.
VRA (with fractions; finding equivalent fractions)	Virtual:		With $\frac{1}{3} = \frac{\_\_}{12}$), 3 is multiplied by 4 to get 12 and hence 1 must be multiplied by 4 to get 4 ($\frac{1}{3} = \frac{4}{12}$). Students were taught to use fact families: $3 \times \_\_ = 12$; hence $12 \div 3 = \_\_$.
VA (with algebra)	Virtual:		$2x + 3 = 11$ $2x + 3 - 3 = 11 - 3$ $2x = 8$ $2x \div 2 = 8 \div 2$ $x = 4$
VR (with multiplication and division)	Virtual		

students demonstrate mastery with the representational phase, they transition to the abstract phase, if a part of the instructional sequence. Likewise, teachers set mastery criteria. The abstract phase involves students using numerical strategies to solve the mathematical problems. Generally, with the manipulative-based graduated sequences of instruction, if a student does not achieve the set level of accuracy for a session they repeated that same learning sheet (i.e., lesson) the next intervention session (i.e., the next day; see Table 5).

Research on Manipulative Based Instructional Sequences

Researchers have explored the CRA instructional sequence for multiple decades (Underhill, 1977; Underhill et al., 1980) and across multiple content areas (Bouck, Satsangi, & Park, 2018). For students with learning disabilities, Bouck, Satsangi, and Park (2018) determined the CRA instructional sequence to be an evidence-based practice. While the research base on the CRA is less for students with ASD/IDD, it still exists. For example, Stroizer et al. (2015) examined the CRA, with base 10 blocks as the concrete manipulative, to teach addition with regrouping, subtraction with regrouping, and multiplication to three elementary students with autism. All students achieved the researcher-set criteria (i.e., six problems correct) for each behavior. Yakubova et al. (2016) also examined the CRA, but in conjunction with video-based instruction to teach number comparison, addition, and subtraction to four elementary students with autism. Students acquired and maintained the mathematical behaviors.

More recently, researchers explored the VRA, VA, and VR instructional sequences, with the research almost exclusively focused on students with IDD/ASD. Predominantly the work of Bouck and colleagues, the mathematics examined with the VRA, VA, and VR instructional sequences has ranged from basic operations (e.g., subtraction with regrouping, multiplication) to fractions (e.g., equivalent and adding with unlike denominators) and algebra (e.g., one and two-step linear algebra) (e.g., Bouck, Park, Satsangi, et al., 2019; Bouck, Park, Shurr, et al., 2018; Bouck, Park, Sprick, et al., 2017. Across the research studies, students acquired the mathematics

Table 5

Sample Schedule for Graduated Sequence of Instruction CRA

Session	Instruction
1	**Concrete session 1** If at least 80% accuracy, move to session 2, if less than 80% accuracy repeat session 1
2	**Concrete session 2** If at least 80% accuracy, move to session 3, if less than 80% accuracy repeat session 2
3	**Concrete session 3** If less than 80% accuracy repeat session 3, when at least 80% on all 3 sessions, move to representational session 1
4	**Representational session 1** If at least 80% accuracy, move to representational session 2, if less than 80% accuracy repeat representational session 1
5	**Representational session 2** If at least 80% accuracy, move to representational session 3, if less than 80% accuracy repeat representational session 2
6	**Representational session 3** If less than 80% accuracy repeat representational session 3, when at least 80% on all 3 representational sessions, move to abstract session 1 *If needed, students can be transitioned back to the concrete phase of instruction to support further conceptual understanding
7	**Abstract session 1** If at least 80% accuracy, move to abstract session 2, if less than 80% accuracy repeat abstract session 1.
8	**Abstract session 2** If at least 80% accuracy, move to abstract session 3, if less than 80% accuracy repeat abstract session 2.
9	**Abstract session 3** If at least 80% accuracy intervention is complete, if less than 80% accuracy, repeat abstract session 3 *If needed, students can be transitioned back to the representational phase of instruction to support further conceptual understanding.
…	**Maintenance** After a period of time probe for maintenance *If needed, students can be transitioned back to concrete, representational, or abstract phases of instruction or boost sessions can be completed to support further conceptual understanding and maintenance of the skills.

taught, but maintenance was not always achieved. Researchers found more success with students maintaining the mathematics if an intervention package was used, involving a virtual manipulative-based instructional sequence and another intervention, such as overlearning (i.e., overlearning refers to teaching students past demonstration of mastery; Bouck, Shurr, & Park, 2020; Park, Bouck, & Fisher, 2020; Shurr et al., 2019).

Implementation of Manipulative-Based Instructional Sequences

Manipulative-based instructional sequences can be used to support students with ASD/IDD across a variety of mathematics areas (e.g., place value, addition/subtraction with regrouping, multiplication, division, fractions, algebra, and more) as well as in a variety of settings. In other words, manipulative-based instructional sequences support providing students with ASD/IDD access to grade-level mathematics (e.g., algebra) as well as foundational skills needed to achieve more advanced mathematics and/or independent living skills. Similar to manipulatives in general, teachers can implement manipulative-based instructional sequences for a whole class, small group, or at the individual level. In addition, manipulative-based instructional sequences can be used to deliver new mathematics content as well as review or reteach previous content. The following section will discuss explicit instruction more in-depth as explicit instruction is the pedagogical approach for teaching the manipulative-based instructional sequences as well as each instructional sequence: CRA, VRA, VA, and VR. Finally, the section will end with additional adaptations that can be made to the manipulative-based instructional sequences to further support students with ASD/IDD.

Explicit Instruction

Explicit instruction is an instructional approach, which involves modeling, guided, and independent phases in its delivery (Doabler & Fien, 2013). When implementing explicit instruction, a teacher begins by modeling how to solve the mathematical problems. The modeling might occur for a few problems (e.g., two) in which the teacher is not only physically demonstrating how to solve the mathematical problem but also with a think-aloud. A think-aloud is a verbal narration in which the thinking and the process by which the teacher solves the problem are made explicit (note, in subsequent sections examples of the verbal narration within the modeling phase of explicit instruction will be provided; Agrawal & Morin, 2016). After a set number of problems modeled (e.g., two), the teacher moves onto the guided portion of explicit instruction (Doabler & Fien, 2013). With guided instruction, the student is asked to solve a problem (or more) independently but the teacher provides prompts or cues as needed if a student makes a mistake or becomes stuck (note, in subsequent sections examples of prompts or cues within the guided phase of explicit instruction will be provided; Agrawal & Morin, 2016). After a set number of problems in the guided phase (e.g., two) and students demonstrate relative independence in the guided phase (i.e., not significant need for prompts or cues), the teacher moves the student into the independent phase of explicit instruction. During the independent phase, students solve a set number of problems (e.g., five, 10) completely independent, meaning the teacher provides no prompts, cues, or assistance (Doabler & Fien, 2013). If students do not demonstrate relative independence in the guided phase, teachers should not move students into the independent phase but either have students engage in more guided practice or return to modeling.

Explicit instruction generally begins with an advanced organizer in which the purpose of the mathematics is briefly verbally explained and the goals identified (Agrawal & Morin, 2016). Next, educators use learning sheets, which include the decided upon number of problems to be modeled, guided, and then done independently (see Table 6 for examples of explicit instruction learning sheets). Feedback is provided to the student during the guided portion but can also be done after the independent practice as a means of helping students learn to self-monitor (Agrawal & Morin, 2016).

As noted, explicit instruction is used to deliver each of the manipulative-based instructional sequences (i.e., CRA, VRA, VA, and VR). At each phase of the manipulative-based graduated sequence of instruction, explicit instruction is used. This means, explicit instruction is

Table 6
Examples of Explicit Instruction Learning Sheets

Math	Modeling	Guided	Independent
Multiplication	$\begin{array}{r}4\\ \times\ 4\\ \hline\end{array}$ $\quad$ $\begin{array}{r}7\\ \times\ 3\\ \hline\end{array}$	$\begin{array}{r}2\\ \times\ 5\\ \hline\end{array}$ $\quad$ $\begin{array}{r}9\\ \times\ 4\\ \hline\end{array}$	$\begin{array}{r}2\\ \times\ 9\\ \hline\end{array}$ $\quad$ $\begin{array}{r}3\\ \times\ 3\\ \hline\end{array}$ $\begin{array}{r}3\\ \times\ 8\\ \hline\end{array}$ $\quad$ $\begin{array}{r}1\\ \times\ 7\\ \hline\end{array}$ $\begin{array}{r}2\\ \times\ 2\\ \hline\end{array}$
Making Change with Coins	Ms. Nickell paid $2.56 for an ice cream. She gave the cashier $3.00. How much change should Ms. Nickell get back? At the store, Alex bought some candy. He spent a total of $0.35. He gave the cashier $1.00. How much change should Alex get back?	At Burger King, Anna's order came to $1.28. She gave the cashier $2.00. How much change should Anna get back? Drake bought a pencil for $0.61. He gave the cashier $1.00. How much change should Drake get back?	At the store, Cate bought a pencil for $0.45. She gave the cashier $1.00. How much change should Cate get back? Noah paid $1.80 for two packs of M&Ms. He gave the cashier $2.00. How much change should Noah get back? At the post office, Ben's order came to $0.72. He gave the postal worker $1.00. How much change should Ben get back? At an ice cream store, Nic's order came to $2.56. He gave the cashier $3.00. How much change should Nic get back? May ordered cheeseburger at McDonalds for$0.96. She gave the cashier $1.00 How much change should May get back?

used to teach students how to solve mathematical problems with a manipulative, to solve with pictorial representations, and to solve with numerical strategies. Note, teachers can also provide explicit instruction to teach students to solve problems with a concrete or virtual manipulative without the intention of implementing a manipulative-based graduated sequence of instruction.

CRA

The CRA instructional sequence is a graduated sequence of instruction that involves students first learning to solve the mathematical problems using concrete manipulatives (i.e., base ten blocks, money, color tiles, fraction tiles, algebra tiles), then to solve using pictorial or drawings to represent the problem (e.g., lines and circles to represent base ten blocks), and finally transitioning to solving the problems using numerical strategies built upon throughout the phases (e.g., counting up for subtraction, repeated addition for single-digit multiplication, or partial products for double-digit multiplication; Agrawal & Morin, 2016; refer to Table 5). The CRA instructional sequence is beneficial for a variety of mathematical problems—place value, addition, subtraction, multiplication, division, making change with coins, and more. As mentioned earlier in the chapter, the CRA instructional sequence is typically taught using explicit instruction which involves modeling, guided practice, and independent phases of instruction (see Table 7 for an example of explicit instruction for the concrete phase of CRA using coins as the manipulatives to solve problems involving making change).

VRA

As mentioned earlier in the chapter, virtual manipulatives also exist to support students in solving a variety of mathematics problems. The VRA instructional sequence is very similar to the CRA, except instead of using concrete manipulatives in the first phase of instruction, students learn to use virtual (computer or app-based) manipulatives to solve the problems. Students first

Table 7

Explicit Instruction for Concrete Phase of CRA for Making Change with Coins

Advanced Organizer: Today, we are going work on making change. We will use plastic money to solve the problems. You will use money throughout many parts of your life like when you want to buy something at a store like food or a new game, when you are saving money to buy something you want, or when you go out to eat at a restaurant. It is important for you to know how to make change so that you know how much money you have, how much money you need, and how much change you should get back when you pay for something at a store.		
Modeling	**Guided**	**Independence**
I am going to show you how to determine the amount of change you should receive when paying for an item using cash or dollar bills and coins. Let's review the coins real quick here [insert review coins] and then I will read the problem. **Problem:** You go to a store to buy a candy bar. The candy bar you want costs $0.86. You give the cashier $1.00. How much change should the cashier give back to you? I know that the candy bar costs $0.86 so I am going to represent $0.86 using our coins. So, I can start with quarters, $0.25, then add another quarter $0.50, I add one more quarter $0.75, then a dime, which is $0.10, to make $0.85, then I can add one penny to make $0.86. Now I have $0.86 in coins, and according to the problem, I gave the cashier $1. To determine how much change, I should get back from my $1, I want to count up from $0.86 to $1. I start at $0.86, let's start by adding pennies. [The teacher models adding the pennies while counting] $0.87, $0.88, $0.89, $0.90. Now, we can add dimes [the teacher models adding the dime while counting] which is $0.10. $0.90 and $0.10 makes $1 Now, we need to count up the coins that we added to find out what our change is. We can start with the dime $0.10, now the pennies, $0.11, $0.12, $0.13, $0.14. My change should be $0.14. I can check my answer by adding together how much the candy bar costs and how much change I should get back. They should equal the $1 that I paid the cashier. $0.86 + $0.14 = $1	Now you are going to try two problems. I will be here to help you if you get stuck, but want you to read the problem carefully and determine the change in these two problems. [Student starts. If a student does not set up the problem correctly (i.e. represents the incorrect money value) the teacher can provide a prompt such as "how much money did you start with?" or "Count how much money you have here, does that match the problem?"] Note, if a student is struggling and needing a lot of prompts or cues, the instructor should go back to the modeling stage before proceeding to the independent stage.	Now that you have tried a couple of problems and I was there to help, if needed, I am going to have you do X (e.g., 5, 10) problems on your own. I will be here, but I will not provide any help.

learn to use the manipulatives in app or computer format (i.e., virtual base ten blocks, virtual algebra tiles, virtual number line, virtual color tiles), transitioning to representing the problem in drawings (see Table 8 for an example of explicit instruction for the representational phase of CRA using drawings to solve subtraction with regrouping problems), and finally using numerical strategies to solve the problem. Like the CRA, each phase of the VRA instructional sequence (i.e., virtual, representation, abstract) is taught via explicit instruction using modeling, guided practice, and independent practice (see Table 9 for an example of explicit instruction for the abstract phase of VRA using numerical strategies to solve addition with regrouping problems).

Table 8
Explicit Instruction for Representational Phase of VRA for Subtraction with Regrouping

Advanced Organizer: Today, we are going work on solving subtraction problems with regrouping. You use subtraction in a lot of different places in your life. Like when you are buying things at a store or are at a restaurant and need to make sure you have enough money, when you are cooking or measuring, and when you are traveling or dealing with time.		
Modeling	**Guided**	**Independence**
Remember how we used base ten blocks on the iPad to help us solve subtraction problems, well this time we are going to draw base ten blocks to help us solve these problems. We can use lines to represent the tens blocks (see |) and squares to represent the ones blocks (see ☐) The problem is 32 − 8 = ___. First, I need to set up our problem. I am going to start by representing our first number. 32 is three tens and two ones, so I will draw three lines in the tens place and two squares in the ones place. I am going to use my ten-and-ones chart (or t-chart) to set it up, just like I used the place value chart with my virtual manipulatives in the app. T | O ||| ☐ ☐ Before I start solving, I am going to check my drawing and make sure that what I drew	Now you are going to try two problems. I will be here to help you if you get stuck, but want you solve these two subtraction problems. [Student starts. If a student does not set up the problem correctly drawing base ten blocks, the teacher might provide a prompt, such as "Do the blocks you drew match the problem?"] [If a student becomes stuck during regrouping, the teacher might provide a prompt such as can you subtract 8 from 2 and get a positive number?] Note, if a student is struggling and needing a lot of prompts or cues, the instructor should go back to the modeling stage before proceeding to the independence stage.	Now that you have tried a couple of problems and I was there to help, if needed, I am going to have you do X (e.g., 5, 10) problems on your own. I will be here, but I will not provide any help.

matches the problem. Now, it is time to solve. Remember, we start in the ones column. I am going to try to subtract my ones column. Can I subtract or take away 8 from 2 and get a positive number? No, I cannot get a positive number so I need to ungroup one of my tens blocks into ten ones. So, I can cross out a tens block from the tens place. Then, I need to draw ten squares in the ones place to show I am ungrouping that ten block.

T	O
||	☐ ☐☐ ☐ ☐☐ ☐ ☐☐ ☐ ☐☐

Now, I have 12 ones blocks. Can I subtract 8 ones from 12 ones and get a positive number? Yes. I need to cross out 8 squares and see how many I have left. (model crossing out 8 squares). 1, 2, 3, 4, 5, 6, 7, 8.

T	O
||	☒ ☒☒ ☒ ☒☒ ☒ ☒☐ ☐ ☐☐

Now, I am going to count how many ones or ones I have left (count the squares): 1, 2, 3, 4. I have 4 squares or ones blocks left so I am going to write 4 in the ones place. Next, I need to find out how many tens I have. I have 2 lines or tens 10 blocks, which means I can write 2 in the tens place. Now, I know that my answer is 24. $32 - 8 = 24$.

I can check my answer by adding. I can add $24 + 8$. If I get 32, I know that I have answered the question correctly.

VA

The VA instructional sequence involves students transitioning from instruction and use of virtual manipulatives to instruction and use of numerical strategies. The VA instructional sequence can be used for any type of mathematical problem but is more advisable to those for whom the representational phase may be more challenging. In other words, for mathematics in which drawing or expressing the pictorial representations can be difficult, such as linear algebra or fractions, the VA instructional sequence may be more appropriate. As with the other instructional sequences, the VA instructional sequence also utilizes explicit instruction (see Table 10 for an example of explicit instruction within the VA) and can be delivered at the individual or small group level. The explicit instruction would be similar in the abstract phase for this, or other, mathematical behaviors (see Table 11 for an example of explicit instruction for the abstract portion for finding equivalent fractions).

VR

The VR instructional sequence involves students transitioning from instruction and use of virtual manipulatives to instruction and use pictorial representations. The VR instructional sequence questions the need for students with ASD/IDD to solve mathematical problems with just numerical strategies (or abstractly) and rather suggests that an appropriate goal is for students to have drawing pictures as a strategy to solve mathematical problems. With a focus on developing students' conceptual understanding of the mathematics through the virtual manipulatives and then providing pictorial representations as a strategy for students to use when manipulatives are not available or appropriate. Any mathematical domains can be taught with the VR instructional sequence. While the VR instructional sequence can also be used with any students with ASD/IDD, it may be particularly beneficial to students who struggle without concrete or pictorial representations, but who also acquire and maintain the ability to draw the pictures. Table 12 provides additional examples of modeling for the virtual and representational phases of a virtual-manipulative instructional sequence.

Table 9

Explicit Instruction for Abstract Phase of VRA for Addition with Regrouping

Advanced Organizer: Today, we are going work on solving addition problems with regrouping. You use addition in a lot of different places in your life. Like when you are adding money to pay for things, when you are determining how many of something you need, and for other math skills like multiplication. We are going to solve these double-digit addition problems using partial sums.		
Modeling	**Guided**	**Independence**
Remember how we used base ten blocks on the iPad and drawings to help us solve addition problems, I am going to teach you how to use different strategies to solve these problems. We are going to start with the problem 36 + 17. See I write it as $$\begin{array}{c|c} T & O \\ \hline 3 & 6 \\ 1 & 7 \end{array}$$ Using by t-chart or tens-and-one chart. We are going to start by adding our ones 6 + 7. We can start at 6 and count up to add 7, 8, 9, 10, 11, 12, 13. 6+7 is 13. $$\begin{array}{c|c} T & O \\ \hline 3 & 6 \\ 1 & 7 \\ \hline 1 & 3 \end{array}$$ 13 is one ten and three ones and I write down 13, as 1 in the tens place and 3 in the ones place. Now, we need to add the tens place. We have 3 tens, plus 1 ten, which equals 4 ten or 40. I write down 40, with 4 in the tens place and 0 in the ones place. $$\begin{array}{c|c} T & O \\ \hline 3 & 6 \\ 1 & 7 \\ \hline 1 & 3 \\ 4 & 0 \end{array}$$ Now, I add my partial sums. So I am adding 3 ones and 0 ones and 1 ten and 4 tens. First, I add 3 ones and 0 ones, which is 3 ones. Then I add 1 ten and 4 tens. Starting with 1, I count up by 4: 2, 3, 4, 5. So, 1 ten and 4 tens is 5 tens. My answers is 5 tens and 3 ones: 53.	Now you are going to try two problems. I will be here to help you if you get stuck, but want you solve these two subtraction problems. [Student starts. If the student starts to count all, encourage to count up. Remember, we can start at 6 and count on by 7.] Note, if a student is struggling and needing a lot of prompts or cues, the instructor should go back to the modeling stage before proceeding to the independence stage.	Now that you have tried a couple of problems and I was there to help, if needed, I am going to have you do X (e.g., 5, 10) problems on your own. I will be here, but I will not provide any help.

Table 10

Explicit Instruction for Virtual Phase of VA for Algebra

Advanced Organizer: Today, we are going to work on solving 2-step algebra problems. Algebra is the language used to describe patterns and relationships in our world. We use algebra throughout many parts of our lives, when we are trying to solve problems with formulas or we are trying to find distance with rate and time, for example.

Modeling	Guided	Independence
The first problem I am going to show you how to solve today is $3x - 3 = 9$. To solve this algebraic equation, we are using the Brainingcamp Algebra Tiles app. This app has many different tiles and tools, but we are going to focus on the 1, -1, x, and –x for our purposes. It is important to keep in mind that the equal sign does not mean answer. The equal sign tells us that both sides of the equation are equal, which I think of like a balance scale. The first thing I am going to do is set up my problem on the app. Notice how the screen has an equal sign and two sides. I am going to start with the left side of the equation and set it up: $3x - 3 = 9$. I need 3 x-tiles, so I am going to pull out 3 x-tiles onto the workspace on the left side of the equal sign. I also need 3 negative one tiles, so I will add 3 negative one-tiles to the left-side of the workspace that contains the 3 x-tiles. The right side of equation is 9, so I will add 9 one-tiles to that side. Before I solve, I want to check that the equation I built on the app matches the equation I am trying to solve ($3x - 3 = 9$). When solving algebraic equations, I like to first start by getting my variable on one side and my numbers or constants on the other. I want to solve for what x equals. As I have numbers right now on the left and right, I want to first get 3x by itself. To do so, I want to do the inverse or opposite operation. The number is -3; hence to remove the -3 – three negative ones – from the left-side I need to add 3 – or three positive ones. I do this by placing 3 one-times on the left. Because an equation is like a balance scale, what I do to one side I must also do to the other. So, I also need to add 3 one-tiles to the right side. I then want to simplify. $3x - 3 + 3 = 9 + 3$ becomes $3x = 12$. I know 3x equals 12, but I want to know what x equals. Again, I am going to look to do the opposite operation or inverse operation. This means I would want to divide 3x by 3 as 3x means 3 times x. On the app, I can also show this by creating rows. I would select 3 rows, as I have 3 x-tiles. I want to distribute my 12 one-tiles across each of the 3 x-tiles evenly; this is similar to dividing 12 by 3. When sharing the 12 one-tiles across the 3xs, I see that each x-tile equals 4 one-tiles, so $x = 4$. I can check my answer, by substituting 4 back into the equation. $3(4) - 3 = 9$. 3 times 4 equals 12 and 12 minus 3 equals 9.	Now you are going to try two problems. I will be here to help you if you get stuck, but want you to solve for x – find the value for x – in two equations. [Student starts. If a student does not set up the algebra tiles correctly, the teacher might provide a prompt, such as "Do your tiles match the equation?"] [If a student becomes stuck balancing the equation, a teacher might cue "Remember an equation is like a balance scale - what we do to one side we need to do the other.] Note, if a student is struggling and needing a lot of prompts or cues, the instructor should go back to the modeling stage before proceeding to the independence stage.	Now that you have tried a couple of problems and I was there to help, if needed, I am going to have you do X (e.g., 5, 10) on your own. I will be here, but I will not provide any help.

Table 11

Explicit Instruction for Abstract Phase of VA for Equivalent Fractions

| Advanced Organizer: Today, we are going work on finding equivalent fractions. We use fractions throughout our daily lives, from baking to building things. Sometimes we may need to know equivalent fractions. For example, if a recipe calls for ½ of a cup of sugar but I only can find my ¼ measuring cup, I may need to know how many fourths are equivalent to one-half. We need to remember that the denominator of a fraction – the bottom number – tells us how many pieces a whole is divided into and the numerator of a fraction – the top number – tells us how many of those pieces we are discussing. |

Modeling	Guided	Independence
This problem is $\frac{2}{3} = \frac{}{12}$. I want to determine how many twelfths is equal to two-thirds. We are trying to determine equivalence, that is, we want the two fractions to have the same value. The first thing I need to do is determine the relationship between the two denominators: 3 and 12. In other words, I need to find if 3 is a factor of 12. I can divide 12 by 3 and get 4; 3 x 4 = 12. Hence, I know the relationship between 3 and 12 is that I can multiply 3 by 4 to get 12. With equivalent fractions, what one does to the denominator, one must also do to the numerator. So, if the denominator is multiplied by 4 so must the numerator. The equivalent fraction is then $\frac{8}{12}$.	Now that I have showed you how I solve two problems, I am going to have you try finding the equivalent fraction yourself. I will be here to provide any help that you may need if you get stuck, but you are going to try to work on the equivalent fractions on your own. [Student begins. If, for example, a student does not find the relationship appropriately, the instructor might cue "What is the fact family? Or do you want to use the calculator to find the factor?] Note, if a student is struggling and needing a lot of prompts or cues, the instructor should go back to the modeling stage before proceeding to the independence stage.	Now that you have tried a couple of problems and I was there to help, if needed, I am going to have you do X (e.g., 5, 10) on your own. I will be here, but I will not provide any help.

Additional Adaptations

Educators can make additional adaptations to the CRA, VRA, or VA instructional sequences. Such adaptations (i.e., moving to an intervention package consisting of more than one intervention) may involve supporting for maintenance within the intervention. Maintenance is the ability to complete a task (e.g., solve a mathematical problem) without instruction proceeding (Alberto & Troutman, 2009). Intervention packages involving the CRA, VRA, or VA plus a practice designed to support maintenance can help students with ASD/IDD not just acquire the mathematics but also maintain it. This is essential given maintenance is significantly important to education.

Table 12
Modeling for VR for Multiplication and Division

Multiplication	Division
Virtual Phase	
The first problem I am going to model for you is 3 × 4. What multiplication means is that I have 3 groups and 4 objects in each group. With the Color Tile app, I going to first draw 3 circles on the app with the colored markers to represent my 3 groups. Next, I am going to drag out and put 4 tiles in each of the 3 circles. I can then either count all the tiles or I can skip count (4 + 4 + 4). I get 12 tiles total, so 3 × 4 = 12.	The first problem I am going to model for you is 15 ÷ 5. What division means is that I have 15 objects and want to evenly distribute these 15 objects among 5 groups. With the Color Tile app, I first drag out my 15 tiles and place at the top of the app. Next, I draw 5 circles on the app with the colored markers to represent my 5 groups. Then, I drag the color tiles one-by-one into each circle, distributing a tile into each circle before adding additional tiles. Finally, I count the number of tiles in each circle and ensure they are the same. The number of tiles in each circle is the answer to 15 ÷ 5, which is 3.
Representational Phase	
The first problem I am going to model for you is 6 × 2. What multiplication means is that I have 6 groups and 2 objects in each group. First, I am going to draw 6 circles on my paper to represent my 6 groups. Next, I am going to draw 2 Xs in each of the 6 circles. I can then either count all the XS or I can skip count (2 + 2 + 2 + 2 + 2 +2). I get 12 tiles total, so 6 × 2 = 12.	The first problem I am going to model for you is 14 ÷ 7. What division means is that I have 14 objects and want to evenly distribute these 14 objects across 7 groups. First, I am going to draw my 14 objects, represented by 14 Xs at the top of my paper. Next, I draw 5 circles on my paper to represent my 7 groups. Then I distributed my Xs evenly into each group, meaning I draw an X into the first circle and cross it out. on top to show I distributed it. I move to the next circle and draw an X, crossing it out at the top. I continue until all my Xs are crossed out and now in each of my 7 circles. Finally, I count the number of Xs in each circle and ensure they are the same. The number of Xs in each circle is the answer to 14 ÷ 7, which is 2.

Interventions designed to support maintenance can include overlearning as well as support fading (Shurr et al., 2019). In overlearning, students are taught past the point of mastery (Shurr et al., 2019). For example, if a manipulative-based instructional sequence involves students demonstrating 80-100% accuracy for three sessions prior to transitioning phase (i.e., C to R or V to A), overlearning could involve setting that threshold at 80 to 100% for five sessions or 100% accuracy for three (see Figure 4 as an example of what data collection might look like using an intervention package of a manipulative-based graduated sequence of instruction and

Figure 4

Data Collection for an Intervention Package

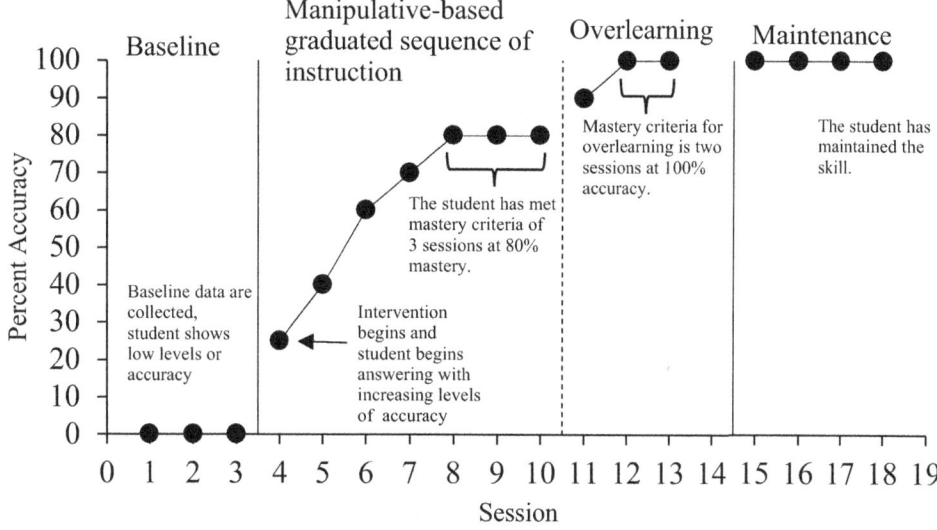

overlearning). Park, Bouck, and Fisher (2020) taught multiplication to one middle school student with autism (and two students identified as having a learning disability although their IQs were 71 and 75) via the VRA instructional sequence paired with overlearning. In this study, overlearning involved each student completing two additional sessions—to 100% accuracy—in each phase when the initial criteria of accuracy at 80% or higher for three sessions was reached. Beyond acquiring how to solve multiplication problems, students also maintained up to four weeks after the intervention ended.

With fading, teachers systematically and gradually reduce supports connected with prompting—either antecedent prompting (i.e., instruction) or response prompting (Collins, 2012; Shurr et al., 2019). For example, Park, Bouck, & Smith (2020) taught middle school students with autism and/or intellectual disability to solve subtraction with regrouping via the VRA instructional sequence paired with fading support. In this study, support was faded through an additional phase after abstract in which students were provided increasingly fewer modeling and/or guided problems within explicit instruction over six sessions). Students in the study maintained their accuracy for up to six weeks.

In another example, which combined both maintenance interventions, Bouck et al. (in press) taught middle school students with intellectual disability multiplication and division using the VR+ instructional sequence, which was the VR instructional sequence with overlearning and fading support. In this case, VR+ meant students received prompting via the system of least prompts in the independent phase of the virtual and first representational phases before transitioning to a representational phase without prompting (i.e., fading supporting). Further, students had to achieve 80% accuracy or higher on five sessions in each phase before transitioning. While the intervention was longer, strong maintenance data were reported for students after intervention ended.

An additional adaptation involves the teaching or delivery of the manipulative-based instructional sequence. Yakubova et al. (2016) examined the delivery of the CRA in conjunction with video modeling to teaching basic operations to elementary students with autism. Prior to completing problems on their own, participants watched first-person point of view videos filmed with narration that shows a teacher's hands solving the problem with manipulatives paired with a verbal narration of how to solve the problem. In their study, the four students acquired the mathematical behaviors as well as maintained them. Video modeling can support the delivery of mathematical interventions for students with ASD/IDD as video-modeling is considered an evidence-based practice (Wong et al., 2015).

Decision-Making

Given the different manipulative-based instructional sequences available (e.g., CRA, VRA, VR), how do teachers make decisions? Decision-making should depend upon multiple factors, including resources available, student preferences and skills, teacher familiarity, and the ultimate goal of student learning. Figure 2 provides a decision-making tree to help teachers in making decisions about what manipulative-based sequence is best for them to implement.

Conclusion

Manipulatives and manipulative-based graduated sequences of instruction offer support and options for teaching mathematics to students with ASD/IDD. And within both a variety of options exist to support students with individual needs, such as students who can achieve to the abstract phase to students who should continue to draw pictorial representations. While the emerging literature is strong, there remains a need for additional research. One need is for additional research that targets the use of virtual manipulatives and virtual manipulative-based instructional sequences with elementary and high school students with ASD/IDD. Another need for additional research is sufficient studies to examine if manipulative-based graduated sequences of instruction are evidence-based practices.

References

Agrawal, J., & Morin, L. L. (2016). Evidence-based practices: Applications of concrete representational abstract framework across math concepts for students with mathematics disabilities. *Learning Disabilities Research & Practice, 31*(1), 34-44. https://doi.org/10.1111/ldrp.12093

Alberto, P., & Troutman, A. (2009). *Applied behavior analysis for teachers* (8th ed.). Pearson.

Bouck, E. C., & Flanagan, S. M. (2010). Virtual manipulatives: What are they and how teachers can use them. *Intervention in School and Clinic, 45*(3), 186-191. https://doi.org/10.1177/1053451209349530

Bouck, E. C., & Park, J. (2018). A systematic review of the literature on mathematics manipulatives to support students with disabilities. *Education and Treatment of Children, 41*(1), 65-106. https://doi.org/10.1353/etc.2018.0003

Bouck, E. C., & Sprick, J. (2019). The virtual-representation-abstract framework to support students with disabilities in mathematics. *Intervention in School and Clinic, 54*(3), 173-180. https://doi.org/10.1177/1053451218767911

Bouck, E. C., Chamberlain, C., & Park, J. (2017). Concrete and app-based manipulatives to support students with disabilities with subtraction. *Education and Training in Autism and Developmental Disabilities, 52*(3), 317-331. https://doi.org/10.2307/26420403

Figure 2
Manipulative-Based Instructional Sequence Decision-Making Tree

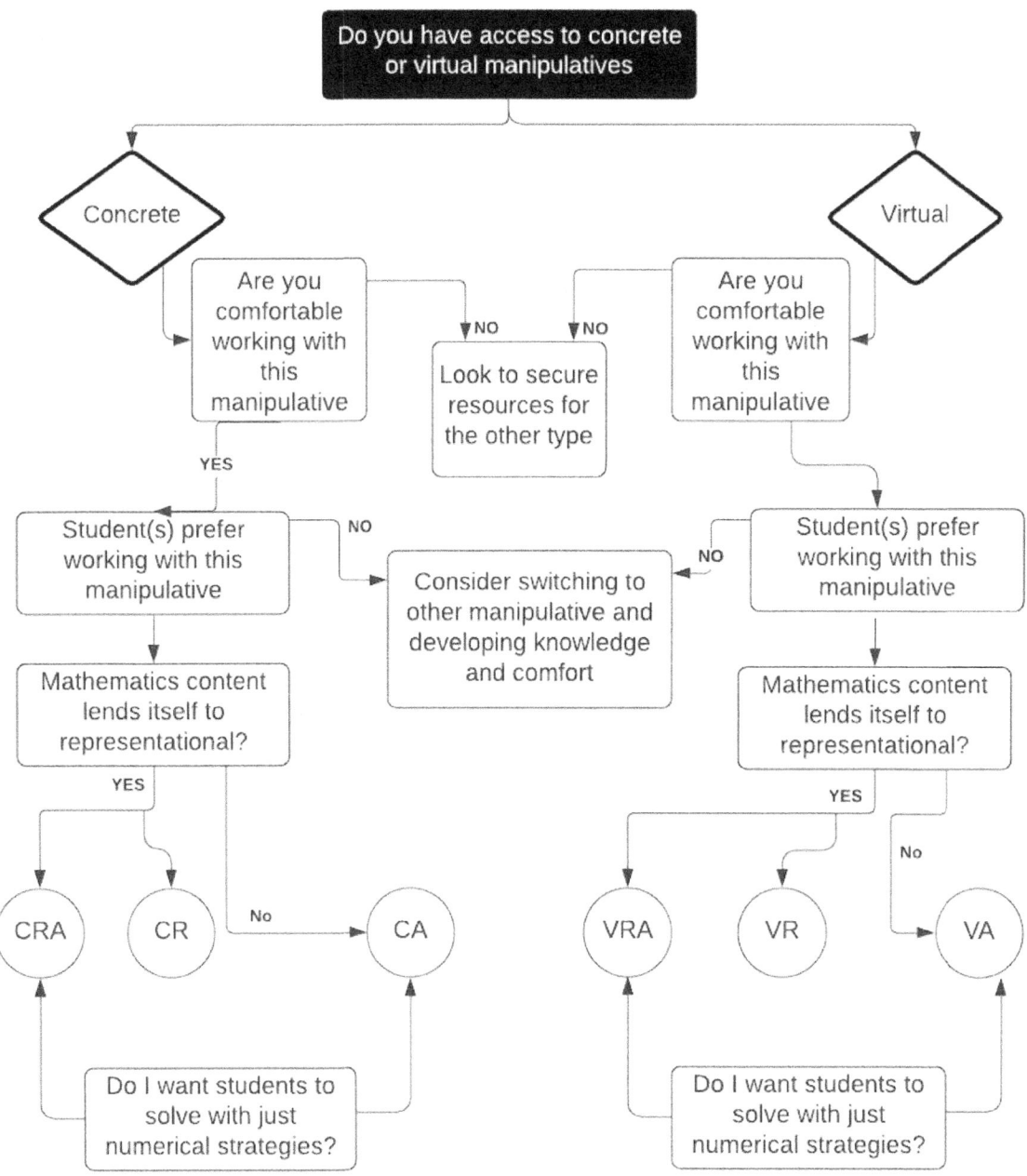

Bouck, E. C., Long, H., & Park, J. (2020). Using a virtual number line and corrective feedback to teach addition of integers to middle school students with developmental disabilities. *Journal of Developmental and Physical Disabilities*. [Advanced Online Publication]. https://doi.org/10.1007/s10882-020-09735-z

Bouck, E. C., Mathews, L. A., & Peltier C. (2020). Virtual manipulatives: A tool to support access and achievement with middle school students with disabilities. *Journal of Special Education Technology, 35*(1), 51-59. https://doi.org/10.1177/0162643419882422

Bouck, E. C., & Park, J. (2020). App-based manipulatives and the system of least prompts to support acquisition, maintenance, and generalization of adding integers. *Education and Training in Autism and Developmental Disabilities, 55*(2), 158-172.

Bouck, E. C., Park, J., Levy, K., Cwiakala, K., & Whorley, A. (2019) App-based manipulatives and explicit instruction to support division with remainders. *Exceptionality*. Advance online publication. https://doi/org10.1080/09362835.2019.1586709

Bouck, E. C., Park, J., Satsangi, R., Cwiaskala, K., & Levy, K. (2019). Using the virtual-abstract instructional sequence to support acquisition of algebra. *Journal of Special Education Technology, 34*, 253-268.

Bouck, E. C., Park, J., Shurr, J., Bassette, L., & Whorley, A. (2018). Using the virtual representational-abstract approach to support students with intellectual disability in mathematics. *Focus on Autism and Developmental Disabilities, 33*(4), 237-248. https://doi.org/10.1177/1088357618755696

Bouck, E. C., Park, J., Sprick, J., Shurr, J., Bassette, L., & Whorley, A. (2017). Using the virtual-abstract instructional sequence to teach addition of fractions. *Research in Developmental. Disabilities, 70*, 163-174. https://doi.org/10.1016/j.ridd.2017.09.002

Bouck, E. C., Satsangi, R., & Park, J. (2018). The concrete-representational-abstract approach for students with learning disabilities: An evidence-based practice synthesis. *Remedial and Special Education, 39*(4), 211-228. https://doi.org/10.1177/0741932517721712

Bouck, E. C., Satsangi, R., Doughty, T. T., & Courtney, W. T. (2014). Virtual and concrete manipulatives: A comparison of approaches for solving mathematics problems for students with autism spectrum disorder. *Journal of Autism and Developmental Disabilities, 44*, 180–193. https://doi.org/10.1007/s10803-013-1863-2

Bouck, E. C., Shurr, J. C., Tom, K., Jasper, A. D., Bassette, L., Miller, B., & Flanagan, S. M. (2012). Fix it with TAPE: Repurposing technology to be assistive technology for students with high-incidence disabilities. *Preventing School Failure: Alternative Education for Children and Youth, 56*(2), 121-128. https://doi.org/10.1080/1045988X.2011.603396

Bouck, E. C., Shurr, J., & Park, J. (in press). Virtual manipulative-based intervention package to teach multiplication and division to secondary students with developmental disabilities. *Focus on Autism and Other Developmental Disabilities*

Bouck, E. C., Shurr, J., Bassette, L., Park, J., Kerr, J., & Whorley, A. (2018). Adding it up: Comparing concrete and app-based manipulatives to support students with disabilities with adding fractions. *Journal of Special Education Technology, 33*(3), 194–206. https://doi.org/10.1177/0162643418759341

Bouck, E. C., Working, C., & Bone, E. (2018). Manipulative apps to support students with disabilities in mathematics. *Intervention in School and Clinic, 53*(3), 177-182. https://doi.org/10.1177/1053451217702115

Cambridge Assessment International Education. (2018). *Global education census report.* Cambridge, United Kingdom: Authors. Retrieved from, https://www.cambridgeinternational.org/Images/ 514611-global-education-census-survey-report.pdf

Carbonneau, K. J., Marley, S. C., & Selig, J. P. (2013). A meta-analysis of the efficacy of teaching mathematics with concrete manipulatives. *Journal of Educational Psychology, 105*(2), 380-400. https://doi.org/10.1037/a0031084

Clements, D. H., & Sarama, J. (2016) Math, science, and technology in the early grades. *The Future of Children, 26*(2), 75-94. www.jstor.org/stable/43940582

Collins, B. C. (2012). *Systematic instruction for students with moderate and severe disabilities.* Paul H Brookes Publishing

Doabler, C. T., & Fien, H. (2013). Explicit mathematics instruction: What teachers can do for teaching students with mathematics difficulties. *Intervention in School Clinic, 48*(5), 276-285. https://doi.org/10.1177/1053451212473151

Jimenez, B. A., & Besaw, J. (2020). Building early numeracy through virtual manipulatives for students with intellectual disability and autism. *Education and Training in Autism and Developmental Disabilities*, 55(1), 28–44.

Maccini, P., & Gagnon, J. C. (2000). Best Practices for teaching mathematics to secondary students with special needs. *Focus on Exceptional Children, 32*(5), 1-22.

Moyer, P. S., Bolyard, J. J., & Spikell, M. A. (2002). What are virtual manipulatives? *Teaching Children Mathematics, 8*(6), 372-377.

National Council of Teachers of Mathematics. (2000). *Principles and NCTM standards for school mathematics.* Author.

Park, J., Bouck, E. C., & Fisher, M. (2020). Using the virtual-representational-abstract with overlearning instructional sequence to support students with disabilities in mathematics. *Journal of Special Education.* [Advanced Online Publication). https://doi.org/10.1177/0022466920912527

Park, J., Bouck, E. C., & Smith, J. P. (2020). Using a virtual manipulative intervention package to support maintenance in teaching subtraction with regrouping to students with developmental disabilities. *Journal of Autism and Developmental Disabilities, 50*(January 2020), 63-75. https://doi.org/10.1007/s10803-019-04225-4

Peltier, C., Morin, K. L., Bouck, E. C., Lingo, M. E., Pulos, J. M., Scheffler, F. A., Suk, A., Mathews, L. A., Sinclair, T. E., & Deardorff, M. E. (2019). A meta-analysis of single-case research using mathematics manipulatives with students at risk or identified with a disability. *The Journal of Special Education.* Advance online publication. https://doi.org/10.1177/0022466919844516

Root, J. R., Browder, D. M., Saunders, A. F., & Lo, Y. Y. (2016). Schema-based instruction with concrete and virtual manipulatives to teach problem solving to students with autism. *Remedial and Special Education, 38*(1), 42-52. https://doi.org/10.1177/0741932516643592

Satsangi, R., & Miller, B. (2017). The case for adopting virtual manipulatives in mathematics education for students with disabilities. *Preventing School Failure: Alternative Education for Children and Youth, 61*(4), 303-310. https://doi.org/10.1080/1045988X.2016.1275505

Satsangi, R., Bouck, E. C., Taber-Doughty, T., Bofferding, L., & Roberts, C. A., (2016). Comparing the effectiveness of virtual and concrete manipulatives to teach algebra to secondary students with learning disabilities. *Learning Disability Quarterly, 39*(4), 240-253. https://doi.org/10.1177/0731948716649754

Shurr, J. C., Jimenez, B. A., & Bouck, E. C. (2019). *Educating students with intellectual disability and autism spectrum disorders: Book 1 Research-based practices and education science.* Council for Exceptional Children.

Stroizer, S., Hinton, V., Flores, M., & Terry, L. (2015). An investigation of the effects of CRA instruction and students with autism spectrum disorder. *Education and Training in Autism and Developmental Disabilities, 50*(2), 223-236.

Underhill, R. (1977). *Teaching elementary school mathematics* (2nd ed.). Merrill.

Underhill, R. (1980). *Diagnosing mathematical difficulties.* Merrill.

Uribe-Flórez, L. J., & Wilkins, J. L. (2010). Elementary school teachers' manipulative use. *School Science and Mathematics, 110*(7), 363-371. https://doi.org/10.1111/j.1949-8594.2010.00046.x

Wong, C., Odom, S. L., Hume, K. A., Cox, A. W., Fettig, A., Kucharczyk, S., ... Schultz, T. R. (2015). Evidence-based practices for children, youth, and young adults with autism spectrum disorder: A comprehensive review. *Journal of Autism and Developmental Disorders, 45*(7), 1951–1966. https://doi.org/10.1007/s10803-014-2351-z

Yakubova, G., Hughes, E.M., & Shinaberry, M. (2016). Learning with technology: Video modeling with concrete–representational–abstract sequencing for students with autism spectrum disorder. *Journal of Autism and Developmental Disorders, 46*(7), 2349–2362. https://doi.org/10.1007/s10803-016-2768-7

Chapter 5: Teaching Problem Solving Using Modified Schema-based Instruction

Jenny Root, Amy Clausen, & Fred Spooner

Problem solving is to mathematics as comprehension is to reading; just as decoding and fluency build an individual's ability to better understand and use text, numeracy and calculation enhance an individual's ability to solve mathematical problems (Spooner et al., 2017). Successful problem solvers are able to activate both conceptual and procedural knowledge in order to model the problem and find the solution. The National Mathematics Advisory Council (2008) recommends emphasis on conceptual understanding, computational fluency, and problem-solving skills across all strands of mathematics with application in real-world situations.

Students with autism spectrum disorder and intellectual and developmental disabilities (ASD/IDD) should have the opportunity to learn mathematical problem solving to: (a) gain skills most adults take for granted; (b) learn methods for solving real-life problems; (c) receive the opportunity to achieve what researchers have shown may be attainable; and (d) have access to the content on which they will be assessed for school accountability (Root et al., 2016). There is growing consensus that increased academic instruction provided to individuals with ASD/IDD will correspond with improved postschool outcomes over prior generations (Spooner & Browder, 2015; Taber-Doughty, 2015). For example, independently leaving a tip for a barista at a coffee shop or determining whether they have enough money for a car wash if they use a coupon may increase autonomy and self-determined behavior.

With increased awareness of the importance of mathematics for students to leave school with the skills needed to function in the 21st century (Kilpatrick et al., 2001) has come greater focus on mathematical problem solving by researchers in the field of special education. In reviewing changes over the last decade in the area of teaching mathematical skills to students with severe disabilities, Spooner et al. (2019) found an increased focus on higher-order skills such as algebra and a decreased emphasis on basic skills such as time and money. Not only is it important that students with ASD/IDD learn mathematical skills beyond basic computation (e.g., numbers and operations), but also that they have the ability to apply those skills in real-life settings. For example, determining how many hours of working at a job that pays $12 per hour will be needed to pay for a concert ticket that costs $80 is a practical context finding a rate of change using an algebraic equation ($\$12x = \$80$). If the individual has already saved $20 toward the ticket, a linear algebra equation can be developed ($\$20 + \$12x = \$80$). Researchers are increasing their attention to problem solving in order to provide teachers with research-based strategies for teaching this critical skill.

Application of mathematical skills is critical to overall quality of life for persons with ASD/IDD, as it will directly influence postschool opportunities for employment, independent living, and leisure skills (Nasamran et al., 2017). Simply teaching calculation without problem solving only shows students how to solve problems and not when or why to apply these skills to everyday life (Browder et al., 2018). Learning to solve word problems is the basis for learning to solve real-world mathematical problems. In the context of word-problem solving, stories present situations requiring a mathematical solution (Van de Walle et al., 2010). The purpose of this chapter is to explain and provide examples of how to teach problem solving skills to learners with ASD/IDD through modified schema-based instruction. Before beginning to discuss the details of problem solving through the use of modified schema-based instruction, it first will be important to examine the term from which the practice was derived, schema-based instruction.

Schema-based Instruction

Problem solving is, by nature, a chained task—one which involves multiple steps (Browder et al., 2018; Spooner et al., 2017). Yet it is not adequate for a student to simply know and apply the steps of a procedure (i.e., procedural understanding). They also must know when to use the appropriate set of steps (i.e., conceptual understanding). What am I solving for? Does the problem require addition or subtraction? Multiplication or division? Is the part or the whole unknown? Often times teachers promote keyword strategies (e.g., "altogether" means add, "share" means divide). The keyword strategy is problematic because keywords are not always associated with the correct operation or problem solving strategy, causing frustration to the students and teacher alike (Powell & Fuchs, 2018). See Table 1 for some examples of why keywords are not a viable strategy.

Table 1
Problematic Keyword Strategies

Common Key Word Associations	Example Problem with False-Association
In All → Addition	Olivia and Matt sold 8 ice cream bars *in all*. If Olivia sold 5 ice cream bars, how many ice cream bars did Matt sell? $(8 - 5 = 3)$
Take away → Subtraction	Abby had some dolls. Her sister *takes away* 1 doll. Abbie has 3 dolls left. How many dolls did she have to begin with? $(3 + 1 = 4)$
Twice → Multiplication	Max stuffed *twice* as many envelopes as Christopher. If Max stuffed 12 envelopes, how many envelopes did Christopher stuff? $(12 \div 2 = 6)$
Each → Division	There are 4 shelves on the bookshelf. Rachel puts 10 books on *each* shelf. How many books did Rachel shelve? $(4 \times 10 = 40)$

A more effective method of teaching problem solving is called schema-based instruction (SBI). SBI is a cognitive-based strategy which teaches students how to follow a problem solving routine to use a schema to model "what is happening" in word problems in order to arrive at the solution. The student reads a word problem, chooses the schematic diagram that matches the problem type, and uses the schematic diagram (e.g., graphic organizer) to solve the problem (Powell, 2011). Students are taught to make sense of quantities and their relationships within the context of the word problems by recognizing patterns (Jitendra et al, 2015). Teachers use explicit instruction to model solving problems by following the problem solving routine (e.g., heuristic, or attack strategy) and provide opportunities for guided and independent practice. In traditional SBI, these heuristics or routines often involve a mnemonic device which helps the student remember the steps to solve a problem. For example, the acronym "RUN" tells the student to **R**ead the problem, **U**nderline the question, and **N**ame the problem type (Fuchs et al., 2014) and "DISC" directs students to **D**iscover the problem type, **I**dentify information in the problem to represent in a diagram, **S**olve the problem, **C**heck the solution; Jitendra et al., 2013).

There are two main types of schemas, or problem types, that have been taught in SBI research: additive and multiplicative. Within the additive schemas, there are combine (e.g., group), compare, and change problem types (see Table 2). Within the multiplicative schemas, there are equal groups, comparison, proportions, and ratio (see Table 3). Schemas orient students to the appropriate problem-solving method beyond simply looking for keywords, by instead having them focus on identifying patterns of the problem type that match the mathematical situation presented in the problem. More information on schemas can be found on the Project STAIR website at https://blog.smu.edu/projectstair/category/educator-resources/tailored-professional-development/word-problem-instruction/.

Table 2
Additive Schemas

Schema	Potential Visual Representation	Example
Combine	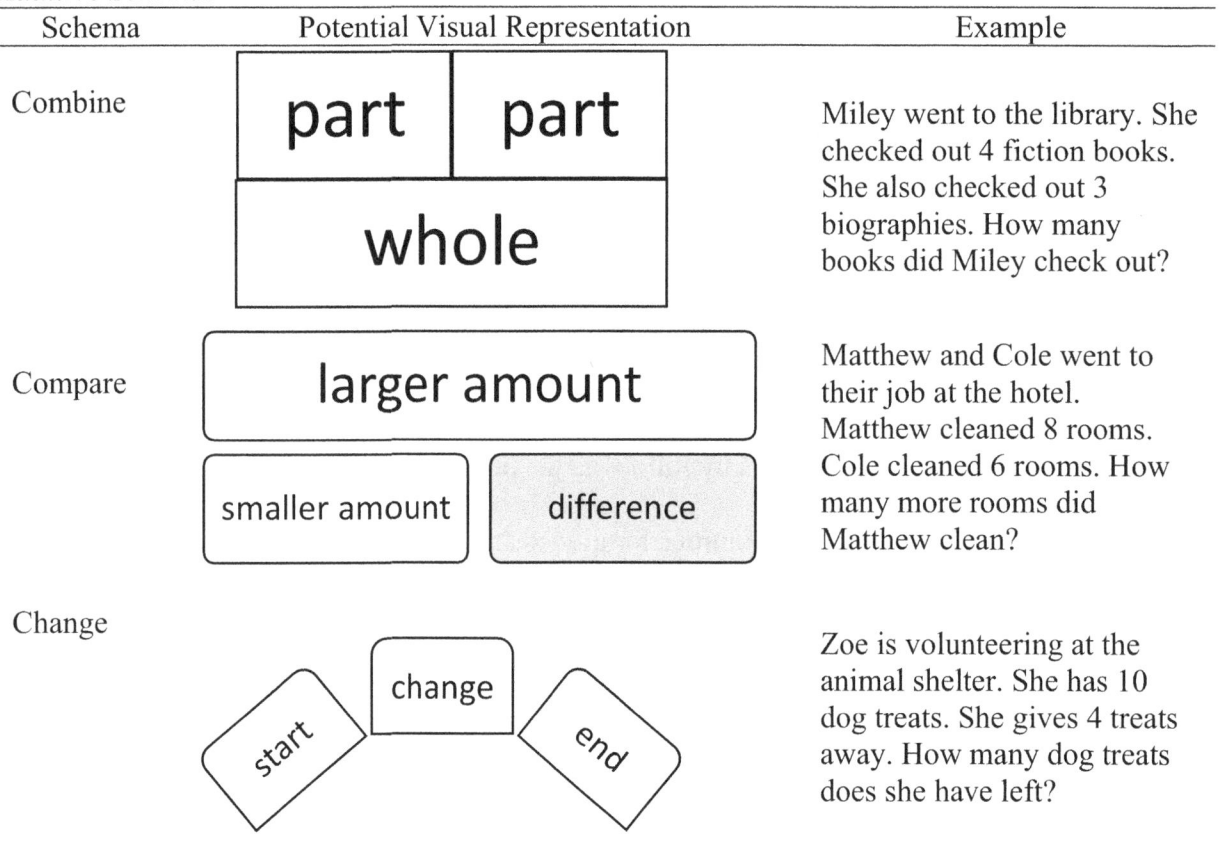	Miley went to the library. She checked out 4 fiction books. She also checked out 3 biographies. How many books did Miley check out?
Compare		Matthew and Cole went to their job at the hotel. Matthew cleaned 8 rooms. Cole cleaned 6 rooms. How many more rooms did Matthew clean?
Change		Zoe is volunteering at the animal shelter. She has 10 dog treats. She gives 4 treats away. How many dog treats does she have left?

Note. Adapted from Powell & Fuchs, 2018

Teachers use explicit instruction to teach the problem-solving routine (Archer & Hughes, 2011). Sometimes known as "I Do, We Do, You Do" or "Model-Lead-Test," teachers use explicit instruction to first present the problem-solving routine, support guided practice with feedback, and then give students the opportunity to independently solve problems. Metacognitive strategy knowledge is the final critical component of SBI. Students "think about what they are doing and why they are doing it, evaluate the steps they are taking to solve the problem, and connect new concepts to what they already know" (Woodward et al., 2012, p. 17.) When modeling the use of SBI, teachers also model their internal processes by using a think-aloud strategy, explicitly telling the students why they chose to use which method. Through these

Table 3
Multiplicative Schemas

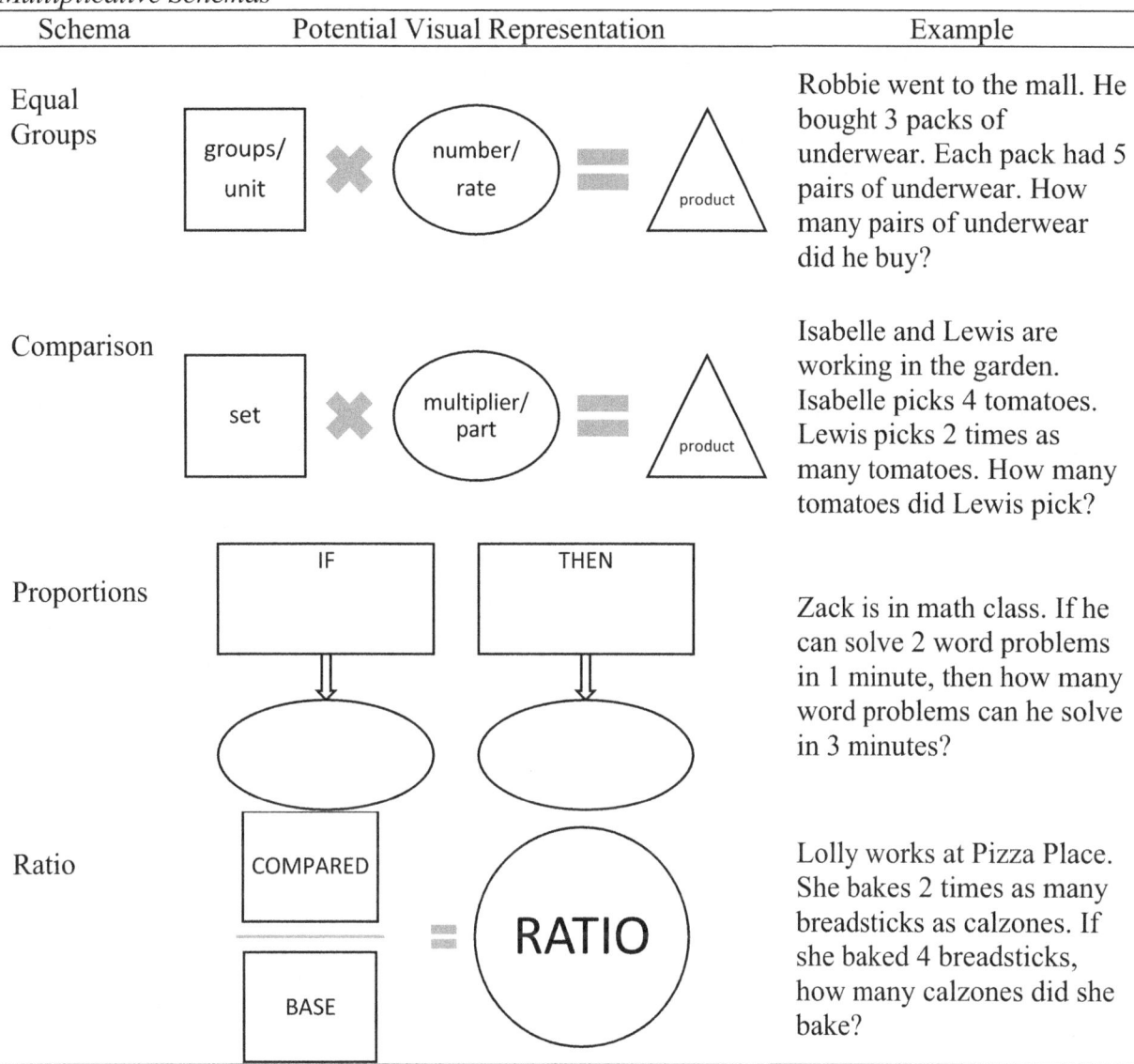

Schema	Potential Visual Representation	Example
Equal Groups		Robbie went to the mall. He bought 3 packs of underwear. Each pack had 5 pairs of underwear. How many pairs of underwear did he buy?
Comparison		Isabelle and Lewis are working in the garden. Isabelle picks 4 tomatoes. Lewis picks 2 times as many tomatoes. How many tomatoes did Lewis pick?
Proportions		Zack is in math class. If he can solve 2 word problems in 1 minute, then how many word problems can he solve in 3 minutes?
Ratio		Lolly works at Pizza Place. She bakes 2 times as many breadsticks as calzones. If she baked 4 breadsticks, how many calzones did she bake?

Note: Adapted from Powell & Fuchs, 2018

think-alouds, students begin to recognize the metacognitive processes behind problem solving and apply them in their own problem solving.

Modified Schema-Based Instruction

SBI is effective for teaching students to solve mathematical problems, particularly those students with learning disabilities (Jitendra et al., 2015; Peltier et al., 2020). On the other hand, students with ASD/IDD may need more supports than those provided in traditional SBI due to poor working memory, language or reading deficits, and overall difficulty with mathematics. Spooner and colleagues (2017) recognized these difficulties and proposed a set of modifications to make SBI more accessible for students with ASD/IDD coined Modified Schema-based Instruction (MSBI). With MBSI, evidence-based practices for teaching students with ASD/IDD are added to core features of SBI, as shown in Figure 1. First, mnemonics, which can be relatively abstract and require advanced language skills, are replaced with more concrete task analyses. Next, color-coded graphic organizers that are provided to students, rather than having them drawn them. Systematic instruction (e.g., system of least prompts) is added to explicit instruction. And finally, students demonstrate metacognitive strategy use through rules that pair words with physical actions rather than relying on student think alouds.

A number of research teams have evaluated MSBI with students at all grade levels, from 1st grade through postsecondary transition programs. There is data to support its effectiveness with students with autism, students with mild intellectual disability, and students with moderate to severe intellectual disability. Students with ASD/IDD have learned to solve problems using all types of schemas, including more complex applications such as percent of change and discount type problems (e.g., Bouck & Long, 2020; Root et al., 2018, 2019; Root et al., in press). Clausen et al. (2020) conducted an evidence-based practice review for MSBI using the quality indicator standards developed by Horner et al. (2005). In general, 11 studies with 39 participants were reviewed to be of high or adequate quality.

We will be using the vignettes presented in Figure 2 and Figure 3 to provide examples of how teachers can use MSBI to teach problem solving to students with ASD/IDD throughout the remainder of the chapter.

Figure 1
Core Features of SBI and MSBI

	What process will students follow? **Problem Solving Routine**		
	Mnemonic	Task Analysis	
Traditional Schema-based Instruction	*How will students represent the numerical relationship?* **Schematic Diagrams**		Modified Schema-based Instruction
	Student-drawn diagrams	Provide graphic organizers with visual supports	
	How will teachers support learning? **Explicit Instruction**		
	Model-Guided Practice-Independent Practice	Model-Guided Practice-Independent Practice + Systematic Instruction	
	How will students monitor and show what they are thinking? **Metacognitive Strategy**		
	Student think alouds	Rules for problem types with words + physical actions	

Planning for MSBI

As shown in Figure 1, there are four decisions teachers need to make as they plan MSBI:

1. The process students will follow (e.g.., problem solving routine)

2. How students will represent the numerical relationship (e.g., schematic diagrams)

3. How teachers will support learning (e.g., explicit instruction)

4. How students will show what they are thinking (e.g., metacognitive strategy).

While these questions are relatively straight-forward, there are a number of nuanced choices teachers can make as they plan and as they consider the individual strengths, needs, and characteristics of their students. MSBI is intended address common learning characteristics of

Figure 2
Elementary Vignette of Problem Solving Instruction—Calvin

Mr. Taylor and Ms. Ibourk co-teach a second grade class at Eaton Elementary school. Their class of 20 students includes several identified with developmental disabilities such as autism and intellectual disability. Calvin is one student in their class who has Cerebral Palsy and a mild intellectual disability which impacts his fine and gross motor skills. They are planning an upcoming unit to address the following state standard:
> CCSS.MATH.CONTENT 2.OA.A.1: Use addition and subtraction with 100 to solve one- and two-step word problems involving situations of adding to, taking from, putting together, taking apart, and comparing, with unknowns in all positions.

All students in the class will be taught using SBI, with some students receiving additional supports in the form of MSBI. During the unit, they will be focusing on the following standards-based IEP goal for Calvin:

Given graphic organizers, a task analysis, and visual supports, Calvin will independently solve word problems using group, compare, and change schemas with the unknown in the final position with 90% accuracy.

Figure 3
Secondary Vignette of Problem Solving Instruction—Jerika

Ms. Robinson is a special education teacher at Noble Middle School. She has 12 students with autism and intellectual disability in her math class who are all working toward alternate-achievement standards. Jerika is one 7th grade student with autism in her class. Although Jerika has memorized her math facts, she struggles with completing independent work, especially if it requires multiple steps. Ms. Robinson plans on differentiating Jerika's task analysis to further support her independence through self-monitoring and goal-setting. The unit will focus on the following standards for her 6th and 7th grade students:
> CCSS.MATH.CONTENT.6.RP.A.3.C: Find a percent of a quantity as a rate per 100 (e.g., 30% of a quantity means 30/100 times the quantity); solve problems involving finding the whole, given a part and the percent.
>
> CCSS.MATH.CONTENT.7.RP.A.3: Use proportional relationships to solve multistep ratio and percent problems.

This aligns with the following standards-based IEP goal for Jerika:

Given a graphic organizer, task analysis, and calculator, Jerika will represent and solve word problems depicting proportional relationships with 90% independence across 3 consecutive opportunities.

students with ASD/ID by adding support to traditional SBI via established evidence-based practices. On the other hand, there should be differentiation within each of these components to tailor instruction to the individual learner. Thinking about potential barriers students may face in solving word problems may help teachers guide these instructional decisions. Teachers can use the UDL framework to identify these barriers in the learning environment and curriculum that may prevent progress and increase opportunities for success by providing multiple options to reach and measure goals (Meyer et al., 2014).

All aspects of planning should be intentional, with understanding that there are many variables that can be altered to increase or decrease support (or challenge), and therefore differentiated to meet student learning goals. As discussed in detail in Chapter 2, teachers should use data to guide this differentiation. We have outlined four considerations to guide teachers' planning as they consider barriers to access, demonstrating conceptual understanding, becoming fluent in procedures, generalizing problem solving, and gaining independence:

1. What are the barriers to accessing the problem?
2. What are the barriers to demonstrating conceptual understanding?
3. What are the barriers to procedural fluency?
4. What are the barriers to independence and generalization?

A blank planning sheet that can be used to document answer to these questions is in the Appendices. These planning worksheets are intended to support teachers in making specific decisions regarding the four questions outlined in Figure 1.

Question 1: What are the barriers preventing students from accessing the problem?

The first barriers that must be considered when planning to use MSBI are those related to access. As outlined in Table 4, these can include reading level, problem structure, quantities or content, and vocabulary. Students may need support with both the literacy and numeracy demands of problem solving.

Reading Level

Accessing the problem itself may be the first barrier preventing students with ASD/ID from making progress in problem solving. The barrier could simply be from not being able to independently decode the word problem, or from not comprehending its meaning. Even emergent readers may struggle to gain meaning from word problems, especially if they are having to spend a great deal of cognitive effort on decoding the text. One strategy emphasized by Spooner et al. (2017) is to use considerate text that includes terminology familiar to students. Students should then be taught to access a read aloud of the problem, either through technology, such as optical character recognition apps (e.g., KNFB reader, Voice OCR), or by asking a peer or adult to read the problem for them. This is an important feature of MSBI because it promotes independence and self-advocacy skills that are beneficial beyond mathematics instruction and can be a building block of self-determination for even elementary learners.

Table 4
Barriers and Solutions to Accessing the Problem

Question 1: What are the barriers to accessing the problem?			
Reading Level	Problem Structure	Quantities/Content	Vocabulary
• Adjust the reading level of the problem by using considerate text • Teach the student to use technology to read the problem or ask for the problem to be read to them	• Limit extraneous information, especially if students are in acquisition phase • Present numerical information in problem in the order students need to use it • Format problem so that it is easy to identify important information (e.g., spacing, separate lines, limited visual supports)	• Align problem structure to problem type • Keep location of the unknown quantity the same across problems while students are in acquisition phase • Use quantities commensurate with student's number sense	• Explicitly teach vocabulary, symbols, and how to label instructional supports

Problem Structure

A second barrier to accessing the problem could be its structure, or the way it is written. Spooner et al. (2017) provide detailed guidelines for writing word problems to increase accessibility for students with ASD/IDD. Writing problems that do not include any extraneous information, presenting math quantities in the order they will be used in the graphic organizer or number sentence, and presenting the question using a common stem "How many ____" are just some of the ways to provide substantive support.

The way a problem appears to the student may also matter. For example, it may be easier to present each sentence of the word problem on a separate line and only include information and quantities relevant to solving the problem. Problems in general education textbooks often contain extraneous information. Beginning with problems that only contain information students need to solve the problem and then adding in extraneous information may increase success and decrease frustration. If problems do contain extraneous information, students should be explicitly taught how to identify and disregard it (Cox & Root, 2020). To increase generalization to real-world applications, teachers can teach students to locate quantities required for problem solving within natural stimuli such as receipts, coupons, screen shots from websites, or sales flyers. Figure 4 shows an example of how Ms. Robinson used receipts to support Jerika's generalization of percent of change problems.

Quantities or Content

Relatedly, the mathematical content addressed in the problem contributes to its accessibility. Conceptual understanding of the targeted mathematics concept is a core feature of MSBI, which directly relates to both how the problem is written, and the graphic organizers used to represent information from the problem (described in more detail below). Understanding essential features of targeted math content (e.g., problem types) is essential to selecting and writing problems for students. MSBI teaches students to understand mathematical relationships within specific problem types (e.g., additive group, additive comparison, additive change) versus rote operations (addition and subtraction). Each problem type has variations depending on the location of the unknown. For example, comparison problems can have the unknown in either the

Figure 4
Example of Percent Increase Word Problem Ms. Robinson Developed for Jerika

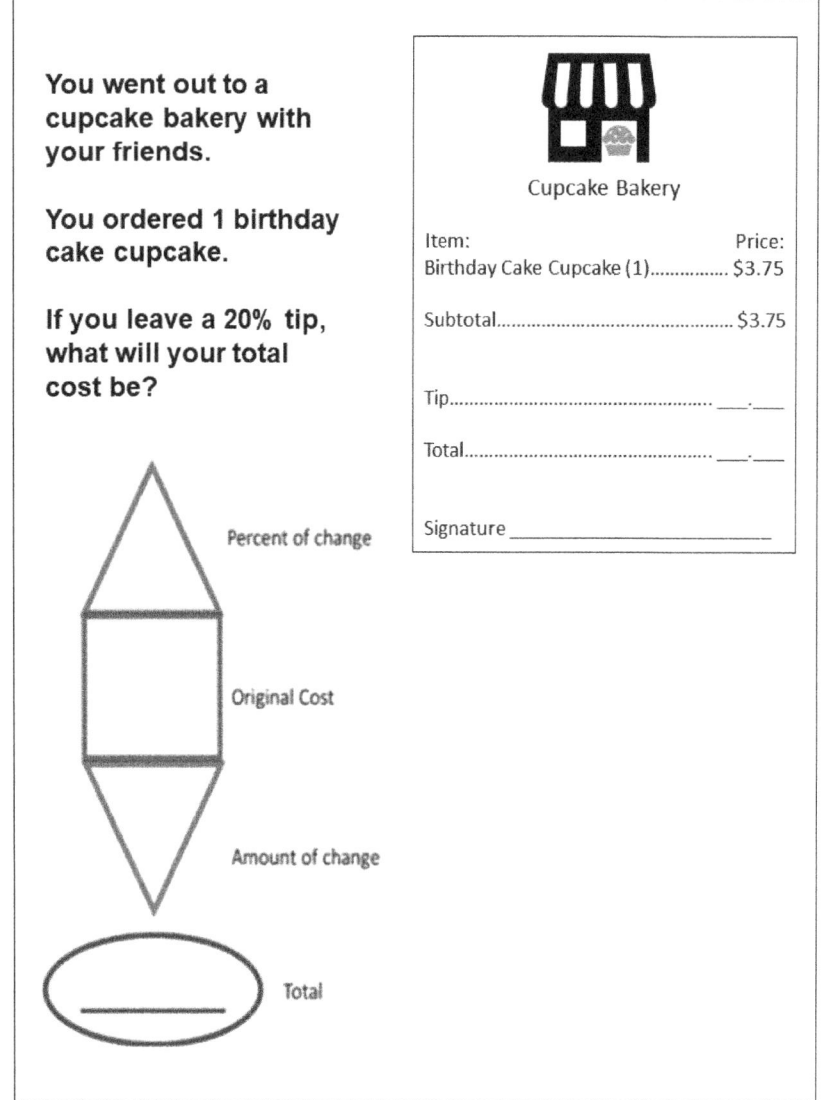

difference, big quantity, or small quantity. For additive problem types, it is easier for the unknown to be the whole (group problems), difference (compare problems), and amount (change problems).

The quantities used should be commensurate with a student's number sense. For example, a student who can identify numerals 1-9 and make sets of 1-9 objects can solve problems involving those quantities. Teachers should use data on student number sense development as they design problem solving instruction. Many word problems found in published commercial curricula or through web-based resources will need to be carefully scrutinized and likely edited in order to be suitable for MSBI instruction with students with ASD/IDD. Figure 5 provides an example of how Ms. Ibourk adapted word problems for her students.

Figure 5
Example of Adapting Word Problems from Basal Curricula

Ms. Ibourk adapts word problems from the 2nd grade curriculum for some of her students with ASD/IDD based on the planning sheet Mr. Taylor filled out. The original problems were written to have the missing lesser amount, like in the following:

At the school fun-run, the 1st grade students ran 4 miles and 2nd grade students ran 5 more miles than Kindergarten students. If Kindergarten students ran 3 miles, how many miles did 2nd graders run?

Based on the planning sheet, Calvin needed problems with a missing difference and no extraneous information. She rearranged the problem to meet his learning needs:

Eaton Elementary had a fun-run on Friday.
Kindergarten students ran 3 miles.
2nd grade students ran 8 miles.
How many more miles did 2nd graders run than Kindergarten students?

Vocabulary and Concepts

Finally, student vocabulary knowledge of both mathematics terms and instructional supports should be considered. As discussed in Chapter 3, the UDL framework emphasizes multiple means of representation, which includes providing options for language and symbols. Students should be explicitly taught mathematics vocabulary (e.g., referent, multiplier, product), symbols (e.g., equals means 'same amount as'), and to label their instructional supports (e.g., graphic organizer, task analysis, number sentence). Constant time delay is an evidence-based practice for teaching vocabulary (Browder et al., 2009) and can be used at the beginning of lessons before problem solving instruction. For example, Root and Browder (2019) began each MSBI instructional session with using constant time delay to teach definitions for the following symbols/terms: addition symbol (combine), subtraction symbol (take away), equal sign (same as), equation (statement that says things are equal), and label (name of group).

Question 2: What are the barriers to demonstrating conceptual understanding?

The second set of barriers teachers should consider are those related to students gaining and subsequently demonstrating conceptual understanding, as detailed in Table 5. The importance of intentionally designing instruction to promote conceptual understanding of mathematical content cannot be overstated. In MSBI, students are taught to use graphic organizers (i.e., schemas) to represent what is happening in the math problem. Manipulatives, drawings, or written numerals are mapped onto the schema to represent understanding of math content and relationships. Rules or chants help students conceptually understand the problem type and connect the problem structure to the graphic organizer. All of these components work together to support students gaining and demonstrating conceptual understanding.

Table 5
Barriers to Conceptual Understanding

Question 2: What are the barriers to demonstrating conceptual understanding?			
Metacognition	Using Diagrams and Manipulatives	Instructional Procedures	Instructional Sequence
• Teach students a "rule" or chant that pairs physical actions with words to reinforce conceptual understanding	• Use color coding in graphic organizers and manipulatives to support executive functioning and executive understanding • Provide students graphic organizers (rather than have them to draw) until they have demonstrated fluency • Provide options for manipulatives	• Use explicit instruction (model, guided practice, independent practice) • Use system of least prompts during guided practice • Use model-retest error correction procedure when students are in acquisition	• Teach one problem type or problem variation at a time, to mastery • Explicitly teach discrimination between problem types or variations in problems using a T-chart and example non-example training • Periodically check maintenance of previously mastered problems

Showing What They Know

Pairing a verbal rule/chant with hand motions is one way to help students show understanding of the relationship between quantities in the problem type. Students with limited vocal abilities can use the hand motions to communicate their understanding. Teachers should accept approximations of both physical and verbal components of rules as long as it is apparent that the student derives meaning from them. Relatedly, if students are not understanding the rule/chant, teachers can break them down or modify them so that they are useful to the learner, as illustrated in Figure 6.

Using Diagrams and Manipulatives

Decisions on the format of the schema and choice of manipulatives are interrelated and

Figure 6
Example of Modifying Rules to Support Conceptual Understanding

Some students in Mr. Taylor's class were having trouble with saying the word "difference" in the compare rule. He taught them to "clap out" the syllables in difference as they said it. Calvin particularly liked this addition to the chant. After a few weeks, he began just clapping three times Since he was completing all of the related steps correctly, Mr. Taylor accepted this approximation because he had evidence Calvin understood the problem type.

should be based on math content, student needs, and available resources. Some students with ASD/IDD may be able to draw schemas for themselves when provided with a model. For other students, this task may either be more effort or time intensive than beneficial, or even impossible due to fine motor difficulties. Providing students with graphic organizers removes this barrier and increases efficiency of instruction. Teachers could print graphic organizers directly onto worksheets (as seen in Figure 4 for Jerika) or provide separately (as shown for Calvin in Figure 7). Researchers demonstrated both paper-based and electronic graphic organizers to be effective (Root et al., in press). However, Root, Browder, et al. (2017) found some students with ASD/IDD were more independent in the virtual condition. This may be because they experienced less fine motor difficulties in the virtual condition. Moving concrete manipulatives on top of laminated graphic organizers may present fine motor difficulties that can be alleviated by using electronic graphic organizers with virtual manipulatives. An alternative solution could be attaching the graphic organizer to either a white board or magnetic slant board and using magnetic manipulatives. Chapter 4 provides more in-depth guidance on using manipulatives and manipulatives-based learning sequences to support conceptual understanding.

Figure 7
Calvin's graphic organizer

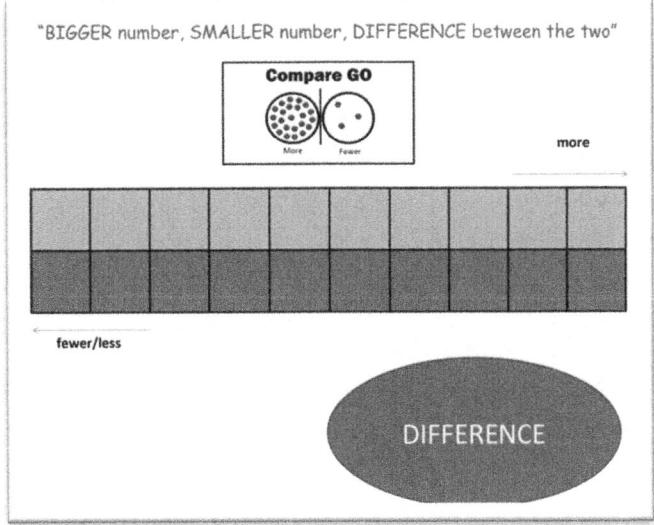

Note: From Browder et al. (2017)

Instructional Procedures

To intensify instruction, teachers can use a system of least prompts. Researchers recommend a 3-level prompting hierarchy, as shown in Table 6. This hierarchy can be modified based on the student and specific mathematics task, but generally should not consist of more than four levels to prevent students from excessively repeating errors. In some cases, it may be more efficient to just use an error correction procedure of a model- retest. The error correction should be brief, based in conceptual understanding of inverse operations, and end with giving the student an opportunity to demonstrate the skill. This model-retest could also involve the teacher modeling completing the skill and then having the student repeat it.

Instructional Sequence

The goal of problem-solving instruction should be discrimination, or the ability to determine what strategy (e.g., graphic organizer, procedure) is appropriate for a given mathematical situation (Browder et al., 2020). The ability to discriminate is the ultimate evidence

Table 6
Hierarchy of Prompting in MSBI

Hierarchy	Description	Example for Calvin	Example for Jerika
Verbal prompt	Verbal reminder of next step in problem solving process by directing attention to heuristic/TA	"Fill in the number sentence."	"Mark and label the original cost."
Specific verbal prompt	Verbal description of how to complete next step of problem solving process by telling how to complete step	"The word problem says Jane had 3 apples. Put 3 in the first box of the number sentence."	"The cupcake costs $3.75. Draw a box around $3.75 and write it in your equation."
Model / retest	Demonstrating how to complete next step of problem solving process with opportunity for student to perform step	"Watch me." *Teacher places the number 3 magnet in the first box of the number sentence and removes it.* "Now your turn."	"Watch me." *Teacher draws a box around $3.75 on the worksheet projected on the interactive whiteboard and then writes $3.75 in the box on the equation template.* "Now your turn."

of conceptual understanding, as it demonstrates the student can make intentional decisions to arrive at a solution to the problem. From the body of research on MSBI, researchers clearly indicated students with ASD/IDD require an intentional instructional sequence in order to demonstrate discrimination, or fluently solve multiple types of problems. In fact, findings have repeatedly shown that most students with ASD/IDD solve problems using the most recently targeted problem type. Based on this information, Spooner et al. (2017) recommend the following instructional sequence for additive problem types: (a) teaching group problem solving to mastery, (b) teaching compare problem solving to mastery, (c) teaching discrimination between group and compare problems to mastery, (d) teaching change addition problems to mastery, (e) teaching change subtraction problems to mastery, (f) teaching discrimination between change addition and subtraction problems to mastery, and finally (g) teaching discrimination between all additive problem types to mastery. Research on multiplicative problem types for students with ASD/IDD is still emerging, but the following sequence would ensure students have a logical foundational understanding of multiplication: equal group, multiplicative comparison, ratio, proportion, and percent of change. Multiplicative problems have variations within problem types just like additive problems (e.g., change addition and change subtraction). Percentages are a special type of ratio, and unit rate is one type of proportion problem. Relatedly, percent of change will include both change increase and change decrease.

Not all students with ASD/IDD will need this explicit discrimination training, as some may independently discriminate between problem types, an indication of maintenance of skills over time. Teachers should conduct maintenance checks of previously mastered problems to help determine whether students need explicit discrimination training. For students who do need this intense instruction, a T-chart sorting activity is efficient and effective (see Chapter 3). Figure 8 gives an example of how Ms. Robinson explicitly taught Jerika to discriminate between percent increase and percent decrease scenarios. This can help students to distinguish relevant features of the problem type (e.g., the rule, graphic organizer, operations, or concepts).

Question 3: What are the barriers to procedural fluency?

The third category of barriers teachers should consider are those related to procedural fluency. Procedural fluency in problem solving is critical to independence. Table 7 outlines strategies for addressing these barriers.

Figure 8
Example of Explicit Discrimination Training

Once per week Ms. Robinson gives her students a problem solving test consisting of 4 problems, including 2 percent increase problems and 2 percent decrease problems. During the problem solving test, Jerika did not find the correct answer to the percent increase problems, even though last week she solved both of them correctly. When analyzing her work, Ms. Robinson saw that she erroneously used the percent decrease rule for all of the problems, and therefore subtracted at step 5. Ms. Robinson used this data to plan a discrimination warm-up activity for the next week. During this activity, students sorted key features of percent increase and percent decrease problems on a T-chart. She then gave them several problems of each type to sort into the two columns using the key features.

Table 7
Barriers to Procedural Fluency

Question 3: What are the barriers to procedural fluency?	
Problem Solving Routine	Performing Operations
• Use a student-friendly task analysis that is appropriate for student's literacy and symbolic level and supports self-monitoring • Model using the task analysis during the problem solving routine by using think-alouds • Reinforce using the task analysis using behavior-specific praise	• Use manipulative-based instructional sequence (e.g., CRA, VRA, VA, or VR) to support acquisition and fluency • Teach students to use a calculator to check their work and support calculation with larger quantities

Problem Solving Routine

Procedural fluency in problem solving is critical to independence. Traditional SBI employs mnemonics as a heuristic to support student progression through a problem-solving routine. Students with ASD/IDD may need more support, at least initially, to make progress in independently following a problem-solving routine. Mnemonics may not break down the problem-solving process into enough steps (e.g., multiple actions chunked into a single step). Further, they rely on literacy skills to associate steps with letters (e.g., D = discover the problem type). The task analysis provided to students in MSBI serves as the heuristic in MSBI. Spooner et al. (2017) characterized it as student friendly, meaning it is formatted in a way that supports independence. Researchers of MSBI found a variety of formats effective (Root, Henning, et al., 2020). When constructing a task analysis, teachers should consider the reading levels of their students and their symbolic levels. These generally include a space for students to check off completed steps (to support self-monitoring) and a brief description of the step paired with an icon or image as a visual support. Teachers should design these to meet the needs of individual students. Some students will require a problem-solving routine with very discrete and incremental steps while others will be able to chunk multiple related behaviors into a single step. Similarly, the presence of visual supports on the task analysis and specific choice of icons or pictures may need to be tailored for individual students. Figure 9 shows examples of task analysis for additive and percent of change problems

Figure 9
Examples of Task Analysis for Additive Problems (Calvin) and Percent of Change Problems (Jerika)

#	Icon	Step
1.		Read the problem
2.		Circle the "whats"
3.		Write the label
4.		Same? Different? More/fewer?
5.		Choose the graphic organizer
6.		Say the rule
7.		Circle the numbers
8.		Fill-in the number sentence
9.		Write + or –
10.		Make sets
11.		Solve and write answer

#	By myself	With help	Step
1.			Talk about the problem out loud ❑ What do we know about the problem? ❑ What do we want to find out? ❑ What kind of problem is it?
2.			Mark and label original cost
3.			Mark and label percent of change
4.			Calculate amount of change
5.			+ or -
6.			Calculate final cost
			Add up totals and graph

Note. Left reprinted with permission from Browder et al. (2017), Right adapted from Root, Cox, et al. (2020).

Performing Operations

Students with ASD/IDD may not have fluency with mathematical operations. As previously mentioned in this chapter and discussed in depth in Chapter 4, manipulative-based sequences of instruction (CRA/VRA, CR, VR, VA) can support students in understanding more abstract representations. However, calculators are a form of assistive technology that can alleviate the cognitive load students experience during problem solving or make higher-levels of mathematics possible. Teachers can use both manipulatives and calculators within problem solving tasks. For example, when initially learning a new operation or problem type, manipulatives should be used with small quantities so that students can see the math relationship. As students gain fluency, they can transition to drawing representations or pictures with small, manageable quantities. After fluency is reached, teachers can introduce larger quantities in the problems and teach calculator use. The danger in only teaching students to use a calculator is that they may just focus on how to make the calculator give them an answer.

Question 4: What are the barriers to independence and generalization?

Although independence and generalization are the final barriers teachers should consider, they are not the least important. In fact, independence and generalization are critical and likely directly measured by student IEP goals. Table 8 identifies the barriers and solutions to supporting these critical skills.

Self-Monitoring

Self-monitoring is an important self-determination skill that increases independence. Self-monitoring generally consists of two processes: self-assessment and self-recording. Students need to receive a cue or prompt that it is time to assess their behavior and have a way to record it. In MSBI, students are taught to use the task analysis as a checklist, marking off each

Table 8
Barriers to Independence and Solutions.

Question 4: What are the barriers to independence and generalization		
Self-monitoring	Engagement	Relevance
• Teach students to self-monitor using the task analysis • Two-column task analysis can support both accuracy and independence • Teach students how to self-graph progress and set goals to support self-determination	• Provide choices with instructional materials • Foster collaboration with partner or small group problem solving	• Feature familiar people, places, and topics in word problems • Allow students to select or even write word problems by providing choices or "fill in the blank" style problems • Use realia (e.g., coupons, receipts, store flyers, screen shots from the internet) to support generalization and connections to real-world applications of math

step as it is completed. As they check off a completed step, their attention is directed to the next step, reinforcing the problem-solving routine. Some students may need more support than just checking off completed to increase independence. A two-column checklist like the one developed for Jerika in Figure 8 can help students self-monitor independence and accuracy, as well as support goal setting. Students can then self-graph their accuracy on paper or electronic graphs using google sheets displayed on a tablet or mobile device.

Engagement

Engagement can be maximized through providing choices and fostering collaboration through group work. When designing word problems to be solved by students, consider developing a pool of problems of similar complexity that students may choose from. Teachers can also provide choices by offering a variety of manipulatives, including concrete and virtual, for the students to choose from (see Chapter 4). Engagement may also be increased through group work. Though students with ASD/IDD may be solving modified word problems, with smaller quantities than their same-age peers, they will still be working towards the same standard and following similar procedural steps. A student with ASD/IDD may participate in their group by monitoring the group's progress using a task analysis, listing the steps of the procedure using an assistive technology device, such as a Step-by-Step™ preprogrammed with the steps, or by entering the number sentence into a calculator to determine the solution.

Relevance

Word problems are often seen as abstract and more difficult to solve than a simple arithmetic number sentence. On the other hand, through the inclusion of familiar people, places, and objects, students will be better prepared to generalize problem solving to real-world situations. Once you have the basic four-sentence model, it is very easy to substitute different components of the word problem to make it more relevant for the student. For example, when writing a word problem for a third-grade student, you may include their classmates, and scenes from their school environment (e.g., Mia and Devonte are collecting pinecones at recess. Mia collects 3 pinecones. Devonte collects 2 pinecones. How many pinecones did Mia and Devonte collect?). When working with secondary students, you might include scenes from their community worksite, or take the opportunity to address some post-school transition skills (e.g., Dani and Michelle are looking for an apartment to rent. They have a budget of $1000 per month. Dani is contributing $600 each month. How much is Michelle contributing?).

Putting It All together

We have provided a blank planning sheet in the Appendix that teachers can use as they plan MSBI. Figures 10 and 11 provide completed examples of the planning sheet for Calvin and Jerika.

Figure 10

Completed Planning Worksheet for Calvin

Potential Barriers	Considerations	Specific Strategies for Calvin
1) Access	Reading level	-Teach to press "Read please" button on AAC device to request peer or adult read problem aloud
	Problem Structure	-No extraneous information -4 line structure -Always with difference unknown (5-3=?)
	Quantities/content	-Limit quantities to whole numbers below 10
	Vocabulary	-difference; subtract
2) Conceptual Understanding	Metacognition	-Compare rule: "**Bigger number** (hands apart with palms facing each other), **smaller number** (move palms closer together), **difference** (clap out syllables) **between the two** (make big circle with pointer finger of right hand)"
	Diagrams and manipulatives	-Laminated color-coded compare schema, taped to magnetic slant board -Magnetic tiles in two colors (one for larger quantity, one for lesser quantity)
	Instructional procedure	-Teacher models, guided practice with peer, independent practice -Peer uses system of least prompts during guided practice
	Instructional sequence	-Teach compare problem type to mastery -Weekly maintenance checks of group problem type
3) Procedural Fluency	Problem-solving routine	-Laminated task analysis taped to magnetic slant board
	Performing operations	-Manipulatives for quantities below 10 -Calculator for quantities above 10
4) Generalization and Independence	Self-monitoring	-Move magnet with check mark down the TA as steps are completed
	Engagement	-Provide a pool of word problems for student to choose from
	Relevance	-Create real-world problems that include names of familiar people and places

Figure 11

Completed Planning Worksheet for Jerika.

Potential Barriers	Considerations	Specific Strategies for Jerika
1) Access	Reading level	-Read aloud of word problem programmed on GoWorksheet app -Teach to tap icon to listen to problem
	Problem Structure	-No extraneous information -Do not put original cost/amount in word problem, needs to locate from real stimuli (e.g., menus, receipts)
	Quantities/content	-n/a
	Vocabulary/ Concept review	-how to read/say monetary values (e.g., $4.50 is four dollars and fifty cents) -how to represent monetary values in calculator / on paper (e.g., $4.50 = 4.5 in calculator)
	Metacognition	-Percent of change rule: "**Percent increase, add** (thumbs up with left hand, use right pointer finger to cross over thumb forming "+" and raise hand upward) **Percent decrease, subtract** (thumbs up with left hand and lower hand downward)"
2) Conceptual Understanding	Diagrams and manipulatives	-Color-coded schema directly on electronic worksheet
	Instructional Procedures	-Model, guided practice, independent practice -Immediate error correction from teacher during guided practice
	Instructional Sequence	-Teach percent decrease to mastery -Weekly percent increase maintenance checks
3) Procedural Fluency	Problem-solving routine	-2-column Task analysis at the top of each electronic worksheet
	Performing operations	-Calculator with % button
4) Generalization and Independence	Self-monitoring	-2-column task analysis – check off whether each step was completed independently or with assistance -Google sheet loaded on iPad with goal setting form and graph
	Engagement	-Allow selection of theme for word problems -Promote collaboration through group work
	Relevance	- Watch short Youtube video at beginning of session related to theme of problem (e.g., nail salon video)

Implementing MSBI

To make progress and move toward independence in problem solving, students with ASD/IDD will need consistent opportunities for learning and practice. Instructional sessions in most research studies lasted between 15-25 minutes, with students having the opportunity to solve between 2-5 problems (Root, Henning, et al., 2020). Most MSBI research studies began instruction with introductory lessons to scaffold introduction to the problem solving process (Root, Henning, et al., 2020). While their exact format and focus varied, they generally include instruction on prerequisite concepts and skills, building conceptual understanding of the problem type by connecting the rule/hand motion to the graphic organizer, and modeling how to solve the problem. Prerequisite concepts and skills should be explicitly taught either prior to or during MSBI. This could be vocabulary or symbols, such as correct terminology for operations (e.g., + = add, - = subtract, % = percent), how to interpret values displayed on calculators (e.g., translating .4 to 40%, or 1.4 to $1.40), or reading math notation correctly (e.g., $1.40 = one dollar and forty cents, 1/5 = one fifth).

Introducing the rule/hand motions and graphic organizers in isolation may support their later use within the problem solving process by reducing cognitive load. That is, students can first just focus on learning the mechanics of the rule/hand motion and how manipulatives are used on the graphic organizer. As a result, students will be in the fluency stage of learning when they begin using them within the problem solving routine. Another way to support students and scaffold problem solving instruction is to use completed problems during introductory lessons. Using problems without any unknown information also gives teachers and students a chance to just practice modeling the problem using the rule/hand motion and graphic organizer. Table 9 gives an example of problems Ms. Singer and Ms. Robinson used in introductory lessons.

Table 9

Example Problems from Vignettes

	Calvin	Jerika
CCSS	2.OA.A.1: Use addition and subtraction with 100 to solve one- and two-step word problems involving situations of adding to, taking from, putting together, taking apart, and comparing, with unknowns in all positions.	7.RP.A.3: Use proportional relationships to solve multistep ratio and percent problems.
Problem Type	Compare	Percent Increase
Word Problem	Eaton Elementary had a fun-run on Friday. Kindergarten students ran 3 miles. 2nd grade students ran 8 miles. How many more miles did 2nd graders run than Kindergarten students?	You went out to a cupcake bakery with your friends. You ordered 1 birthday cake cupcake. If you leave a 20% top, what will your total cost be?
Graphic Organizer		
Task Analysis		

Browder et al. (2018) recommended only a few days of these introductory lessons. The majority of instructional sessions should be focused on providing students repeated opportunities to practice problem solving with graduated levels of support. As discussed previously, teachers can use explicit instruction and the system of least prompts to balance the need for students to receive instruction with opportunities to practice the skill on their own. Data should then drive instructional decisions regarding enhancing or reducing support and facilitating progression through the phases of learning. Chapter 3 discusses this data-based decision-making progress in depth, along with corresponding instructional changes.

Incorporating technology, particularly computers, tablets, or interactive whiteboards, can increase the effectiveness and efficiency of MSBI, as well as student engagement. Spooner and colleagues (2019) found technology-assisted instruction to be an evidence-based practice for teaching math skills to students with ASD/IDD. Technology provides many opportunities to address the principles of UDL (CAST, 2018). For example, video simulations of real-world contexts for solving problems can be used to optimize relevance, value, and authenticity (UDL guideline 7.3) as well as activate or supply background knowledge (UDL guideline 3.2). Root, Cox, et al. (2020) taught young adults with autism to use an Augmented Reality app on a mobile device to access social story videos explaining the process and rationale for leaving a tip at various locations in the community prior to solving problems.

Several researchers used digital worksheets with text-to-speech features and online calculators (e.g., Gilley et al., 2020; Root et al., 2019; Saunders, 2014). This provides multiple means of representation by offering alternatives for auditory information ([UDL guideline 1.2](#)) support for decoding of text, mathematical notation and symbols ([UDL guideline 2.3](#)), and multiple means of action by varying methods for response and navigation ([UDL guideline 4.1](#)) and multiple tools for construction and composition ([UDL guideline 5.2](#)). Other teams investigated the use of virtual manipulatives and graphic organizers (Root, Browder, et al., 2017; Saunders, 2014), which provided multiple means of action by building fluencies with graduated levels of support for practice and performance (UDL guideline 5.3). Additionally, Gilley et al. (2020) and Root, Cox, et al. (2020) taught students to self-monitor by graphing their progress on Excel spreadsheets. This supported students executive functioning by guiding appropriate goal setting (UDL guideline 6.1), supporting planning and strategy development (UDL guideline 6.2), and enhancing capacity for monitoring progress (UDL guideline 6.4). Root, Cox, et al. (2020) provide extensive details on how MSBI can align to the UDL framework. For more resources on UDL, visit cast.org.

Conclusion

The purpose of this chapter was to discuss how to teach problem solving skills to learners with ASD/IDD. In doing so, we have outlined the importance of mathematics and the impact that solving everyday life problems has on postschool outcomes such as independence and overall quality of life. SBI is an evidence-based practice for teaching students with high incidence disabilities mathematical problem solving. Frequently, however, students with ASD/IDD may need more supports than those provided in traditional SBI. Based on these additional supports, modified schema-based instruction was developed. We go on to identify the similarities and differences between SBI and MSBI, how to incorporate technology in the application of MSBI, how to plan for MSBI, and then address four potential barriers to implementation: (a) accessing the problem, (b) demonstration of conceptual understanding, (c) procedural fluency, and (d) independence and generality.

References

Archer, A. L., & Hughes, C. H. (2011). *Explicit instruction: Effective and efficient teaching.* Guilford Press.

Bouck, E. C., & Long, H. (2020). Teaching students with intellectual and developmental disabilities to calculate cost after discounts via schematic diagrams. *Research in Developmental Disabilities, 102.* https://doi.org/10.1016/j.ridd.2020.103656

Brosh, C. R., Root, J. R., Saunders, A. F., Spooner, F., & Fisher, L. B. (2018). Embedding literacy in mathematics problem solving instruction for learners with intellectual and developmental disability. *Inclusion, 6*(2), 81-96. https://doi.org/10.1352/2326-6988-6.2.81

Brosh, C. R. (2018). *Effects of a multi-component intervention package on academic skills for students with severe disabilities* (Publication No. 10791865) [Doctoral dissertation, University of North Carolina at Charlotte]. ProQuest Dissertations and Theses Global.

Browder, D. M., Ahlgrim-Delzell, L., Spooner, F., Mims, P. J., & Baker, J. N. (2009). Using time delay to teach literacy to students with severe developmental disabilities. *Exceptional Children, 75*(3), 343-364.

Browder, D. M., Spooner, F., & Lo, Y.-y. (2017). *The solutions project manual.* U.S. Department of Education, Institute of Education Sciences. https://access.uncc.edu/sites/access.uncc.edu/files/media/solutions/TheSolutionsProject_Manual%20For%20Dissemination.pdf

Browder, D. M., Spooner, F., Lo, Y.-y., Saunders, A. F., Root, J. R., Ley Davis, L., & Brosh, C. R. (2018). Teaching students with moderate intellectual disability to solve word problems. *The Journal of Special Education, 51*(4), 222-235. https://doi.org/10.1177/0022466917721236

Browder, D. M., Spooner, F., & Courtade, G. R. (2020). *Teaching students with moderate and severe disabilities* (2nd ed.). Guilford Press.

Buncher, A. G. (2019). *Effects of modified schema-based instruction on addition and subtraction word problem solving of students with autism spectrum disorder and intellectual disability* (Publication No. 27692341) [Doctoral dissertation, University of Cincinnati]. ProQuest Dissertations and Theses Global.

CAST. (2018). *Universal design for learning guidelines* (version 2.2). Retrieved from https://udlguidelines.cast.org

Clausen, A. M., Tapp, M. C., Teasdell, A., Pennington, R. C., & Spooner, F. (2020). *Establishing the evidence for modified schema based instruction to teach mathematical problem solving to students with moderate and severe disabilities* [Manuscript submitted for publication]. Cato College of Education, University of North Carolina at Charlotte.

Cox, S. K. (2019). *The development of mathematical practices through word problem solving instruction for students with autism spectrum disorder* [Doctoral dissertation, Florida State University]. Retrieved from http://purl.flvc.org/fsu/fd/2019_Summer_Cox_fsu_0071E_15264

Cox, S. K., & Root, J. R. (2020). Modified schema-based instruction to develop flexible mathematics problem-solving strategies for students with autism spectrum disorder. *Remedial and Special Education, 41*(3), 139-151. https://doi.org/10.1177/0741932518792660

Fuchs, L. S., Powell, S. R., Cirino, P. T., Schumacher, R. F., Marrin, S., Hamlett, C. L., Fuchs, D., Compton, D. L., & Changas, P. C. (2014). Does calculation or word-problem instruction provide a stronger route to prealgebraic knowledge? *Journal of Educational Psychology, 106*(4), 990-1006. https://doi.org/10.1037/a0036793

Gilley, D. P., Root, J. R., & Cox, S. K. (2020). Development of mathematics and self-determination skills for young adults with extensive support needs. *The Journal of Special Education.* Advance online publication. https://doi.org/10.1177/0022466920902768

Jitendra, A. K., Peterson-Brown, S., Lein, A. E., Zaslofsky, A. F., Kunkel, A. K., Jung, P.-G., & Egan, A. M. (2015). Teaching mathematical word problem solving: The quality of evidence for strategy instruction priming the problem structure. *Journal of Learning Disabilities, 48*(1), 51–72. https://doi.org/10.1177/0022219413487408

Jitendra, A. K., Star, J. R., Dupuis, D. N., & Rodriguez, M. C. (2013). Effectiveness of schema-based instruction for improving seventh-grade students' proportional reasoning: A randomized experiment. *Journal of Research on Educational Effectiveness, 6*(2), 114-136. https://doi.org/10.1080/19345747.2012.725804

Kilpatrick, J., Swafford, J., & Findell, B. (2001). *Adding it up: Helping children learn mathematics*. National Academy Press.

Ley Davis, L. (2016). Effects of peer-mediated instruction on mathematical problem solving for students with moderate/severe intellectual disability (Publication No. 10111913). [Doctoral dissertation, University of North Carolina at Charlotte]. ProQuest Dissertations and Theses Global.

Meyer, A., Rose, D. H., & Gordon, D. T. (2014). *Universal design for learning: Theory and practice*. CAST Professional Publishing.

Nasamran, A., Witmer, S. E., & Los, J. E. (2017). Exploring predictors of postsecondary outcomes for students with autism spectrum disorder. *Education and Training in Autism and Developmental Disabilities, 52*(4), 343-356.

National Mathematics Advisory Panel. (2008). *Foundations for success: The final report of the National Mathematics Advisory Panel*. US Department of Education.

Peltier, C., Sinclair, T. E., Pulos, J., M., & Suk, A. M. (2020). Effects of schema-based instruction on immediate, generalized, and combined structured word problems. *The Journal of Special Education, 54*(2), 101-112. https://doi.org/10.1177/002246691988339

Powell, S. R. (2011). Solving word problems using schemas: A review of the literature. *Learning Disabilities Research & Practice, 26*(2), 94-108.

Powell, S. R., & Fuchs, L. S. (2018). Effective word-problem instruction: Using schemas to facilitate mathematical reasoning. *TEACHING Exceptional Children, 51*(1), 31-42. https://doi.org/10.1177/00400591877250

Root, J. R., & Browder, D. M. (2019). Algebraic problem solving for middle school students with autism and intellectual disability. *Exceptionality, 27*(2), 118-132. https://doi.org/10.1080/09362835.2017.1394304

Root, J. R., Browder, D. M., & Jimenez, B. (2016). Algebra instruction for students with severe disabilities. In B. S. Witzel, & P. J. Riccomini (Eds.), *Arithmetic to algebra gap: Instructional and intervention recommendations*. Council for Exceptional Children.

Root, J. R., Browder, D. M., Saunders, A. F., & Lo, Y.-y. (2017). Schema-based instruction with concrete and virtual manipulatives to teach problem solving to students with autism. *Remedial and Special Education, 38*(1), 42-52. https://doi.org/10.1177/0741932516643592

Root, J. R., Cox, S. K., & Gonzalez, S. (2019). Using modified schema-based instruction with technology-based supports to teach data analysis. *Research and Practice for Persons with Severe Disabilities, 44*(1), 53-68. https://doi.org/10.1177/1540796919833915

Root, J. R., Cox, S. K., Hammons, N., & Davis, K. (in press). Contextualizing mathematical problem solving instruction for secondary students with extensive support needs. *Research and Practice for Persons with Severe Disabilities*.

Root, J. R., Cox, S. K., Hammons, N., Saunders, A. F., & Gilley, D. (2018). Contextualizing mathematics: Teaching problem solving to secondary students with intellectual and developmental disabilities. *Intellectual and Developmental Disabilities, 56*(6), 442-457. https://doi.org/10.1352/1934-9556-56.6.442

Root, J. R., Cox, S. K., Saunders, A., & Gilley, D. (2020). Applying the universal design for learning framework to mathematics instruction for learners with extensive support needs. *Remedial and Special Education, 41*(4), 194-206. https://doi.org/10.1177/0741932519887235

Root, J. R., Henning, B., & Cox, S. K. (2020). Evidence-based practices for teaching mathematical word problem solving to students with autism spectrum disorder. *Manuscript under review.*

Root, J. R., Henning, B., & Boccumini, E. (2018). Teaching students with autism and intellectual disability to solve algebraic word problems. *Education and Training in Autism and Developmental Disabilities, 53*(3), 325-338.

Root, J., Saunders, A., Spooner, F., & Brosh, C. (2017). Teaching personal finance mathematical problem solving to individuals with moderate intellectual disability. *Career Development and Transition for Exceptional Individuals, 40*(1), 5-14. https://doi.org/10.1177/2165143416681288

Saunders, A. F. (2014). *Effects of schema-based instruction delivered through computer-based video instruction on mathematical word problem solving of students with autism spectrum disorder and moderate intellectual disability* (Publication No. 3636163) [Doctoral dissertation, University of North Carolina at Charlotte]. ProQuest Dissertations and Theses Global.

Spooner, F., & Browder, D. M. (2015). Raising the bar: Significant advances and future needs for promoting learning for students with severe disabilities. *Remedial and Special Education, 36*(1), 28-32. https://doi.org/10.1177/0741932514555022

Spooner, F., Root, J. R., Saunders, A. F., & Browder, D. M. (2019). An updated evidence-based practice review on teaching mathematics to students with moderate and severe developmental disabilities. *Remedial and Special Education, 40*(3), 150-165. https://doi.org/10.1177/0741932517751055

Spooner, F., Saunders, A. F., Root, J. R., & Brosh, C. (2017). Promoting access to common core mathematics for students with severe disabilities through mathematical problem solving. *Research and Practice for Persons with Severe Disabilities, 42*(3), 171-186. https://doi.org/10.1177/1540796917697119

Taber-Doughty, T. (2015). STEM for students with severe disabilities. *School Science and Mathematics, 115*(4), 153-154.

Van de Walle, J. A., Karp, K. S., & Bay-Williams, J. M. (2010). *Elementary and middle school mathematics: Teaching developmentally* (7th ed.). Pearson.

Woodward, J., Beckmann, S., Driscoll, M., Franke, M., Herzig, P., Jitendra, A., Koedinger, K. R., & Ogbuehi, P. (2012). *Improving mathematical problem solving in grades 4-8: A practice guide* (NCEE 2012-4055). Institute of Education Sciences, U.S. Department of Education. http://ies.ed..gov/ncee/wwc/PracticeGuide.aspx?sid=16

Chapter 6: Embedded Instruction

Bree Jimenez

The number of students with autism and intellectual and developmental disabilities (ASD/IDD) taught within the inclusive classroom has continued to increase in recent years (Morningstar et al, 2017). As more students are included in the math classroom working towards grade-aligned math standards, educators must continue to consider how they will incorporate research- and evidence- based practices (EBPs) for students with ASD/IDD within the inclusive math lessons.

While Universal Design for Learning (UDL) offers the potential to reduce learning barriers within the math lesson for all learners (CAST, 2017), students with ASD/IDD will most likely continue to need explicit and intensive instruction designed to support additional learning goals. The UDL math classroom prioritizes the learning goals for the math lessons and identifies how all students will be able to engage in the lesson, how the information and math concepts will be represented so that all students can understand and gain access, and finally how all students will 'show what they know.' For more on UDL, see Chapter 3 of this book. This chapter will address an additional strategy that can be used within the Universally Designed classroom to support the individualized learning needs of students with disabilities.

What is Embedded Instruction?

There are three basic trial formats in which learning opportunities can occur; massed trials (occurring consecutively), spaced trials (opportunity to respond, wait time to listen to others before receiving another trial on the same skill), and distributed trials (opportunity to respond to target skill interspersed with practice on other tasks; Collins, 2012). Embedded Instruction (EI) is designed to distribute instructional trials (i.e., learning opportunities) within the ongoing routine and activities of the classroom environment. Essentially, distributed trials and EI are the very similar; however, trials may be considered embedded rather than simply distributed when they occur within the on-going, naturally occurring general education context. In comparison to other forms of trial delivery formats, EI may provide a more feasible way to support Tier 2 and Tier 3 interventions for students with ASD/IDD within the general education classroom (Jimenez & Barron, 2019). Please see Chapter 3 for a more in-depth discussion of tiers and MTSS for mathematics for students with ASD/IDD. Although research supports the use of all three formats, educators may find it difficult to use massed trials within the general education lesson, as this format typically requires an individual time and place.

Researchers demonstrated EI to be an effective strategy in supporting the use of EBPs (i.e., systematic instruction) for students with ASD/IDD within the general education classroom across various academic areas (Jimenez & Kamei, 2015; McDonnell et al., 2014; see Table 1 for examples of research on EI). Additionally, demonstrated across each of the chapters of this book, we are able to see the effectiveness of well-designed mathematics instruction that includes grade-aligned outcomes, as well as systematic instruction (e.g., constant time delay, least to most prompting). EI provides an opportunity for educators to plan instruction that includes instructional trials for learners based upon explicit learning goals they need, naturally within the math lesson.

What does EI look like?

Teachers plan when and how many trials are distributed across the learning activities and who will embed each trial. Basically, the educational team identifies prioritized learning goals for a specific student, then finds ways in which they can 'embed' opportunities to explicitly teach this new skill throughout their lessons. For example, Mr. Artican has 17 students in his 6th grade

Table 1
Embedded Instruction Research Examples

Math Content	Participants	Who Embedded	Research
Addition word problems with sums less than five	Elementary students with moderate and severe disabilities	General education teacher	Bowman et al. (2019) • Embedded simultaneous prompting with feedback • 10-step task analysis to solve word problems, with graphic organizer and manipulatives • Students generalized to untaught word problems
Number identification, tell time 15 and 30 minutes past the hour	Elementary students with developmental disabilities	General education teacher	Polychronis et al. (2004) • Embedded instruction package: constant time delay with instructional trials across 30 min. (one lesson) and 120 min (multiple lessons); both successful. • Generalized to natural stimuli in the classroom
Grade-aligned math and early numeracy goals (i.e., extending patterns, use multiplication chart, simple addition and subtraction)	Elementary students with ASD and/or intellectual disability	Special education, general education, and teacher assistants	Jimenez & Barron (2019) • Educational team planning was effective to determine alternate assessment grade-aligned academic goal and additional early/pivotal learning goals needed to be embedded. • Significant increase in individualized 'lesson-specific' learning goals embedded within inclusive lesson.

math class. While teaching a lesson on fractions, decimals and percentage he knows that two of his students, Tony and Kasik, have not yet mastered the vocabulary of fractions. Periodically (i.e., at least 6 planned opportunities throughout the 45-minute lesson), he and his paraprofessional will ask Tony and Kasik to identify:

- the numerator
- the denominator
- identify which represents the "parts we have"

- identify which represents "how many equal parts the item is divided into"

By identifying four additional learning outcomes for this unit of math that both Tony and Kasik need to help build their understanding of converting fractions, decimals, and percentage, Mr. Artican is able to plan and implement explicit and systematic instruction during the ongoing math lesson; rather than a separate time in the day. Using EI is not only effective in supporting the student's needs; if is a feasible and easy tool for Mr. Artican. Tony and Kasik are provided individualized instruction within the ongoing math lesson, building their math skills in the context of the grade aligned math lesson.

Because EI is explicit and systematic, it is important for educators to work together to plan what, how and when they will embed learning trials. Consideration should be made to the learning goals needed, classroom context and instructional team members strengths. Recently, Jameson et al. (2020) published a step-by-step guide to planning for EI in the general curriculum classroom for students with intellectual and developmental disabilities. This chapter will use those steps to outline the use of EI to support mathematics instruction, specifically to support early numeracy instruction within the grade-aligned math lessons (see Figure 1).

Chapter 2 outlines the need for ongoing progress monitoring and data-based decision making to support student mathematics progress. Beginning with identified learning goals, Cox and colleagues identify students with ASD/IDD will likely need both prerequisite (e.g., early numeracy) and facilitating skill (e.g., subitizing) development aligned to the general curriculum content. EI can support the development of those skills that are necessary to being able to independently complete the task, as well as facilitating skills that may increase efficiency or decrease cognitive load.

Figure 1
Designing and Implementing Embedded Instruction

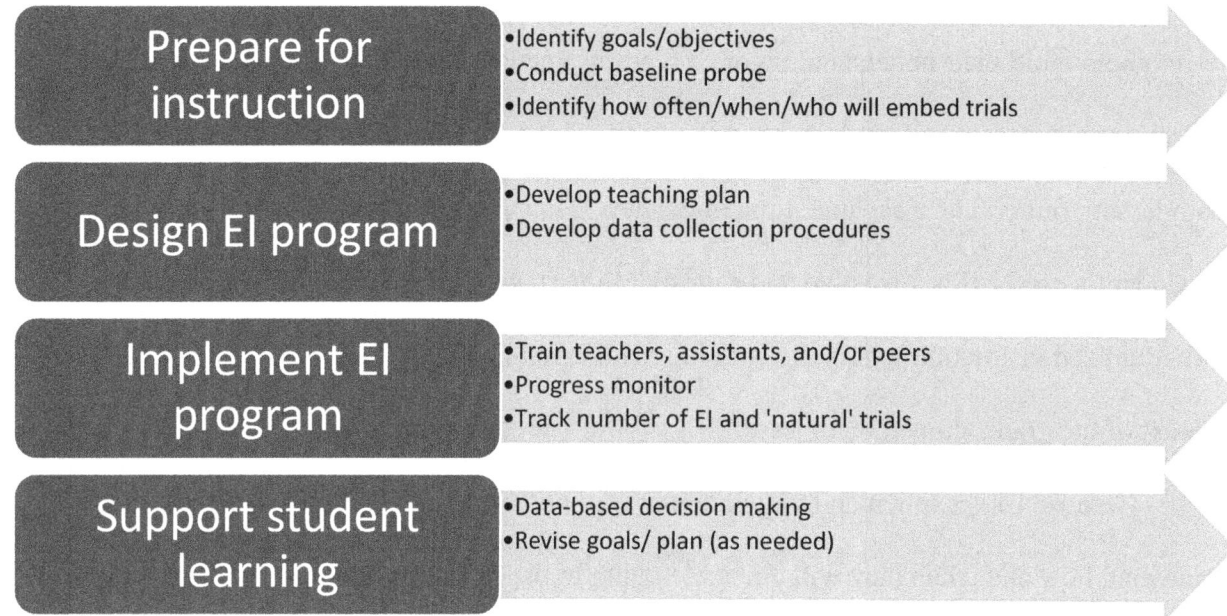

Note: Modified from Jameson et al., 2020. Figure 1.1

Early Numeracy Instruction

Numeracy—basic number concepts and skills—is the basis of all mathematics instruction and is imperative to student later math and life-long success (National Mathematics Advisory Panel, 2008). A challenge many educators face when planning for grade-aligned math lessons for students with ASD/IDD is student's prior learning and math skill acquisition. Often students have not gained mastery of earlier number concepts and skills (e.g., number identification, 1:1 correspondence, simple addition) along typical mathematics learning trajectories (see Figure 2). A learning trajectory has three parts: the mathematics goal, the developmental path children take to reach that goal, and the instruction surrounding depth of thinking along that path (Clements & Sarama, 2015).

Figure 2
Example Early Numeracy Learning Trajectory for Composing 2D Shapes

Math Goal: Compose (put together) two-dimensional shapes to make other shapes, solving puzzles or making pictures or designs, or decompose ("take apart") shapes into parts (simpler shapes).
Developmental Path:

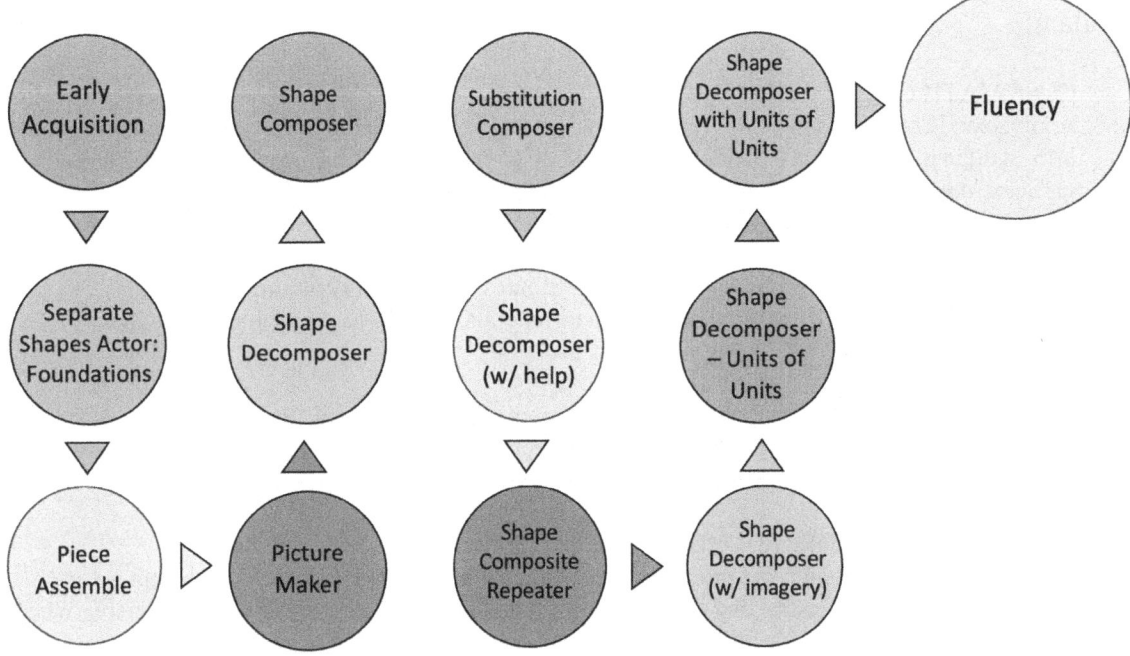

Note: Based upon Clements & Sarama (2017/2019) Composing 3D Shapes Learning Trajectory

As mentioned in Chapter 1, students with ASD/IDD should be provided with grade-aligned instruction; however, we would be remiss if we ignored the fact that many students with ASD/IDD are currently working on various levels within numeracy learning trajectories, even within the same inclusive classroom. In Figure 2, the example of composing 2D shapes is typically taught within early childhood curriculum; however, many students with ASD/IDD may not have mastered or even been exposed to instruction along numeracy trajectories (Browder et al., 2011; Root et al., 2020). It may be necessary to embed instruction on prerequisite skills and concepts for students with ASD/IDD within the general curriculum to provide students greater access to grade-aligned priority learning goals. For example, this one learning trajectory includes prerequisite skills and concepts aligning to multiple math standards across both elementary and secondary curriculum. Here are a few standards in which steps of the developmental path of composing 2D shapes could be embedded to support student access to the grade-aligned curriculum:

> CCSS.MATH.CONTENT.K.G.B.4
> Analyze and compare two- and three-dimensional shapes, in different sizes and orientations, using informal language to describe their similarities, differences, parts (e.g., number of sides and vertices/"corners") and other attributes (e.g., having sides of equal length).
>
> CCSS.MATH.CONTENT.2.G.A.1
> Recognize and draw shapes having specified attributes, such as a given number of angles or a given number of equal faces.[1] Identify triangles, quadrilaterals, pentagons, hexagons, and cubes.
>
> CCSS.MATH.CONTENT.5.G.B.3
> Understand that attributes belonging to a category of two-dimensional figures also belong to all subcategories of that category. For example, all rectangles have four right angles and squares are rectangles, so all squares have four right angles.
>
> CCSS.MATH.CONTENT.7.G.A.2
> Draw (freehand, with ruler and protractor, and with technology) geometric shapes with given conditions. Focus on constructing triangles from three measures of angles or sides, noticing when the conditions determine a unique triangle, more than one triangle, or no triangle.

Prerequisite math skills should not be a barrier to including students within the inclusive math classroom and grade level curriculum; rather an opportunity to think about how to plan for explicit individualized instruction during the mathematics lesson and/or unit. We can help students access the general curriculum content, and also continue to support student growth along the numeracy learning trajectories at the same time. Because EI specifically identifies priority learning goals for the learner (or small group of learners), it is possible to identify numeracy goals students may still be working towards, even though they are not typically taught within that grade level. In Figures 3, 4, and 5, multiple vignettes are provided to highlight examples that will be used throughout the rest of this chapter of how EI may be utilized to support various students with ASD/ID across the grade levels and mathematical learning.

Figure 3
Embedded Instruction Vignettes—Lochlan

Lochlan is a Kindergartener with ASD. His general education teacher conducted a baseline assessment of all of his students at the beginning of the year and realized Lochlan is missing some key concepts and skills regarding patterning and counting that are typically mastered prior to coming to school. Although his special education teacher is also working on some of these skills with Lochlan individually; his teachers decide they will develop an EI plan to embed trials of these specific patterning and counting skills into the general math lessons to provide Lochlan the instruction and practice he needs as often as possible.

Figure 4
Embedded Instruction Vignettes—Sunny

Sunny is a 7th grade boy with an intellectual disability and Cerebral Palsy. His current IEP lists math goals such as identify numerals to 10, and make sets to 10 items, tell time to the hour. In planning for the upcoming math unit of work, his educational team (i.e., general education teacher, special education teacher, and paraprofessional) meet together to identify the learning outcome he will work towards that are grade-aligned and appropriate. They also identify numeracy skills he is currently working towards and other math concepts he may not already have (e.g., concept of more/less) that will be also be important for him to gain access to the curriculum being taught.

Figure 5
Embedded Instruction Vignettes—Fayola

Fayola is a 10th grade high school student with Autism who participates in math instruction within the general education classroom, as well as in a transition course designed specifically for application of 'everyday math' in the community. Fayola's math teachers meet quarterly to determine numeracy skills she would benefit from learning (e.g., rounding to the nearest dollar, calculator skills, place value) and then determine what units and lessons they can best be embedded within to support her in Algebra I and Transition Math class.

When teachers prepare for instruction, they include the identification of the priority skills and concepts that will be embedded. However, just as important, is the decision of how often learning trials should be embedded into the math lesson and activities. EI can occur during these activities and everyday school routines. Depending on the learning being embedded, it may make sense to embed trials during the lesson itself, and also within other parts of the school day (e.g., using the Next Dollar strategy to pay for lunch). The more practice a student has to learn something new, the faster they will learn it. Therefore, it is important for education teams to identify how many instructional trials will be presented to a student within a lesson. Jameson et al. (2020) suggested teachers determine the number of potential embedded trials by listing the natural (i.e., instructionally, such as text, worksheets, collaborative groups) and supplemental (other times a trial could be embedded; e.g., transitions, independent work) teaching opportunities. Once these opportunities have been identified, teachers can estimate how many trials could be embedded during that part of the class period. Finally, all the trials are added together to determine the total number of potential trials the educational team will try to embed. Professional judgement is important here based on the student's current level of skill and how many trials are feasible to be embedded within the lesson and other natural opportunities (see Table 2 for examples of various considerations).

Repeated Opportunities

Students with disabilities benefit from multiple opportunities to learn new content and skills. While quality instruction should include models and multiple learning trials with feedback (see Figure 6 for an example of systematic instruction and feedback), some students may need more trials to practice skills other students have already mastered. EI provides the option for educators to embed as many trials as needed (and appropriate) for the learner. For example, Sunny's teacher, Mr. Timar, may decide to embed five trials of the prerequisite skill of 'set making with quantities to 10', within the ongoing math lesson because he knows Sunny will need the repeated practice every day while in the acquisition stage of learning. However, he

Table 2
Designing EI Instructional Trials

# Goals & Trials	Classroom Context & Team Members	Factors & Considerations
Four learning goals; embedded 3x each	Elementary math class, 1 student; General education teacher; special educator periodically in class during lessons	The student in this class has four prerequisite math goals embedded in each lesson. Typically, the general education teacher is the only one available to embed trials; therefore 4 goals, 3x per lesson is a significant number of trials for the teacher to embed. Because these four goals include skills, such as number identification and 1:1 correspondence, the teacher is able to embed trials as they naturally occur to support the grade-aligned content the student is working towards.
Two learning goals; embedded 5x each	Middle school math class, 3 students; general educator, paraprofessional	Each of the three students have been identified by the special and general educators to need additional repeated practice of a few early numeracy skills they are also receiving Tier 3 intensive instruction in (also on their IEP). The paraprofessional and general educator make a plan to embed at least five trials across all math lessons, allowing the student more repeated practice with error correction and feedback. They feel that embedding more than five trials may begin to feel unnatural to the lessons; they believe they can seamlessly embed five trials into ongoing activities all students are completing.
Two learning goals; embedded 3x each	High school math class, 1 student; special educator and peers	The special education teacher, in consultation with the general education teacher have identified three prerequisite skills the student would greatly benefit from mastering to have better access to the grade-aligned curriculum (e.g., the concept of repeat and rotation to build tessellations). During small group activities, peers will embed at least 3 opportunities for the student to 'repeat' or 'rotate' a shape to collaboratively design a tessellation. The special education teacher will support peers in systematic prompting procedures.

plans to fade the number of trials as Sunny progresses across the stages of learning (see Figure 7; Shurr et al., 2019).

Figure 6
Planning for Systematic Embedded Instruction Embedded Instruction for Lochlan.

In Lochlan's kindergarten class, his teacher decides that he will embed at least 3 opportunities each for Lochlan to identify patterns, make sets, and rote count during each math lessons. Lochlan's teacher also plans to embed at least 2 more opportunities to make sets throughout the school day during transitions and natural activities (e.g., counting a set of four pencils for his group). While developing an EI program for an upcoming Geometry unit, Lochlan's teacher determines parts of the lessons in which the EI trials can be embedded (e.g., rote count to get class started during warm-up activity, identify which set of shapes on the board is in a pattern, make a set of 3 squares). Lochlan's teacher has found it easiest to use the systematic instruction strategy of System of Least Prompts (SLP). This is the same strategy his special education teacher uses most often during individualized instruction sessions.

Math Unit: 'Analyze and compare two- and three-dimensional shapes'
During lessons, multiple shapes will be places on the classroom Smartboard for students to analyze, describe, and compare.

Example procedure for embedding learning trials for: **Identify a Pattern**

	Which one of these sets are in in a pattern?	Praise correct answer OR Provide non-specific verbal
Natural Cue:		
Non-specific verbal:	Look at both sets. Remember a pattern is 'repeating design'. Which one of these sets is in a pattern?	Praise correct answer OR Provide verbal prompt
Verbal:	Look at set one 'square, square, circle, triangle'. Look at set two 'square, triangle, square, triangle'	Praise correct answer OR Provide model prompt
Model:	(touching set two) I see a repeating design here. This is a pattern. 'square, triangle, square, triangle' Now you show me, which one is a pattern?	Praise student for touching set two, guide student to towards set two and continue with lesson.

Figure 7
Example of Fading Embedded Trials across Stages of Learning

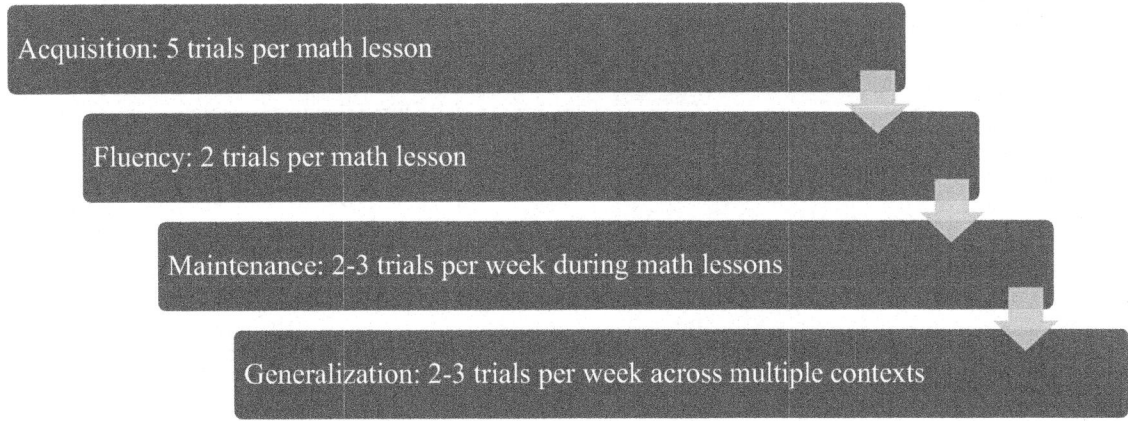

There is not a true and tried equation to use to determine the number of trials that should be embedded within a lesson or activity. Educational teams must determine how often, when and what type of prompting system fits best in the math context. For example, Fayola's special education teacher may decide that the paraprofessional who supports Fayola in the general education math classroom can embed both prerequisite and facilitating skills during independent work time, whole group activities, and during activity transitions. Using an MTSS model to plan Fayola's math instruction, they identify priority math goals within Tier 1, 2 and 3 (refer to Chapter 3 for additional information regarding MTSS, mathematics, and students with ASD/IDD). Refer to Figure 8 to see how Fayola's educational team identified how EI could support instruction within both Tier 2 and 3, as well as other formats for learning.

The exciting thing to remember about EI is that for any skill a student individually needs more instruction and practice in can be embedded within the naturally occurring lessons and activities of the classroom. When planning for EI and identifying the instructional objectives for a specific student, it is helpful to think about what additional (other than planned for the whole class) learning trials or skills would the student benefit from during the lesson or unit.

Figure 8
Example of Embedded Instruction within the MTSS Model for Fayola

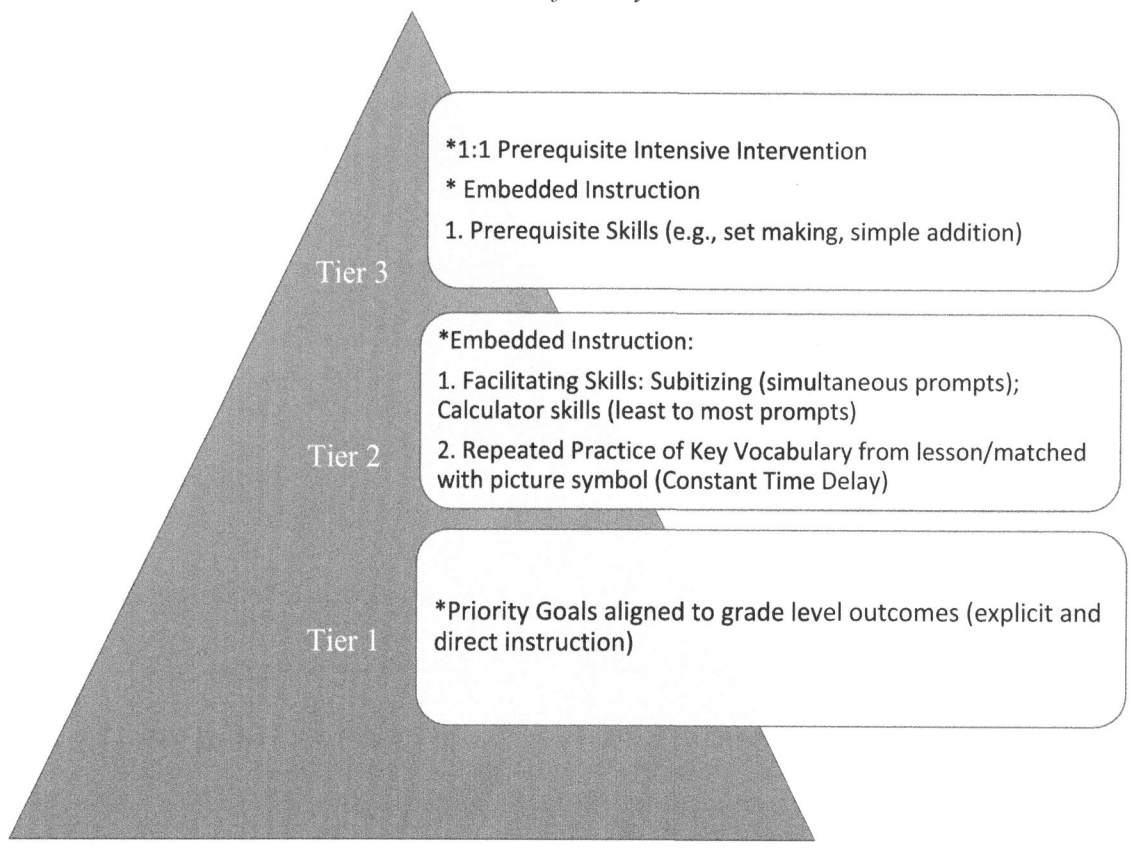

Pivotal Math Concepts

Mathematics is made up of skills and concepts that build upon each other (Clements & Sarama, 2019). Rather than waiting for students to master each and every skill and concept, Chapter 1 stresses the importance of aligned instruction. When planning for instruction, educators should think about the necessary concepts that students should have in order to truly master the skill being taught. For example, in a math unit on calculating the area and perimeter of polygons, the concepts of measurement (e.g., length, height), inside or around would be necessary (pivotal) to engage in the lesson with depth and functionality. The standard of calculating perimeter is typically taught in 3rd grade (CCSS.MATH.CONTENT.3.MD.D.8) and students would have mastered the concepts of length, height, inside and around in preschool and/or kindergarten. However, if James (as student with IDD) does not know these concepts, rather than teaching a separate lesson surrounding these pivotal concepts, his teacher can embed learning trials of these concepts into the ongoing lessons (See Table 4).

Communication, Social and Behavioral Goals

EI has been used to support multiple learning goals for students across the grade levels. While the focus of this chapter is mathematics, it is important to think about other academic readiness skills that may impact the learners' success in math education. Many students with

Table 4

Example of Embedded Pivotal Skills in Math Lesson on Perimeter

Student: JAMES

Planned Activities	Pivotal Math Concept(s)	Example of Embedded Teacher Script
Define Perimeter	Around	To whole class: Perimeter is the distance around a two-dimensional shape. To James: Which one of these is <u>around</u>?
Define Area	Inside	To whole class: Area is the size of a surface, the amount of space inside the boundaries of the two-dimensional shape. To James: Color in the <u>inside</u> of this square.
Teacher models measuring polygon	Width Height	I want to start by measuring the width of my rectangle, James show me the <u>length</u>?
Students measure sides of polygon	Width Height	To whole class: Measure the sides of your rectangle. To James: Show me the <u>height</u> of this rectangle.

ASD/IDD also have IEP objectives or classroom goals in communication, social skills, and/or behavior. These types of goals should be taught explicitly across the school day, extended into the community and home. Rather than only teaching these skills in isolation, embedding them into the natural routines of the math lessons provides learners increased opportunities to learn; increasing the speed and likelihood of mastery and fluency. Furthermore, embedding communication and/or behavior goals into math lessons also builds generalization of skills across settings or situations. Notice in Figure 9, the goals for Sunny extend past his math related IEP goals. While his IEP goals are embedded throughout the math lesson, he also building mathematical conceptual understanding and communication goals, while working within the grade-aligned standards.

Sunny's educational team needs to know when to embed the learning trials. They identify potential opportunities during the math period for each of the embedded goals and agree on who is responsible for embedding trials (Figure 10). The EI plan is used to proactively design instruction but teachers will be on the look-out for additional natural opportunities to embed additional trials or modify the delivery of EI. Planning for EI supports the student by spreading out explicit instruction on individual learning goals across ongoing classroom routines. This gives students specially designed instruction without separating them from their peers.

Data Collection & Progress Monitoring

Data-informed decisions are necessary to ensure student learning and are an essential component of systematic instruction (Collins, 2012). With EI, student progress can be monitored during the ongoing daily routine or through data-collection assessment probes at a later time. Either of these procedures are appropriate, as long as student progress is monitored and instructional decisions are made based upon how students are doing in meeting their learning

Figure 9
Planning Embedded Instruction Across Priority Goals

Student: Sunny
7th grade Math Standard: Analyze proportional relationships and use them to solve real-world and mathematical problems.
Objective: Compute unit rates associate with ratios of fractions.

Instructional Area	Concepts/Skills	Instructional Procedures
Pivotal Math Concepts	-Whole -Half -More -Less	Constant Time Delay Procedure
Communication Goals	When presented with his AAC device (Dynovox) on home screen, will navigate to Math – Numbers screen.	Task Analysis of steps with Least to Most Prompting
Behavior Goal	When he doesn't know an answer, ask for help by touching HELP icon on desk (rather than refuse to do work)	Least to Most Prompting
Early Numeracy Skills	-Compose sets to 10 -Time to the hour	Task-Analysis of steps with Least to Most Prompting
	-Numeral ID to 10	Constant Time Delay

goals (see Chapter 2). One strategy to help educators keep track of the number of learning trials they have embedded into a lesson, is to develop data collection sheets that record student responses for each planned trial. For example, in the sample data sheet in Figure 11), four trials of each of the learning goals were embedded across the lesson. The teacher marked each of the trials as he embedded them and tracked the student's responses (+ for independent correct, - for no response/incorrect). He may have embedded them in any order, as planned in his EI Planning

Figure 10
Planning for Embedded Instruction for Sunny

Lesson Components	Skills / Who will embed trials
1. Introduction to Lesson	-open AAC to numbers page **LM** -identify time – log in journal **LM**
2. Guided Practice Intro of terminology, Smartboard examples	-concept of whole/half **LM/TR** -concept of more/less. **LM/TR** -identify numbers on fractions (e.g., denominator). **LM/TR**
3. Group Activity Small groups of 3; Manipulation of fractions with manipulatives, C (concrete)-R (Representational) moving into A (abstract)	-concept of whole/half **LM/TR/G** -make sets of manipulatives, identify numeral. **LM/TR/G**
4. Independent Practice Manipulation of fractions with manipulatives, C (concrete)-R (Representational) moving into A (abstract)	-open AAC to numbers page. **LM** -concept of more/less **LM** -make sets of manipulatives, identify numeral. **LM**
5. Group Lesson Closure	-identify time-log in journal **LM** -identify number on fractions (e.g., numerator) **LM**

LM – paraprofessional, TR – teacher, G-small group/peers

Sheet, or as they naturally occurred within the learning environment. After each lesson, Fayola's teacher circled the total number of correct responses, then draws a line from one day's data to the next. This visual graph allows him to track Fayola's trend (level of progress over time). Refer to Chapter 2 for more information on data collection procedures and progress monitoring, as well as making data-based instruction decisions.

In the vignette example of Fayola in Figure 5, a high school student who is taking two math courses, her teachers also developed one data sheet they both use to track her progress on one of her facilitating math skills: use of a calculator (Figure 12). Both her Algebra I and her Transition Math teachers record data on separate data sheets but enter their data into an online spreadsheet 2-3x per week. They are then able to meet together and report her progress on her individualized math goals, as they are embedded into both courses across topics/units for the entire semester. Early in their planning, they identified that Fayola needs quite a bit of repetition before she is able to acquire a new skill and use it with fluency, so they decided that she would need at least 3 trials of each of her learning goals daily. Quarterly, they meet with Fayola to formally discuss her progress on her specifically identified individualized goals. They review a graph that visually displays her progress and make instructional decisions together. Because her teachers are both inputting data online several times a week, they are also able to keep track of her progress across classes weekly.

Conclusion

Students with ASD/IDD experience multi-faceted learning needs in the math classroom. Researchers consistently show EI to be an effective way to meet support individualized learning within the large group lesson or daily routines of the classroom (Jimenez & Kamei, 2015;

Figure 11
Progress Monitoring of Embedded Math Goals

Student: ___Fayola_____

Interventionist Initials	T	P	P	T	T	P	T	T	P	P		
Date	2/1	2/2	2/4	2/6	2/8	2/8	2/10	2/11	2/13	2/15		
Round to nearest dollar	8 −	8 −	8 −	8 −	8 −	8 +	8 +	8 −	8 +	8 +	8	8
Round to the nearest dollar	7 +	7 −	7 −	7 −	7 −	7 −	7 −	7 −	7	7	7	7
Round to nearest dollar	6 −	6 −	6 −	6 −	6 −	6 −	6 −	6 −	6 −	6	6	6
Round to nearest dollar	5 −	5 −	5 −	5 −	5 −	5 −	5	5 +	5 −	5	5	5
ID Place Value	4 −	4 +	4 +	4 +	4	4 +	4	4 −	4 +	4 +	4	4
ID Place Value	3 −	3	3	3	3 +	3	3 +	3 +	3 +	3 +	3	3
ID Place Value	2	2	2 −	2 +	2	2 +	2 +	2 +	2 +	2 +	2	2
ID Place Value	1 −	1 −	1 +	1 +	1 −	1 +	1 −	1 +	1 +	1	1	1
TOTAL INDEPENDENT CORRECT:	2	2	3	4	2	3	4	5	7	6		

McDonnell et al., 2014). Through tiered instruction, students with ASD/IDD are able to receive high quality UDL instruction, and also receive personalized instruction through one-on-one, small group, and embedded learning opportunities. We know explicit and systematic instruction is effective in teaching students with ASD/IDD new skills; therefore, it is important to identify how EI can be used to support math instruction across math strands and grades.

Figure 12
Progress Monitoring of Embedded Math Goal Across Teachers

Student: __Fayola__
Goal: Use personal cell phone calculator to add or subtract two price amounts under ten dollars.

	Interventionist Initials	RR	AT	AT	P	RR				
Step	Date	10.2	10.6	10.7	10.9	10.10				
	S Response:									
10. States total	Reads total amount	10	10	10	10	10	10	10	10	10
9. Finds answer	Locates = symbol and presses	9	9	9	9	9	9	9	9	9
8. Enters cents	Locates numbers and presses buttons	8	8	8	8	8	8	8	8	8
7. Enters decimal (.)	Locates decimal button and presses	7	7	7	7	7	7	7	7	7
6. Enters dollar amount	Locates number and presses buttons	6	6	6	6	6	6	6	6	6
5. Enters operation	Locates + or – symbol and presses button	5	5	5	5	5	5	5	5	5
4. Enters cents	Locates numbers and presses buttons	4	4	4	4	4	4	4	4	4
3. Enters decimal (.)	Locates decimal button and presses	3	3	3	3	3	3	3	3	3
2. Enters dollar amount	Locates number and presses buttons	2	2	2	2	2	2	2	2	2
1. Find Calculator app and press	S finds app on her phone and opens	1	1	1	1	1	1	1	1	1
	TOTAL INDEPENDENT CORRECT:	1	4	6	7	7				
Notes:		She asked for help, rather than trying		Very motivated by sunglasses she was purchasing in the stories	Mr. G was absent - worked with peer	Used today on her own in cafeteria - self motivated				

References

Bowman, J. A., McDonnell, J., Ryan, J., Coleman, O., Conradi, L. & Eichelberger, C. (2019). Effects of general education teacher-delivered embedded instruction to teach students with intellectual disability to solve word problems. *Education and Training in Autism and Developmental Disabilities, 55*(3), 318–331.

Clements, D. H., & Sarama, J. (2015). Discussion from a mathematics education perspective. *Mathematical Thinking and Learning, 17*(2-3), 244-252. doi: 10.1080/10986065.2015.1016826

Clements, D. H., & Sarama, J. (2017/2019). *Learning and teaching with learning trajectories [LT]^2.* Retrieved from Marsico Institute, Morgridge College of Education, University of Denver. Website: www.LearningTrajectories.org

Collins, B. (2012). *Systematic instruction for students with moderate and severe disabilities.* Brookes.

Jameson, M. J., McDonnell, J., Riesen, T., Polychronis, S. (2020). *Embedded instruction in the general education classroom for students with intellectual and developmental Disabilities.* Council for Exceptional Children.

Jimenez, B. A., & Barron, T. (2019). Learner-centered professional development: A model to increase inclusion for students with moderate intellectual disability. *Inclusion, 7*(2), 125-139. doi.org/10.1352/2326-6988-7.2.125

Jimenez, B. A. & Kamei, A. (2015). Embedded Instruction: An evidence-based practice to support academic achievement in inclusive core academics. *Inclusion, 3,* 132-144.

National Mathematics Advisory Panel. (2008). *The Final Report of the National Mathematics Advisory Panel.* Washington, DC: U.S. Department of Education

McDonnell, J., Jameson, M. J., Riesen, R., Polychronis, R. (2014). Embedded instruction in inclusive settings. In D. M., Browder & F. Spooner (Eds)., *Language arts, math, and science for students with significant cognitive disabilities* (pp. 15-36). Paul H. Brookes.

Morningstar, M., Kurth, J., and Johnson, P. E. (2017). Examining national trends in educational placement for students with significant disabilities. *Remedial and Special Education, 38,* 3-12. doi.org/10.1177/0741932516678327

Polychronis, S. C., McDonnell, J., Johnson, J. W., Riesen, T., Jameson, M. (2004). A comparison of two trial distribution schedules in embedded instruction. *Focus on Autism and Other Developmental Disabilities, 19,* 140-151. doi.org/10.1177/10883576040190030201

Appendices

Chapter 1

Steps for Instructional Planning using Alignment and Contextualized Math

	Steps for Planning	**Activities/Examples**
1	Select, understand, and prioritize standards	
2	Give standards a real-world context	
3	Use evidence-based and research-based practices to teach	
4	Select instructional supports	
5	Monitor Progress	

See Chapter 1 Table 3 for Example filled out

Contextualized Mathematics Planning Form

Grade-aligned standard:	IEP Goal:	Contextualized Math Activity:	Instructional Methods:	Measurement Method:

See Chapter 1 Table 4 for Example filled out

Chapter 5

Planning Worksheet for MSBI

Potential Barriers	**Considerations**	**Specific Strategies for Student**
1) Access	Reading level	
	Problem Structure	
	Quantities/content	
	Vocabulary	
2) Conceptual Understanding	Metacognition	
	Diagrams and manipulatives	
	Instructional procedure	
	Instructional sequence	
3) Procedural Fluency	Problem-solving routine	
	Performing operations	
4) Generalization and Independence	Self-monitoring	
	Engagement	
	Relevance	

See Chapter 5 Figures 10 and 11 for example filled out

Chapter 6

Blank Embedded Instruction Planning Chart

Part 1.

Student:
Math Standard:
Learning Objective:

	Goal(s):	Teaching/Prompts Procedure
Pivotal Math Concepts		
Communication, Social, and/or Behavior		
Early Numeracy		

Part 2.

Lesson Components	Skills / Who will embed trials
1.	
2.	
3.	
4.	
5.	

Part 3. Data Collection

Student: _____
Goal:

	Interventionist Initials									
	Date									
Step	**S Response:**									
10		10	10	10	10	10	10	10	10	10
9		9	9	9	9	9	9	9	9	9
8		8	8	8	8	8	8	8	8	8
7		7	7	7	7	7	7	7	7	7
6		6	6	6	6	6	6	6	6	6
5		5	5	5	5	5	5	5	5	5
4		4	4	4	4	4	4	4	4	4
3		3	3	3	3	3	3	3	3	3
2		2	2	2	2	2	2	2	2	2
1		1	1	1	1	1	1	1	1	1
	TOTAL INDEPENDENT CORRECT:									
Notes:										

Glossary

Abstract representations: In mathematical problem-solving abstract representations are problems solved with numerical strategies only. This phase of instruction is often the final step in an instructional sequence.

Accommodations: Accommodations are alterations to the materials, setting or evidence of learning that are individualized based on student need. Accommodations do not change what is taught or assessed, only how it is taught or assessed.

Acquisition: Acquisition is the initial phase of learning; students are taught a new skill or behavior that the student has not mastered.

Alignment: Alignment in special education instruction refers to consistent goals between instructional strategy, grade aligned standards, assessment tools and IEP goals.

Anecdotal records: Anecdotal records in education refer to teacher notes based on observation of student behaviors. These records can be used for assessment.

Chained task: A chained task is a task or skill which involves multiple steps or sub-tasks.

Concrete manipulatives: Concrete manipulatives are physical objects that can be moved to represent quantities or concepts during instruction.

Concrete representations: In mathematical problem-solving concrete representations are problems demonstrated and solved with manipulatives. These manipulatives are physical, such as concrete manipulatives. This phase of instruction is often the first step in an instructional sequence that utilizes concrete manipulatives.

Contextualized math: In contextualized math instruction, instructional planning begins with prioritizing grade level standards and identifying real-world applications within which the standards can be taught

Considerate text: Considerate text is written at a student's instructional level, using high-frequency sight words and common vocabulary, without unnecessary extraneous details

Constant time delay: Constant time delay is an evidence-based practice in which a teacher presents a controlling prompt (i.e., prompt that models the expected response) simultaneously with the instructional cue (e.g., 0-s round) during initial teaching trials, and then in subsequent teaching trials the prompt is provided after a delay interval (e.g., 4-s) in order to give the student an opportunity to independently respond.

Curriculum based measurement: Curriculum based measurement was developed by Deno (1985) and uses a protocol for frequent formative assessments of student performance on content from the current curriculum.

Data-based decision making: Data-based decision making occurs when teachers monitor student progress and use subsequent data to adjust instruction.

Direct observation: Direct observation occurs when teachers watch students as they perform tasks.

Error analysis: Error analysis occurs when teachers observe student behavior or permanent products (e.g., worksheets) to determine a pattern of errors in order to adjust instruction

Discrepancy analysis: Discrepancy analysis compares performance to typically developing same-age peers in order to identify discrepancies between current and desired skill level. This allows educators to identify and prioritize skills to target and determine what supports a student will need to be successful.

Discrete skills: Discrete skills are behaviors that require a single response.

Embedded Instruction (EI): Embedded instruction is designed to distribute instructional trials within the ongoing routine and activities of the classroom environment.

Error correction: Error correction is a process in which the teacher blocks the student from making an error (if possible) and redirects them to the correct answer, using a model-retest procedure.

Evidence-based practice (EBP): EBPs are interventions and strategies with sufficient quantity of high-quality research to support their effectiveness for specific populations of students.

Executive function: A persons executive functioning refers to a set of skills related to self-monitoring, cognitive flexibility, and inhibition.

Explicit instruction: Explicit instruction includes breaking complex skills into individual components that can be mastered and learned in logical sequence by providing multiple opportunities to practice and frequent, formative feedback. Often called "I Do, We Do, You Do", "Model-Lead-Test", or "Model, Guided Practice, Independent Practice"

Flexible grouping: Teachers use flexible grouping by reviewing data and grouping students based on identified needs for a specific instructional period. Student groups are fluid and change frequently.

Fluency: Fluency refers to how easily and efficiently a learner can complete a behavior and is often measured in terms of duration or latency in addition to accuracy.

Formative assessment: Formative assessment is frequent and informal and informs instructional decisions based on student need. Formative assessment is used during instruction and can include a single skill or several.

Generalization: Generalization occurs when the student can apply skills or knowledge to an untaught context or setting.

Graduated sequence of instruction: Graduated sequence of instruction is an instructional approach that uses three sequenced steps to teach problem solving. Often the first stage involves concrete or virtual manipulatives, followed by pictorial representations drawings and then an abstract phase that involve solving problems with numerical strategies.

Graphic organizer: In mathematics, graphic organizers use visual representations (i.e., diagrams, schemas, number lines) to represent mathematical relationships to promote conceptual understanding

Heuristic: A heuristic is an attack strategy, often consisting of a mnemonic device to help students remember the steps of a procedure.

Inclusion: An inclusive educational setting supports students with and without disabilities participating in the same educational activities with support to master appropriate, individual learning goals. Inclusive classrooms recognize that disability is part of the human continuum and the classrooms reflect natural proportions of students with and without identified needs (Giangreco et al., 2020).

Indirect observation: Indirect observation occurs when teachers collect data from sources other than directly measuring the student's performance themselves, such as observing work samples or interviews with teachers, peers, or caregivers

Instructional trials: unit of instruction that includes an antecedent (e.g., request, discriminative stimulus), behavior (e.g., response), and consequence (e.g., prompt, reinforcement).

Intensive instruction: Intensive instruction refers to a process, driven by data, characterized by increased intensity and individualization. When teachers use intensive instruction they provide tailored instruction to meet identified needs of a small group of students with increased duration and frequency when compared to peers.

Iterative planning process: The iterative planning process makes data informed changes to an instructional plan during the instructional unit. The process often uses an assess, teach, assess process to determine appropriate next steps for individual learners.

Keyword strategy: The keyword strategy is a problematic word problem solving strategy in which students are taught to equate specific "keywords" in a word problem with specific mathematical operations (e.g., more = addition).

Learning trajectory: A learning trajectory has three parts: the instructional goal, the developmental path students take to reach that goal, and the instruction surrounding depth of thinking along that path.

Maintenance: Maintenance is the learner's ability to perform a behavior with appropriate speed and accuracy over time after the reinforcement is faded and instruction has stopped.

Manipulative-based sequence of instruction: In mathematics instruction a manipulative-based sequence of instruction is used to scaffold student learning by starting with concrete or virtual manipulatives and moving towards pictorial representations and finally numerical strategies, as appropriate.

Modified Schema-Based Instruction (MSBI): MSBI is a cognitive-based strategy to teach mathematical word problem solving that is derived from schema-based instruction. Explicit and systematic instruction is used to teach students to use a heuristic (e.g., task analysis) to model information from word problems on a schematic diagrams (e.g., graphic organizers).

Multi-Tiered System of Supports (MTSS): Multi-tiered system of support includes both response to intervention (RtI)—an academic MTSS—and positive behavior intervention and supports(PBIS)—a behavioral MTSS. MTSS involve provides multiple tiers of supporting students who struggle.

Overlearning: Overlearning is the process of continuing to practice a skill after mastery has been reached.

Performance deficit: A performance deficit occurs when students have demonstrated the ability to complete a task independently, but they are not doing so consistently. Performance deficits may be related to a lack of motivation, unclear expectations, or inadequate reinforcement.

Permanent product: A permanent product is evidence of student work that can be used for assessment. In math instruction it is often a worksheet.

Positive behavioral interventions and supports (PBIS): Positive behavioral interventions and supports is a three-tier framework for improving teacher and student outcomes by integrating school practices, data and systems.

Progress monitoring: progress monitoring refers to the use of formative assessments to measure the degree to which students are making progress toward learning goals

Procedural fluency: Procedural fluency is a student's ability to apply a set of procedures to solve a problem in an efficient manner.

Prompting hierarchy: Prompting hierarchies are a systematic sequence of prompts, typically ordered from least intrusive to most intrusive (e.g., system of least prompts, least intrusive prompting) or most to least.

Reinforcement: A reinforcement is any consequence that increases the likelihood of the preceding behavior reoccurring.

Representational representations: In mathematical problem-solving representational representations are student made drawings used to demonstrate and solve problems. This phase of instruction is often the second step in an instructional sequence.

Scaffolds: Scaffolds are supports offered to guide a learner towards independent completion of academic tasks. Scaffolds should be removed as the learner demonstrates independence.

Schema: In mathematics problem solving, schema refers to a category, often paired with a visual representation, which allows students to accurately identify the appropriate set of steps to solve a problem.

Schema-based instruction: Schema-based instruction is a cognitive-based strategy to teach students how to solve mathematical word problems using schemas (e.g., graphic organizers), heuristics, explicit instruction, and metacognitive strategy instruction.

Summative assessment: Summative assessment is a form of mastery assessment that occurs at the end of a unit of learning or a specified amount of time. Summative assessments evaluate the overall progress students have made and typically include multiple skills.

Systematic instruction: Systematic Instruction is based on the principles of Applied Behavior Analysis (ABA). Begins by defining the targeted skill(s), defining methods to use during instruction, directly teaching, and reviewing progress to modify instruction (Collins, 2012).

Task analysis: Task analysis breaks complete tasks into discrete steps or teachable components that are chained together. Task analysis can be used for instruction and assessment.

Technology-assisted instruction (TAI): Technology-assisted instruction is an evidence-based practice in which technology (e.g., computers, tablets, interactive whiteboards, software) plays a central role in instruction

Theory of Mind: Theory of mind is the ability to understand the perspectives of others, along with the ability to explain and predict the behaviors of others.

Think-alouds: Think-alouds are a process in which a teacher verbally explains their thinking to model for students the cognitive processes involved when solving a problem.

Universal Design for Learning (UDL): Universal design for learning is a framework for teaching and learning where barriers are minimized for all learners through explicit planning for representation, engagement, and expression.

Virtual representations: Virtual representations are virtual manipulatives, which can be used as part of a virtual manipulative instructional sequence. This can be used in place of concrete manipulatives.

Virtual manipulative: A virtual manipulative is a dynamic image used in technology that can be manipulated in a similar way to traditional physical manipulatives. Virtual manipulatives are interactive and allow learners to construct mathematical knowledge (Moyer, et al., 2002).

Visual representations: Visual representations are image or pictures—provided or created by a student—to aid in understanding and solving mathematical problems. Examples include schemas, pictures or drawings representing a problem.

Weak Central Coherence: Weak central coherence is a theory developed by Frith and Happe (1994) to explain the tendency for individuals with ASD to focus on details rather than the whole picture.

Made in the USA
Columbia, SC
14 August 2022